Symptomatic Affective Disorders

This is a volume in

PERSONALITY AND PSYCHOPATHOLOGY
A Series of Monographs, Texts, and Treatises

Under the Editorship of David T. Lykken

A complete list of titles in this series appears at the end of this volume.

Symptomatic Affective Disorders

A study of depression and mania associated with physical disease and medication

F. A. Whitlock, MA, MD, FRCP

Professor Emeritus of Psychiatry
University of Queensland

1982

ACADEMIC PRESS

A Subsidiary of Harcourt Brace Jovanovich, Publishers

Sydney   New York   London
Paris   San Diego   San Francisco   São Paulo   Tokyo   Toronto

616.89
W6145

ACADEMIC PRESS AUSTRALIA
Centrecourt, 25–27 Paul Street North
North Ryde, N.S.W. 2113

United States Edition published by
ACADEMIC PRESS INC.
111 Fifth Avenue
New York, New York 10003

United Kingdom Edition published by
ACADEMIC PRESS, INC. (LONDON) LTD.
24/28 Oval Road, London NW1 7DX

Printed in Australia

National Library of Australia Cataloguing-in-Publication Data

---

Whitlock, F. A. (Francis Antony), 1916–.
Symptomatic affective disorders.

Bibliography.
Includes index.   85-0805
ISBN 0 12 747580 X.

1. Affective disorders.   I. Title. (Series :
Personality and psychopathology; no. 31).

616.85'2

Library of Congress Catalog Card Number: 81-71780

Contents

Foreword

During the past few decades, it has become increasingly plain to psychiatrists and physicians that emotional disturbance or frank mental illness and physical disease occur together in a relatively high proportion of patients. And evidence has slowly accumulated to indicate that this association is of considerable importance for the clinical practice and the science of medicine and psychiatry alike. It has long been known that emotional disorder may present mainly in the form of prominent physical symptoms, but only in recent years has a beginning been made in defining the causal relationships between psychiatric and somatic disease. Evidence has been adduced that depressive illness in particular may be the early harbinger of covert physical disease and may for long periods dominate the total clinical picture. It is to the evaluation and synthesis of the findings in this new area of psychiatry and medicine that Professor Whitlock's book is devoted.

As the evidence he has brought together makes clear, the extent of the overlap between somatic and psychiatric disorders is greater than can be explained by chance. Moreover, in addition to its importance for diagnosis, the presence of prominent depression or anxiety has been found to have an adverse affect upon the course, outcome and treatment response of a wide range of illnesses, ranging from viral infections to cancer. Similar observations have been made in relation to the results of cardiac surgery. But causes and effects are difficult to disentangle, and such findings rarely admit of simple interpretations. This is perhaps one reason why these new observations have received so little attention despite their significant implications for clinical practice and medical science.

But they have probably been overlooked for other reasons. Conventionally trained physicians and surgeons are liable to focus selectively on physical symptoms and signs, so that any emotional concomitants of illness go unnoticed. Should they be observed, they may be interpreted as unimportant epiphenomena or as "functional overlay" and be brushed aside as lying beyond the proper range of interest and duty. In contrast, conservatively reared psychiatrists will have been taught that it is only those mental disorders in which the psychiatric features conform to an "organic" picture, with clouding of consciousness and defects of memory and cognition, that can be deemed to have any physical causes. The hope had long been entertained that, in such "functional" disorders as manic-depressive illness and schizophrenia, cerebral causes in the form of subtle biochemical lesions might one day come to light. But the possibility that a whole range of conditions (e.g. infections, carcinomas, drugs, focal cerebral lesions) might contribute in varying degrees and along different pathways to the causation of affective disorders could not be readily accommodated within a simple "all or none" concept of the functional–organic dichotomy.

The early contributions towards a changed outlook began about thirty years ago with a number of studies. It was Hinckle and Wolff who showed in 1952 that physical and mental disorders were not randomly distributed throughout the span of life. Over years of observation they proved to cluster with one another and to correlate with the degree of perceived psychological stress emanating from the life situation of patients. Within a few years, a number of contributions, initially from studies of aged people, noted that the prevalence of physical disease among depressed patients was greater than could be expected by chance. The possibility that biassed selection was the explanation was excluded by the markedly increased mortality found in elderly people diagnosed as suffering from depressive and related disorders compared with mentally well subjects in community samples. But the direction of causality remained unclear, and a large number of other questions posed by the findings remained unsolved. For example, Feighner and his colleagues in St. Louis included under their rubric of "secondary" depression conditions closely associated with serious and life-threatening disease. But the extent of the contribution made by physical disease alone, as distinct from hereditary predisposition to emotional disorder, premorbid personality and concomitant life events remained unclear.

The problems are of great complexity. People with physical diseases may become depressed as a result of metabolic disturbance, through a direct interference with cerebral function, or as a consequence of the special psychological meaning the disability has for them. The emotional disorder may follow from physical disease or it may cause or aggravate it. There is an intricate interplay of many factors such as genetic predisposition to affective disorder, the patient's premorbid personality, and his attitudes to illness and its implications for his future social and family life. In the case of some forms of physical illness, men appear to be affected with a selective severity. Is this response rooted in biological causes, or does the threat of impaired virility and physical disablement prove particularly stressful for the male of the species?

In this monograph, Professor Whitlock presents a comprehensive review of the contributions that have been made to this growing area of psychiatric research, including an account of his own important studies. Although knowledge in this field is at a relatively early stage of development, the facts have begun to form themselves into orderly patterns. For example, as Professor Whitlock points out, in the case of depressive episodes that develop in old age, an hereditary component is stronger in those cases where the depression is of a recurring type, having occurred earlier in life, than in those depressions occurring for the first time. Correspondingly, exogenous factors, including physical illness, are found in significant excess in affective disorders and can be judged to be among the causes of illness. He concludes that a similar situation exists in respect of cerebral lesions. Hereditary factors do not figure among the causal agents, and he concludes that the lesion can be regarded as the sole cause of the associated depression. In the case of temporal lobe epilepsy, depressive states, often of a severe nature and carrying a considerable hazard of suicide, are the commonest psychiatric complication observed between attacks. As the lesion is located in structures concerned with the regulation of emotional life, the hypothesis that it is entirely responsible is plausible. But the reason why some of these patients suffer from severe depressions while others are immune remains unexplained.

In other symptomatic cases, as in those related to drug effects and endocrine disturbance, the evidence favours interaction with an inherent and possibly hereditary predisposition to affective disorder. A good example is provided by reserpine and other antihypertensive drugs, where only a minority of those treated, albeit a substantial one, develop depressive disorders. The task set for scientific enquiry is to define the enzyme deficit or other neurochemical abnormality in which the underlying genetical factors are expressed. Any success achieved could be expected to shed new light on the aetiological basis of the more serious forms of depressive, and possibly manic-depressive, illness.

Symptomatic Affective Disorders highlights other opportunities for scientific enquiry into depressive illness. One further example must suffice. Having regard to the steep rise in the prevalence of depressive illness in old age and the evidence for a relatively low contribution to causation by genetical factors, Professor Whitlock suggests that subtle cerebral lesions may be among the causative factors. This would have been an idle hypothesis twenty years ago, but recent refinements in post-mortem neuropathology, and the discovery that even hours after death the brain remains packed with valid neurochemical information, have made it possible to submit it to stringent investigation.

Symptomatic depressions also have many lessons to teach about the practice of clinical medicine and psychiatry. In neither discipline is tunnel vision compatible with satisfactory standards of practice. The psychiatrist cannot function effectively in the management of the commonest illnesses that present in clinical and community practice unless he is reasonably competent as a physician. The physician, in turn, has not only to be ready to take note of isolated emotional symptoms, but must have enough expertise to assess whether they represent an understandable transient response to disability or an affective illness that passes beyond explanation in such terms. It is essential that he should be able to do this, for the depressive part of a chronic and incapacitating physical illness, though rooted, in part, in the patient's life situation, may prove to be more susceptible to appropriate treatment than any other part of the condition.

Professor Whitlock's book is timely and valuable because it builds bridges between psychiatry and medicine and poses questions regarding the ground common to them that are susceptible to empirical enquiries.

Sir Martin Roth
CAMBRIDGE
JULY 1982

Preface

The word "depression" conjures up in many minds a clinical picture in which misery and hopelessness predominate, often in response to some major misfortune. The very term "reactive depression" implies that the patient's symptoms are an understandable consequence of events which might have aroused similar feelings in oneself had one been exposed to the same set of circumstances. On the other hand, a diagnosis of endogenous depression suggests an aetiology involving some inherent defect in the individual's make-up or presumed inheritance from which there is no greater chance of escape than is granted to one fleeing from the Eumenides.

Without necessarily questioning the correctness of these interpretations, it soon becomes apparent to the practising psychiatrist that many patients suffer from affective disorders which would not have occurred had they not developed a major physical illness or been exposed to one or more powerful drugs. These drugs, it is presumed, cause changes in mood, because they interfere with cerebral biochemistry thought to be involved in the maintenance of normal affect in the healthy individual.

The diagnosis of a reactive depression is commonly made in aged patients particularly liable to these mood disturbances. Understandably, it has been assumed that the problems of retirement, bereavement, financial stringency, and declining physical health and strength are sufficient to account for any sustained depression exhibited by elderly persons, an assumption based more on commonsense than on scientifically demonstrated fact. Accepting the unity of brain and mind, it would, of course, come as no surprise to find that the ageing brain was less able to withstand emotional shock and stress and that severe stress in younger patients should activate mechanisms capable of producing the clinical picture of endogenous depression, despite an assumed intactness of brain structure and function.

With some of these considerations in mind, it has to be admitted that current classifications of affective disorder are unsatisfactory, partly because they tend to ignore an essential ingredient — depression caused or precipitated by physical disease. All clinicians will have treated patients whose affective disturbances have followed a severe viral infection or developed in the course of a major endocrine disease. Others may have treated patients for depression which gratifyingly disappears when the cerebral tumour, of which it was the principal manifestation, has been removed. The questions arise: how frequent are these symptomatic affective disorders, and what is their pathogenesis?

Although a belief in multi-factorial aetiology has become almost axiomatic in psychiatry, some examples of depression could be the result of single, identifiable and treatable causes. This appears to be most apparent in patients with certain brain diseases, following some infections, or as syndromes arising as part of an endocrinopathy. In the case of drug-induced depression, the relationship is often complicated by an earlier personal or family history of affective illness. Furthermore, in the event of depression or mania following the use of a drug, can one say with absolute certainty that it is the drug and not the disease, or the patient's response to disease, which is the prime cause of the mood disturbance? These are difficult and perplexing problems, but ones requiring answers if progress is to be made.

The existence of symptomatic affective disorders presupposes biochemical and neuroanatomical mechanisms, the disruption of which would give rise to the major signs and symptoms of psychiatric illness. It would be premature to claim that this pathogenetic relationship has been clearly demonstrated, but enough is known to make the assumption that such a relationship is a reasonable basis for explaining the nature and origins of depression occurring in the course of a physical disease.

This topic has been a major interest over a number of years, but the opportunity to consider it in depth did not come until 1978 when I was granted a period of sabbatical leave by the University of Queensland. This enabled me to write the first draft while enjoying the hospitality of Professor Sir Martin Roth at the University of Cambridge and Dr Peter Sainsbury, Director of the Medical Research Unit at Graylingwell Hospital, Chichester. I am particularly grateful to them for advice and encouragement during this period.

Progress was slowed over the next two years by the exigencies of routine work and other matters, but during this time a number of major changes and additions were made. These enabled me to include recent work which was still appearing when the final draft had been completed.

I am grateful to Professor Brian Shanley, Professor of Medical Biochemistry in the University of Queensland, for reading the earlier draft of Chapter 2 and for his critical comments. Needless to say, he is not responsible for any errors in the final draft, but as knowledge of the biochemistry of affective disorder increases almost exponentially each year, it is likely that my own writing will be outdated by the time this book gets into print. I am also grateful to Professor W. A. Lishman for permission to quote from his valuable monograph *Organic Psychiatry* (1978), which was a major stimulus to my own writing. I also acknowledge permission from the publishers and editors of the *Medical Journal of Australia* to reproduce the table from Selecki's paper which appears in Chapter 5.

Finally, I am grateful to Mrs V. Donovan, Mrs E. Poropat and Mrs B. Bratchford, who patiently and competently typed and retyped the manuscript and the long list of references. Any errors in these now must be my responsibility.

1

Symptomatic Affective Disorder: The Nature and Extent of the Problem

The numerous classifications of affective disorder pay remarkably little attention to the onset of mania and depression in association with physical disease or following the use of certain drugs. None the less, as will be shown later, some 20 to 30 per cent of patients with serious depression fall into the category of what will be referred to as symptomatic or "organic" affective disorder (D.S.M. III, Spitzer, 1978). The St. Louis group (Robins and Guze, 1972; Feighner *et al.*, 1972) used the term "secondary depression" to designate affective illnesses complicating the course of schizophrenia, alcoholism, drug addiction, psychopathy, Briquet's syndrome and a number of neuroses. However, Feighner *et al.* (1972) include under the rubric of secondary depression patients with affective illnesses in a setting of organic brain disease or with serious or incapacitating medical illnesses, as well as those whose affective disorders occur in conjunction with neurosis, personality disorder, psychosis, etc. Such a classification ignores patients whose affective illnesses appear in association with the consumption of certain drugs, or in the course of illnesses which would not generally be regarded as serious or life-threatening. On the other hand, Akiskal and McKinney (1975), in their valuable review, observe that depression can also be secondary to a number of physical illnesses. They postulate a diencephalic final common pathway for melancholia to be reached via numerous routes, clinical, experiential and behavioural. After considering the possible relationship between drugs and illness on the one hand and genetic and developmental mechanisms on the other, they comment that the mechanisms may theoretically be bypassed by

1

some stressors on account of their capacity to induce physiochemical changes of a kind regarded as important in the aetiology of affective disorder.

Clearly, despite the passage of some 50 years since the contributions of Mapother (1926) and Lewis (1934), controversy over the classification of affective disorders continues unabated. Whereas the dichotomy between "endogenous" and "reactive" depression provides a useful if somewhat illogical distinction, the place of symptomatic depression has yet to be considered. More recently attention has been given to the term "reactive mania" as applied to mania or hypomania in a setting of physical disease or in response to medication (Krauthammer and Klerman, 1978), but in what way symptomatic depression or mania relate to the broader concepts of manic-depressive psychosis has hardly been considered. For example, Kendell (1976), after reviewing the various classifications of affective illnesses, says very little about depression or mania in the course of physical disease or precipitated by drugs. Kielholz (1972) included a category of somatogenic depression, subdivided into organic and symptomatic, but it is not entirely clear what is included under this heading. Klein (1976), without giving many details, mentions organic and toxic illnesses as well as major psychotic syndromes as causes of secondary "dysphoric" disorders.

Given the fact that symptomatic affective illnesses can and do occur, it has to be admitted that their status is psychiatry is far from clear. For example, when faced by a patient with depression associated with a physical condition, how does one decide whether this implies a causal or a coincidental relationship? Is the depressed mood to be regarded as an understandable response to pain, disability and the seriousness of the prognosis? Can depression of this kind be distinguished from the normal human reactions of grief and despondency? Is it the disease or its treatment which has caused the affective change? In what percentage of patients can one say that a physical or biochemical disturbance has *caused* or *precipitated* depression in a patient who, in some hitherto undeclared way, is predisposed to this type of reaction? Is depression associated with physical illness in older patients caused more by changes occurring in the ageing brain than by the accompanying disease? Patients do not always develop physical or psychiatric disorders whose origins are unrelated to preceding or continuing psychosocial stresses. These may contribute to the affective or other psychiatric illnesses in conjunction with physical disease to a greater extent than the disease itself (Cutting, 1980). Finally, what should be the criteria for a diagnosis of symptomatic depression?

Unfortunately, although many authors mention depression as a complication of numerous medical conditions, all too often they fail to provide sufficient details to enable the reader to reach conclusions about what has been observed. Taking the criteria for primary affective illness as stated by Feighner *et al.* (1972), it seems reasonable to include as cases of symptomatic depression only those patients whose affective states constitute a syndrome rather than an isolated symptom of lowered mood. Weissman *et al.* (1977), comparing the symptoms of patients with primary and secondary depression, and using the Feighner criteria for both conditions, found little distinction between them, although patients with secondary depression appeared to be less seriously impaired. Wood *et al.* (1977) came to a similar conclusion.

In order to separate affective disorders which can be regarded as reactions to physical illness from those in which such illnesses are playing major aetiological roles, the features of the symptomatic depressions need to be clearly stated. For the purposes of further discussion the criteria for primary depression will be those resembling the symptoms and signs of patients with severe endogenous depression or the depressive phase of manic-depressive psychosis. Patients with feelings of sadness, anxiety and lack of drive in response to physical illness of some weeks' or months' duration clearly do not fall within the boundaries of endogenous depression as generally described. The major psychological symptoms will be hopelessness and despair of a fairly unremitting kind, psychomotor agitation or retardation, impaired concentration, loss of interest in normal pursuits, feelings of guilt and self-reproach with, in some patients, suicidal thoughts or behaviour. They may also develop frank delusional symptoms generally referring to their bodily state or sense of unworthiness. In addition, they will experience fatigue, weakness, anorexia, marked loss of weight, a characteristic disturbance of sleep, decline in sexual activity and, particularly in older patients, constipation. It must be admitted that many of these so-called vegetative symptoms can equally well be caused by major physical disease but, when combined with at least five of the psychological symptoms, a diagnosis of an endogenous-type depression can be safely made. Physically ill patients who do not show these features should not be classed as suffering from symptomatic depression even when they experience a down-turn in spirits as a transitory or more persistent mood change. In these patients, anxiety and evidence of a vulnerable, unstable personality prone to respond adversely to misfortune and difficulties in the past may provide useful clues to the reactive nature of their symptoms.

Two other issues need to be discussed in some detail before considering the symptomatic depression syndrome in the context of specific physical disorders: the frequency of the condition and its relationship to the major categories of affective illness.

The incidence of physically caused depression varies considerably according to the author and the period when observations were made. For example, Kraepelin (1921) claimed that depression in male patients was associated with alcoholism in 25 per cent and with syphilis in 8 per cent. In contrast, one finds Bonhoeffer (1909, 1912), in his discussion of exogenous reactions, declaring that pure depressive states of exogenous origin presenting with the symptomatology of the depressive phase of manic-depressive psychosis are extremely rare. He stated that he had never come across such a case which he could so categorize with certainty. Such an observation would hardly be confirmed today, although Kielholz (1959) felt that only in 5 per cent of patients did somatic factors appear to be causes or precipitants. Herridge (1960), surveying the frequency of physical disorders in 209 psychiatric patients, found that 58 had endogenous and 22 reactive depressions. Twenty-one per cent of the total number of patients were considered to be psychiatrically ill partly on account of their physical illnesses. Eleven patients presented as "functional" syndromes but were found to have physical illnesses. Of these, 4 were depressed, 2 of whom had undiagnosed neoplasms, with the other 2 suffering from presenile dementia and cerebrovascular disease respectively. G. P. Maguire and Granville-Grossman (1968) examined 200 psychiatric admissions of whom 54 were severely and 41 moderately depressed. Sixty-seven patients had physical as well as psychiatric illnesses, a finding which increased with the ages of the patients. Twenty-one of the 54 depressed patients had physical illnesses of varying degrees of severity and seriousness, but the relationship between the two conditions was not discussed beyond noting that those with organic brain disease had a higher incidence of physical illness. Mitchell-Heggs (1971), in her study of 200 depressed patients, found that 20 per cent had developed a physical illness within 8 weeks prior to the onset of depression, and Koranyi (1979), in an investigation of 2,090 psychiatric clinic patients, found that 43 per cent were also suffering from one or more physical disorders, half of which had not been diagnosed by the referring agency. Sixty-nine per cent of these physical illnesses were contributing significantly to the aetiology of the psychiatric symptoms. In 18 per cent of the patients the physical condition was considered to be the sole cause of the psychiatric disorder. The percentage of patients with depressive illnesses was not stated. Hays (1980), who examined 150 patients with typical features of endogenous depression, found that 19 had become ill during the puerperium, 5 were depressed in association with menopausal symptoms, 3 were taking reserpine, one was on sulfonamides, one patient had recurrent pancreatitis, while 14 had sustained preceding brain damage from strokes or head injuries. Thus, nearly one-third of these cases of "endogenous" depression originated with a physical condition or use of a drug known to cause depression in some patients.

Looking at the problem from the point of view of the general physician, Schwab *et al.* (1967) reported on 153 medical patients and, using clinical assessment and rating scales, found that 22 per cent were depressed, a figure rather lower than the 28.7 per cent obtained by Moffic and Paykel (1975), who examined 150 medical inpatients. Twenty-six had affective illnesses secondary to their physical disorders, but they had less frequently suffered from depression in the past. The patients with physical illnesses were less severely depressed and suicidal, although the physical signs and symptoms of depression were much the same as those observed in endogenous depression. Altschule (1975), after reviewing current biochemical theories of affective disorder, commented on the frequency of depression in patients on certain drugs or suffering from a variety of central nervous system, endocrine and metabolic diseases.

On the evidence presented it appears that some 20 to 30 per cent of patients with endogenous-type depressions will also have one or more physical conditions which might be contributing wholly or partly to the aetiology of the psychiatric illness.

The question of whether the physical illness causes or precipitates depression in predisposed patients must now be considered. Pollitt (1972), who compared patients with endogenous ("physiological") depression following physical disturbances with those whose illnesses followed psychological stress, found a lower genetic loading in the physically caused depressions. Patients aged 35 and over also had less frequent family histories of affective disorder. In an earlier study, Pollitt (1971a) commented that the symptomatology of patients with physically precipitated depression did not differ from those with psychologically caused illnesses. He also found (1971b) that depression in patients aged 40 and over, compared with younger patients, was more likely to be caused by physical than psychological factors. Despite these findings, Pollitt appears to regard depression following physical illness as being precipitated rather than caused by infections, endocrine disorders, drugs, etc. (Pollitt, 1965). This surely presupposes a significant genetic or constitutional loading in such cases, although this appears not invariably to be the case. Other writers (Roth and Kay, 1956; Post, 1969; Mendelewicz, 1976) appear to agree that patients who develop depression in later life are more likely to do so in association with physical disease and will have lower genetic loadings for affective illness than younger patients.

Winokur *et al.* (1969) also considered physical factors to be precipitants rather than essential causes and, in patients with puerperal depression, those with a previous history of manic-depressive psychosis were more liable to recurrences after delivery. Other writers tend to regard depression in a setting of major physical diseases as an understandable response to the illnesses (Stewart *et al.*, 1965). In some cases the quality of depression appears to be less severe when compared with patients with the depressive phase of manic-depressive psychosis. Suicidal ideation and behaviour, for example, are unusual. Lloyd (1977) listed a number of possible relationships between psychiatric and physical illness but concentrated mainly on the possibility that the physical disorder uncovered some latent predisposition to psychiatric illness; in short, that it acted as a precipitant rather than as an essential cause.

Nonetheless, regardless of the precise relationship, this matter, as Klerman (1975) points out, is one of some importance. "Theoretically," he writes, "the secondary depressions are of tremendous research significance." He goes on to elaborate on how better understanding of drug and endocrine disturbances might provide some clues to the possible pathogenesis of other types of affective disorder. This whole problem is given further consideration by Roth (1977, p. 190) when he notes the frequency of depression following viral infections, as part of an endocrinopathy or as a consequence of certain drugs. "Many of those affected," he writes, "have no previous experience of psychiatric disorder nor any history of it in their family. The remission that follows in the wake of treatment will be complete and depressive symptoms in such cases generally do not occur until, perhaps, a further attack of infectious disease." If this is correct, it does appear that in some instances the physical disease or drug is an essential cause rather than a precipitant, but a clear-cut either-or relationship is improbable. It remains to be seen what kind of relationships can be detected in a very large number of physical disorders associated with major affective disturbances.

2

Symptomatic Affective Disorder: Some Anatomical and Biochemical Considerations

Regardless of other factors, it is a reasonable presumption that the onset of a symptomatic affective disorder will probably be the result of some structural or functional alteration in the brain. Consequently, a discussion of the neuroanatomical and biochemical substrates of affect and its expression might provide some understanding of the pathogenesis of affective states following damage to or temporary functional impairment of the central nervous system. Nevertheless, the heterogeneous nature of affective disorders implies that any explanation of their origins solely in terms of neuroanatomy and biochemistry will be inadequate.

NEUROANATOMY

It is generally agreed that the limbic system as described by Papez (1937) and MacLean (1955) is the area most concerned with the expression and experience of emotional states. The essential elements of the system have been described in detail by a number of authors (Fulton, 1951; Smythies, 1966; Girgis, 1971; Kelly, 1973). From the point of view of affective disorder, the areas of particular significance are the orbital surface of the frontal lobe, the cingulate gyrus, the dorsomedial nucleus of the thalamus and the hypothalamus. The orbital surface of the frontal lobe receives afferent fibres from the dorsomedial nucleus of the thalamus while its efferent connections are mainly with the hypothalamus and reticular formation via the medial forebrain bundle. It also projects via the cingulum to the hippocampus. The cingulate gyrus receives fibres from the anterior nuclei of the thalamus and from the orbitofrontal cortex. It projects to the anterior and other thalamic nuclei, and also to the hippocampus and hypothalamus.

According to Girgis (1977, p. 14), "The functional importance of the dorsomedial thalamic nuclei would seem to depend very largely upon their connections with both higher and lower brain centres. In other words, they provide a mechanism whereby the highest functional levels of the brain are enabled to control the more primitive elements of mental activity such as emotional reactions and instinctive impulses". Kelly (1973) comments on how the functions of the limbic system are modulated by higher cortical control, particularly from the frontal lobe. It is known that severance of connections between the frontal lobe and the limbic system is sometimes effective in cases of intractable anxiety and depression. Stimulation of different parts of the Papez circuit results in affective and autonomic changes. The cingulate gyrus, with its connections with the rest of the circuit, is of particular significance as excision of this part of the brain will also cut its connections with the orbito-frontal cortex and has been shown to be of value in relieving the symptoms of severe and intractable depression. Whereas the older prefrontal leucotomy sometimes abolished symptoms of depression, its unwanted consequences in terms of major personality change led to more accurate localization of areas in the frontal lobe whose excision or severance would produce the desired therapeutic effects without causing permanent, unwanted changes of personality and behaviour. Initially, orbital under-cutting or limited section through the lower medial quadrant were effective in the treatment of depression, anxiety and obsessional neuroses. In addition, ablation of the anterior part of the cingulate gyrus was sometimes successful. More recently, the operation of subcaudate stereotactic tractotomy, which divides connections between the anterior cingulate region and posterior fronto-orbital cortex, as well as fronto-hypothalamic fibres, has produced good results in 50–60 per cent of cases of severe depression. The fact that such a lesion is effective still leaves us some distance from understanding the precise origins of depressive states and the way in which they are related to the controlling action of the neocortex upon the limbic system as a whole.

Smythies (1966, p. 12) has speculated that "if the physiological malfunction of depression has its main locus in the amygdala or hypothalamus this may send 'depression laden' abnormal schemata around the meta-organizational system in which the hippocampal circuits are inseparably entwined". He considers that this might be the anatomical substrate for delusional beliefs of guilt, etc. This may be correct, but it still leaves more or less unexplained what part is being played by the orbitofrontal cortex and cingulate gyrus in originating and perpetuating severe depression. Notwithstanding the controlling and modulating effects these areas may have on the limbic mechanisms, causing profound disturbance of sleep, appetite and weight, as well as a number of important endocrine changes, it is still unknown how these influences become pathological and why the division of fibres to and from these areas sometimes gives the most gratifying relief for patients who may have been incurably ill for years. A better understanding of the process may be provided by considering the central role of the hypothalamus as the core of the mechanism of emotional expression. Of particular relevance are the connections between the posterior orbital gyri and the hypothalamus, as cutting these fibres abolishes a number of autonomic effects in experimental animals (Fulton, 1951). It must also be noted that the principal septal nuclei in man are located in the postero-medial part of the orbital surface of the frontal lobe with connections to other structures in the limbic system. As Smythies writes (1966, p. 22), "The main septal region in man is not the thin septum pellucidum . . . but it is the subcallosal (para-olfactory) area, a small region under the corpus callosum on the medial aspect of the frontal lobe. The human homologue of the lateral septal nuclei in animals is the thin plate of grey matter on the lateral surface of the septum pellucidum." The septal region has two-way connections with the hippocampus, amygdala, hypothalamus and reticular formation; also, by the stria medullaris, to the reticular formation and to the amygdala via the diagonal band of Broca. It connects directly with the dorsomedial and other thalamic nuclei.

On the basis of the inter-connections between the cingulum, the orbital surface of the frontal lobe, the hypothalamus and other parts of the limbic system, it is reasonable to conclude that these interconnections play an important part in controlling emotional expression and experience. Dividing these connections by placing lesions under the head of the caudate nucleus has been of value for the relief of severe depression and anxiety states. Precisely how or why these areas of the frontal and cingulate cortex influence these affective states is far from clear, but as understanding of the relationship between psychic function and brain mechanism is very imperfect, our failure to determine the neural basis of severe affective disorders is not entirely surprising.

BIOCHEMISTRY

Although relatively little attention has been given in recent times to the anatomical substrate of affective disorder, the same cannot be said for biochemical disturbances associated with severe depression or mania. Following the introduction of antidepressant drugs, attention has been concentrated on changes in neurotransmitters which might be influenced by these drugs. There is, of course, nothing new about this, as ill-defined changes in the blood and brain were regarded as causes of melancholia by writers like Laurentius, Willis and Boerhaave (Jobe 1976). In the past 15 years a number of theories involving transmitter amines in the brain have been propounded as explanations of the aetiology of affective disorders and their responses to treatment with antidepressant drugs. Of these theories, the well known biogenic amine theory correlating depression with deficiencies in catechol-amines and indole-amines in the brain (Schildkraut, 1965; Coppen, 1967) continues to be widely but not uncritically accepted. An alternative hypothesis put forward by Janowsky *et al.* (1972), supported by a good deal of circumstantial evidence, suggests that an imbalance between adrenergic and cholinergic mechanisms resulting in a preponderance of adrenergic or cholinergic activity is the cause of mood changes of the manic-depressive kind. Dopamine, in comparison with its possible role in the aetiology of schizophrenia, has been relatively neglected as a biochemical variable in depression but, as Van Praag (1978) has stated, there are sufficient indications to justify further research on this substance. Changes in electrolytes, particularly sodium and calcium (Coppen, 1965; Frizel *et al.*, 1969; Carman *et al.*, 1977), may be directly relevant, although some could well be secondary to more fundamental endocrine changes involving the hypothalamic–pituitary axis (Carroll, 1977). The great interest shown recently in the endorphins and enkephalins might throw additional light on the aetiology of affective disorders. Genetic factors are fundamental to the biochemical abnormalities thought to be causes of mood change. The evidence for the inheritance of major affective disorders has been fully assessed by many investigators and for that reason alone consideration of the family histories of patients with symptomatic depression or mania is of considerable importance. Aberrant enzyme activity in the brains of these patients, resulting in deficiencies of transmitter amines, is likely to be genetically determined unless directly affected by abnormal metabolites, drugs or poisons.

Although it is not proposed that the numerous biochemical theories should be discussed in detail, it is essential that they should be considered critically so that some of their short-comings can be evaluated. Before doing so, however, it is worth examining the various cerebral structures and their connections which have specific neurotransmitters for their functions. A number of writers have reviewed these pathways (Lloyd, 1978; Farley *et al.*, 1978; Morgane and Stern, 1974; Curzon, 1976).

Neurotransmitter Pathways

Curzon has briefly outlined some of the structures and pathways with specific neurotransmitters.

Noradrenalin

Two ascending systems arise, one from cells in the medulla and pons terminating in the lower brain stem, mid-brain and diencephalon, the other originating in the locus coeruleus which connects with the lower brain stem, cerebellum, the cortex and the hippocampus. This system appears to have an important role in arousal and sleep mechanisms.

Dopamine

Fibres arising from the substantia nigra ascend through the hypothalamus to terminate in the caudate nucleus and putamen, which contain the greatest dopamine fraction of the brain. A second pathway, the mesolimbic tract, originating from cells dorsal to the nucleus interpeduncularis terminates in the nucleus accumbens and olfactory tubercle. The third tract, the tubero-infundibular system arising from the hypothalamus innervates the external layer of the median emminence. Its function is intimately concerned with the control and release of a number of pituitary hormones.

5-Hyrodxytryptamine (5-HT or Serotonin)

Serotonergic fibres originate from the median raphe nuclei in the pons and mid-brain to terminate in the hypothalamus and preoptic area. Lateral ascending pathways terminate in the cortex and caudate nuclei.

Acetylcholine

Morgane and Stern (1974), who have described cholinergic pathways, observe that cortical arousal is attended by an increased release of acetylcholine from the cerebral cortex. Cholinergic mechanisms are found in the brain stem and basal forebrain areas and along the forebrain–limbic–mid-brain circuits. Cholinergic tracts of the ascending reticular system can be divided into the dorsal and ventral tegmental pathways. The former of these terminate in the tectal, pretectal, geniculate and thalamic areas, whereas the latter connect with, amongst other structures, the hypothalamus and basal area of the forebrain. The forebrain cortex is innervated by cholinergic fibres.

In discussing the cholinergic limbic system Morgane and Stern note a close relationship between the ascending reticular system and the hippocampus, whose out-flow is mainly non-cholinergic, although this impinges on cholinergic cells whose efferent fibres will also be cholinergic. Such pathways connect with the forebrain and mid-brain, but at present relatively little is known about the interaction between adrenergic and cholinergic mechanisms in the hypothalamus. It has been claimed that cholinergic neurones localized in the medial aspect of the septum connect with the hippocampus, but there are additional monoaminergic fibres ending in the septum. In this context De Feudis (1974) has observed that destruction of the septum in rats leads to a decrease in acetylcholine with a concomitant effect on emotionality. The function of the septum may involve reciprocal relationships between cholinergic and adrenergic mechanisms and, as such, may be relevant to the concept that affective disorders are due to a relative loss of adrenergic activity with a preponderance of cholinergic activity in the limbic brain and, more particularly, in the hypothalamus. The element of speculation in such an hypothesis must be acknowledged, although recent work (Carroll *et al.*, 1980a) gives it some experimental support.

In summary, there is strong evidence for the existence of adrenergic, serotonergic and cholinergic mechanisms in the limbic brain and its connections, but at this stage the precise inter-relationships between these systems and their relevance to severe depression are uncertain. For better understanding we must now consider some of the current biochemical theories of depression and mania with particular attention being paid to the functions of noradrenalin, 5-hydroxytryptamine, acetylcholine, electrolytes, the neuro-endocrine changes associated with depression and, more speculatively still, the roles of the opiate peptides which have receptor neurons in the limbic brain and hypothalamus (Extein *et al.*, 1980).

Chemical Transmitters

Noradrenalin

Simply put, it is postulated that depression is a consequence of a functional depletion of noradrenalin at synaptic–receptor sites in the brain and that mania develops when there is an excess of this transmitter amine. Quite obviously such a theory is far too simple to explain all the varying facets of affective disorder. Nonetheless, although the theory, as originally formulated, is no longer accepted in unmodified form, it continues to have a profound influence on current thinking about the biochemical basis of affective disturbance.

Observations on the effects of certain drugs on mood led to investigations of their actions on the biochemistry of the central nervous system. Reserpine, for example, which depletes catecholamines in the brain, causes depression in about 10–15 per cent of patients. It was also found that drugs used in the treatment of tuberculosis, such as isoniazid and iproniazid, had euphoriant effects. They were found to inhibit the activity of monoamine oxidase. In initial trials of monoamine-oxidase inhibiting drugs, relief of depression in some patients undoubtedly occurred, the consequence, it was thought, of decreased destruction of catecholamine transmitters leaving greater amounts available in the synaptic cleft. In addition, the tricyclic antidepressant drugs were found to inhibit the re-uptake of catecholamine neurotransmitters, again with beneficial results in patients who more often showed the features of endogenous or vital depression. It seemed logical in the face of this evidence to conclude that catecholamines, particularly noradrenalin, if depleted, would lead to depression, whereas correction of this deficit by drugs would reverse the course of the illness.

There are some fairly formidable objections to such an hypothesis, and for consideration of these the reader is referred to the numerous reviews on the topic (Baldessarini, 1975a, 1975b; Akiskal and McKinney, 1975; Green and Costain, 1979; Berger and Barchas, 1975). It is enough at this point to comment that reserpine, which not only depletes catecholamines and serotonin, but also releases acetylcholine in the brain, was more likely to cause depression in patients with a past personal history or family history of affective disorder. In other patients a picture of apathy, fatigue and inertia, the direct consequences of the sedative action of the drug, could easily be mistaken for depression. Tricyclic antidepressants also have pronounced anticholinergic actions, sufficient at least to leave room for argument that, in conjunction with their amine reuptake-blocking effect, the benefit observed in depressed patients could be caused partly by the correction of an imbalance between noradrenergic and cholinergic mechanisms, particularly in the hypothalamus and limbic brain. Furthermore, although tricyclic antidepressants such as imipramine and amitriptyline block the re-uptake of indole and catecholamines, the newer antidepressants such as mianserin and iprindole do not. Mianserin, in comparison with amitriptyline, etc., also has considerably fewer anticholinergic effects. Nevertheless, both mianserin and iprindole are effective antidepressants, but their precise modes of action are not fully understood.

Selective reduction of catecholamine synthesis by alpha–methyl para-tyrosine (AMPT) does not, according to Mendels (1974), cause depression in medical patients, although it can cause sedation and fatigue. On the other hand, this substance aggravated the condition of three depressed patients and also had some beneficial effects on manic patients. However, as Baldessarini comments (1975a, p. 385) "In relation to the basic biology of behaviour and psychiatric illness it also seems that aminergic systems are particularly likely to be involved if only secondarily or incidently in disturbances of mood, drive, initiative, sleep and diurnal rhythmicity, as well as hypothalamic–adrenal functions . . .". But, as he goes on to point out, "One very broad criticism of the amine hypotheses is that they have often not adequately taken into account the physiology of central neurotransmitters; a consequence of the relatively primitive state of our knowledge of their functions."

Dopamine

In contrast with noradrenalin there is relatively little evidence of changes in dopaminergic activity in patients with severe depression. Clearly this is very different from the part thought to be played by dopamine in schizophrenia and Parkinson's disease, but giving L-dopa to depressed patients is of no obvious benefit (Klerman *et al.*, 1963). Van Praag *et al.* (1975) have shown that treating depressed patients with dopamine improves motor retardation without obvious benefits to their psychological status. Dopamine inhibits prolactin-releasing factor, but tricyclic antidepressants do not affect prolactin levels in man (Melzer, 1980) so presumably dopaminergic release of prolactin is not altered by antidepressant drugs. In any case there is no clear evidence that prolactin plays any significant role in the aetiology of depression, and Sachar *et al.* (1973) concluded that high prolactin levels in some depressed patients were non-specific responses to stress as shown by rises in this hormone after electroconvulsive therapy (ECT) (Öhman *et al.*, 1976; O'Dea *et al.*, 1978). However, it is worth mentioning that dopamine levels are high in the nucleus accumbens, the lateral hypothalamus and diencephalon (Farley *et al.*, 1978), all areas concerned with neuroendocrine and emotional control.

5-Hydroxytryptamine (5-HT or Serotonin)

5-HT has been the other main contender for a primary role in the aetiology of depression. As originally formulated, it was considered that a loss of available serotonin at the synapse was the basic biochemical lesion but, as Baldessarini has commented (1975b), more recent work suggests that behavioural depressant effects are associated with an *excess* of that transmitter amine, whereas decreased availability is associated with a variety of "excited" behaviours. An alternative point of view proposed by Van Praag and de Haan (1980) is that, although depression can hardly be regarded as a homogeneous diagnostic entity, in some patients with vital (endogenous) depression there is a persistent defect in available 5-HT which can be corrected by clomipramine, a strong inhibitor of 5-HT re-uptake. Presumably, once again, one has to seek a genetic basis for such a defect, as parachlorphenylalanine (PCPA), a selective inhibitor of tryptophan hydroxylase, the rate-limiting enzyme in the synthesis of 5-HT from tryptophan, does not generally cause depression despite the lowering of 5-HT in the brain.

Three studies have claimed that levels of 5-HT are diminished in brains of suicides obtained post mortem (Shaw *et al.*, 1967; Pare *et al.*, 1969; Lloyd *et al.*, 1974), but other investigators (Beskow *et al.*, 1976; Gottfries, 1980) have been unable to confirm these findings. No doubt technical and methodological difficulties are likely to affect results from studies of this kind.

Serotonin also plays a part in the release of various pituitary hormones. Loading doses of 5-HT can release growth hormone, which is also under dopaminergic control, but this response is decreased in depressed patients. Similarly, growth hormone release in response to amphetamines is diminished in depressed patients (Brown and Seggie, 1980). Sachar *et al.* (1980a) have pointed out that 5-HT and acetylcholine stimulate the release of cortisol via the hypothalamic corticotropin-releasing factor (CRF), but that 5-HT is not increased in depression. Hence, it is difficult to account for the abnormal cortisol levels in depressed patients by reference to the possible actions of 5-HT in the hypothalamus. If noradrenalin is the amine responsible, along with gamma-aminobutyric acid (GABA), for the inhibition of CRF in the hypothalamus, one can hardly hold a *deficiency* of 5-HT responsible for increased cortisol release in depression. An observation which is not in keeping with an excess of 5-HT being a major cause of depression is that slow-wave sleep appears to be under the control of serotonergic mechanisms in the brain stem and hypothalamus and that one of the more characteristic symptoms of severe depression is a relative loss of stage 4 slow-wave sleep. In this context the finding by Lloyd *et al.* (1974) of reduced levels of 5-HT in the median raphe nuclei might be particularly relevant. Furthermore, Carlsson *et al.* (1980) have demonstrated seasonal and circadian levels of 5-HT in the hypothalamus and that the circadian changes have a reciprocal relationship with cortisol secretion. Possibly noradrenaline and 5-HT are involved in the release of cortisol via hypothalamic activity.

Although Van Praag (1977) favours a serotonergic defect as having a particular significance for the aetiology of depression, he also points out that considering this transmitter amine alone without reference to other substances probably does scant justice to the complexity of the biochemical basis of affective disorders. Hence, he favours a monoaminergic "profile" as one likely to be more fruitful. Furthermore, whereas a deficiency of serotonin in one part of the brain (e.g. brain stem) might be responsible for some depressive symptoms, an excess in other areas may contribute to disturbed hypothalamic function in depressed patients.

Acetylcholine

Acetylcholine is widely distributed in the central nervous system, being particularly high in the limbic system and nucleus accumbens. Antipsychotic drugs increase acetylcholine turnover and release in the striatum due to inhibition of dopaminergic receptors but not in the limbic region (Lloyd, 1978). Rather surprisingly, up to relatively recent times, cholinergic mechanisms were not thought to play any significant role in the aetiology of affective disorder until Janowsky *et al.* (1972) proposed that an imbalance between adrenergic and cholinergic mechanisms, resulting in a relative excess or defect of available noradrenaline, could explain some of the phenomena of mania and depression. This is similar to the disparity between acetylcholine and dopamine in the pathogenesis of Parkinsonism (Hornykiewicz, 1966), and it is worth commenting on the high incidence of depression in Parkinsonian patients possibly caused by an imbalance between noradrenalin and acetylcholine in the striatum and nucleus accumbens. There is clinical evidence showing that the administration of anticholinesterases such as physostigmine will ameliorate symptoms of mania and aggravate those of depression (Rowntree *et al.*, 1950; Bowers *et al.*, 1964; Oppenheim *et al.*, 1979), and that giving choline, an acetylcholine precursor, will cause severe depression in some patients (Tamminga *et al.*, 1976). Fink (1966) has reviewed evidence for ECT being followed by a release of acetylcholine into the CSF with a corresponding fall in acetylcholine levels in the brain and, more recently, Checkley (1980) has discussed the mechanisms controlling the release of growth hormone, prolactin and adrenocorticotropic hormone (ACTH), and other hormones, where the findings tend to favour overactivity of cholinergic and a defect of alpha-adrenoceptor functions in patients with endogenous depression, but not in those with reactive (neurotic) depression.

Girgis (1979) has shown that amitriptyline and scopolamine will reduce high voltage spike-and-wave discharges induced by an anticholinesterase substance, physostigmine, injected intracerebrally into the septum, amygdaloid and other limbic areas in experimental animals. The precise significance of these experiments for the role of acetylcholine in ordinary depression is uncertain, although they could well be relevant to the episodic affective psychoses described by Monroe (1979).

Additional data supporting the cholinergic theory of affective disorder come from a recent study by Carroll *et al.* (1980b), who gave physostigmine to a group of healthy volunteers and found that this resulted in a rise in cortisol previously suppressed by dexamethasone. They concluded that acetylcholine has some part to play in maintaining the abnormal cortisol levels in patients with endogenous depression, but that its site of impact might be at some point in the limbic system higher than the median eminence of the hypothalamus.

Electrolytes

Electrolyte changes in affective disorder have been reviewed by Baer (1973), who found that most studies show that sodium is retained during depression with reversion to normal when the patient recovers. Coppen (1965) found a high residual, probably intracellular, sodium in depression and also in mania, and Coppen and Shaw (1963) discovered that there was a significant decrease in intracellular sodium on recovery from depression. Baer *et al.* (1970) also found sodium retention in depression, with loss of sodium on recovery without any significant changes in potassium. Lithium treatment, on the other hand, resulted in a loss of water, sodium and potassium. To what extent these changes in sodium are primary or secondary to endocrine change is far from clear, and although abnormalities in sodium and potassium are associated with a variety of psychiatric syndromes, particularly in older patients (Taylor 1979), their mode of action is obscure.

The role of calcium in depression has been considered by Carman *et al.* (1977), who recorded a fall in CSF and serum calcium after a short course of ECT. It is known that the high levels of serum calcium found in patients with parathyroid tumours can be associated with major depressive symptoms and that reduction of calcium following removal of the tumour appears to correlate well with improvement in mood (Jimerson *et al.*, 1979). Frizel *et al.* (1969) observed a fall in magnesium in patients treated with ECT but no changes in calcium. Fink and Ottosson (1980), when propounding a theory of the effects of ECT in patients with endogenous depression, comment that calcium is essential for the metabolism and release of hypothalamic and pituitary hormones. ECT causes a fall in extracellular calcium which may be associated with a rise in intracellular calcium. This, however, could be but one of the mechanisms affected by ECT, and there is no clear reason for singling out a change in calcium metabolism as the sole, or even the major, contribution to the aetiology of depression.

Histamine

The possible role of histamine as a neurotransmitter and, therefore, as a putative contributor to the biochemistry of affective disorder has only recently been considered. Rand and McCulloch (1977) mention that tricyclic antidepressants block histamine receptor sites and Kanof and Greengard (1978) found that both iprindole and mianserin shared this property. Histamine-sensitive adenylate cyclase is present in the hippocampus and neocortex. Its activity is blocked by the H2 receptor antagonist, metiamide. All antidepressants and some phenothiazines block H2 receptors, but it would be premature to suggest that antidepressant drugs exert their effects through this mechanism. In any case, cimetidine, which is said not to cross the blood–brain barrier, can apparently precipitate depression in some patients taking it for the treatment of peptic ulcer (see Chapter 8).

Endorphins and Enkephalins

The very great interest shown in endogenous opioids since their discovery by Hughes *et al.* in 1975 inevitably has led to speculation about their possible role in the aetiology of the functional psychoses. Evidence scattered through the scientific literature gives some indication of endorphins being involved in the aetiology of affective disorders, but it would be unrealistic to say at this stage that any clear linkage has been demonstrated. The following observations may be relevant.

(a) Guillemin *et al.* (1977) found that both beta-endorphin and ACTH are secreted together by the pituitary gland in response to stress. Indeed, as Cleghorn (1980) has commented, this makes physiological sense in terms of the body's preparedness to cope with a stress. Both substances appear to originate from the same precursor molecule present in the same cells in the anterior pituitary.

(b) The distribution of endorphins and enkephalins corresponds closely with the distribution of opiate receptor sites in the brain, but there appear to be at least two types of receptor (Kosterlitz, 1979). Beta-endorphin receptors are found in the hypothalamic–pituitary axis and in the mid-line regions of the diencephalon and anterior pons, whereas the short-chain enkephalins are more widely distributed in the brain. Snyder (1978) has also commented on the diverse functions of opiate receptors, with some being concerned with the modification of pain and others with mood. Exogenous opiates produce at least two effects, relief of pain and euphoria, but there is very little indication that the euphoriant effect is of any value in the treatment of severe depression.

(c) There is evidence that relatively small quantities of tricylic antidepressants can relieve chronic pain secondary to diabetic neuropathy (Davis *et al.*, 1977; Gade *et al.*, 1980; Massey and Riley, 1980; Turkington, 1980), post-herpetic neuralgia (Woodforde *et al.*, 1965; Mersky and Hester, 1972; Taub, 1973; Castaigne *et al.*, 1979), terminal cancer (Hugues *et al.*, 1963; Kocher, 1976; Kocher, 1978; Ribèyre and Facchin, 1979) and severe arthritis (MacDonald Scott, 1969; Gringras, 1976). The possible mechanisms underlying this phenomenon have been discussed in a number of reviews (Sternbach *et al.*, 1976; Lee and Spencer, 1977; Clarke, 1979; Gonzalez *et al.*, 1980; Whitlock, in press), and it appears that drugs such as zimelidine and clomipramine, which are more potent inhibitors of presynaptic uptake of 5-HT, are most effective for the treatment of intractable pain, whereas drugs like mianserin and maprotiline, which inhibit the reuptake of noradrenalin, are less useful. Johansson *et al.* (1980) report that zimelidine causes a reduction in CSF levels of endorphins and 5-hydroxyindoleacetic acid (5-HIAA) with concomitant relief of symptoms in some patients with intractable pain. Pain perception can also be reduced by giving a 5-HT precursor such as l-tryptophan (King, 1980) which also potentiates endogenous opioids (Lee *et al.*, 1979), whereas reserpine, which lowers both noradrenalin and 5-HT in the brain, increases pain awareness and accelerates tolerance to morphine (Sparkes and Spencer, 1971). In contrast, noradrenalin reduces the antinocioceptive effect of morphine, so that drugs like maprotiline and mianserin, understandably, do not benefit patients with chronic pain. The possibility that dopaminergic mechanisms are involved is raised by the apparent usefulness of nomifensine whose main effect is on dopaminergic activity (Gonzalez *et al.*, 1980).

(d) Although Almay *et al.* (1978) claim that patients with psychogenic pain have higher CSF levels of endorphins than patients with organic pain, there is no evidence that the measurements in the psychogenic patients were higher than those in healthy volunteers. They also claim that the endorphin levels in the patients were correlated with the degree of depression in these patients, but as the term "depression" in this context is unclear, one might conclude that a full-blown syndrome of endogenous depression was not present. On the other hand, Lindström *et al.* (1978) found that patients with manic-depressive psychosis had greater amounts of CSF endorphins than normal volunteers, with the highest measurements being made in patients with mania. This is a rather paradoxical finding, bearing in mind the frequency with which depressed patients complain of pain. Ward *et al.* (1979) found that all 17 of their patients with unipolar depression had at least one chronic pain symptom with headache predominating. The origin of the raised levels of endorphins in affective disorder is unclear, but could, one might speculate, be associated with the increased ACTH secretion found in a percentage of depressed patients. Gerner *et al.* (1980), after reviewing some of these rather conflicting findings, treated 10 depressed patients with intravenous endorphin and obtained a temporary improvement which was better than intravenous placebo. On the other hand, a similar study by Kline *et al.* (1977), who treated three depressed patients with endorphins, could hardly be said to be successful as any changes observed were transitory and were not repeated with second courses of the peptide. Terenius *et al.* (1977) gave naloxone to a small number of depressed patients refractory to treatment with ECT and clomipramine but obtained no clear benefits; rather, the patients' depression worsened. Biegon and Samuel (1980) note that tricyclic antidepressants bind to a number of brain receptors and can be displaced by naloxone or morphine. In experimental animals tricyclic antidepressants raise pain thresholds, but possibly species' differences might explain the association of apparently lowered pain thresholds in depressed patients with raised CSF endorphins. At this stage it seems likely that tricyclic antidepressants and endorphins have at least two functions which are not necessarily related to one another. Pain relief is clearly mediated by both substances, but whether excess endorphines cause depression has yet to be determined. A pointer to this possibility comes from the report by Pullan *et al.* (1980) who describe three patients with Cushing's syndrome caused by ectopic ACTH secretion from carcinoid tumours. One patient was manic and the other two seriously depressed. In conjunction with the raised ACTH, increased levels of beta-endorphin and methionine enkephalin were found in the carcinoid tissue. When the tumours were removed, the psychiatric symptoms and features of Cushing's syndrome cleared up. The authors consider the possibility that the high levels of endorphin and enkephalin in these tumours would modify the patient's experience of pain. On the other hand, their affective psychoses could be related either to the high endorphin and enkephalin output or to the other hormonal disturbances occurring as part of the Cushing's syndrome.

Additional evidence in support of differential effects of endorphins in depression comes from the study of Gold *et al.* (1980). Giving intravenous methadone to a number of depressed patients resulted in a fall in the abnormally high levels of cortisol in these patients. This was greater than the fall in cortisol following placebo injection. Possibly methadone and, one might presume, endogenous opiates can cause a negative feedback effect on the hypothalamic–pituitary axis, although if this was the case the higher levels of endorphins observed in depressed patients by the Swedish investigators should correct this abnormality, unless they are secondary to events occurring in some other region of the limbic brain where opiate receptors are also present. Possibly these can regulate catecholaminergic transmitter systems. Giving morphine to depressed patients does not cause a rise in prolactin output in contrast with normal volunteers (Extein *et al.*, 1980). This seems to indicate some failure in noradrenergic and serotonergic receptors which are said to modulate prolactin secretion, although this is inhibited in the first place by dopamine.

On balance the evidence for any direct relationship between endorphins, depression and antidepressant drugs is tenuous. If antidepressant drugs can relieve severe intractable pain in a time as short as 48–72 hours when given in relatively s nall a nounts (e.g. 10–25 mg of amitriptyline three times daily), it seems improbable that the relief is brought about solely by the drug's antidepressant properties. There is no clear evidence that endorphins or enkephalins are relevant to the pathogenesis of depression, although possibly potentiation of serotonin availability by antidepressants is sufficient to boost the action of endogenous opioids without the need for a prior alteration of mood. At present, therefore, one has to conclude that endorphins and enkephalins are not important contributors to the biochemical aetiology of affective disorder.

ENDOCRINE CHANGES IN DEPRESSION

The profound physiological changes associated with severe depression imply disturbances of hypothalamic function and endocrine activity. Consequently, it is not surprising that a good deal of attention has been paid to alterations in hormonal secretion, an area of research which has increased now that it has become possible to measure very small quantities of hormones and hypothalamic peptides controlling pituitary activity.

Of the various hormones whose output is known to change in severe depression, cortisol is of particular importance. This topic has been fully reviewed by Sachar (1975) and by Carroll (1976b, 1977), and for fuller details the reader is referred to these papers. The most frequently discussed abnormality involving cortisol secretion in depressed patients is the failure of levels to fall during the night-time hours and a lack of response to dexamethasone suppression in about 50 per cent of patients. Normal subjects respond to 2 mg of dexamethasone by complete suppression of cortisol output over the ensuing 24 hours. It appears that in endogenous depression — but not in neurotic (reactive) depression — the normal feedback mechanism of circulating cortisol on the output of ACTH is in abeyance. The hypothalamic–pituitary mechanism for controlling the output of ACTH is through the CRF whose release is inhibited by noradrenalin and GABA but promoted by acetylcholine and 5-HT (Krieger, 1973; Sachar *et al.*, 1980a). Carroll *et al.* (1980b) observed that in a patient with Cushing's disease the use of a 5-HT receptor blocking drug, cinanserin, improved the response to dexamethasone, a finding which would be consistent with the CRF releasing effect of 5-HT. They also found that the normal dexamethasone suppression effect in healthy volunteers escaped when they were given the anti-cholinesterase drug, physostigmine, which presumably increased the levels of acetylcholine in the brain and, more particularly, in the median eminence of the hypothalamus. Somewhat conflicting findings have been observed on the effect of amphetamine on cortisol levels in patients with endogenous depression. Sachar *et al.* (1980b) found that, when healthy volunteers were given amphetamine, there was a brief rise in cortisol followed by a later fall. This response is not prevented by 5-HT receptor blockade with pimozide. In depressed patients, amphetamine causes a consistent fall in cortisol without a prior rise, suggesting a defect in noradrenergic receptors. Checkley and Crammer (1977) found that the cortisol response of depressed patients to amphetamine was lower compared with the output after recovery. They consider alpha-adrenoceptor neurons to be responsible for the normal reaction of patients to amphetamines, as this is prevented by alpha adrenoceptor blockading drugs. Checkley (1980) has recently reviewed his earlier findings and observed that patients with endogenous depression showed a significantly lower corticosteroid output in response to amphetamine compared with patients with reactive depression and other psychiatric disorders. It is evident that Checkley's depressed patients did show a transient small rise in cortisol following intravenous amphetamine, whereas Sachar *et al.* (1980b) found a more consistent fall. In discussion (Checkley, 1980), it was considered that these findings were not incompatible as Sachar *et al.* were using smaller doses of amphetamine. One might conclude that in depression either the noradrenoceptor neurons are too depleted of noradrenalin to respond to amphetamine or there is some defect in the neurons themselves. However, it is by no means certain that the primary defect is in the hypothalamus itself for, as already mentioned, Carroll *et al.* (1980a) consider that the abnormal dexamethasone suppression test in depression indicates some associated disturbance in the limbic system as well as in the hypothalamic–pituitary axis.

Output of other hormones such as growth hormone and prolactin are also disturbed but, compared with cortisol, it is unlikely that these changes are directly relevant to the aetiology of depression. Matussek *et al.* (1980) have found that growth hormone output is lower in depressed patients following the induction of insulin hypoglycemia or taking amphetamine, a finding which again appears to indicate a reduced availability of noradrenalin or reduced post-synaptic receptor sensitivity to this hormone. Clonidine, which is an alpha adrenoceptor agonist causes a rise in growth hormone in normal subjects, whereas endogenous depressive patients show a low response. This and other findings led this group to consider that there may be two sub-types of depressed patients, those with low levels of noradrenalin which are insufficient to act on post-synaptic receptors, and those with relative insensitivity of adrenoceptors, thus preventing a normal response to noradrenalin stimulation. This is similar to the hypothesis formulated by Ashcroft and his colleagues (1972) when they concluded that in depression there may be a reduction in amine-mediated synaptic sensitivity associated with normal levels of neurotransmitters or, alternatively, a lower output of amines with, as a consequence, low levels of their metabolites in the cerebrospinal fluid. Possibly patients with neurotic depressive reactions have abnormally sensitive adrenoceptors causing them to react adversely to stressful situations.

CONCLUSIONS AND SUMMARY

It should not be assumed that this survey has done more than touch on some of the neurochemical and anatomical findings thought to be relevant to the aetiology of affective disorder. A full and critical appraisal of all the facts would require a book rather than a chapter, and in any case it must not be assumed that, in the hierarchy of causes, genetic, developmental and psychosocial factors are irrelevant. Biochemical abnormalities and altered receptor sensitivity to the various neurotransmitters are likely to be genetically determined, thus setting the scene in some patients for symptomatic depression to occur. This is particularly so with drugs which appear capable of causing this type of psychiatric illness predominately in patients with some constitutional or genetic loading, as witnessed by previous attacks of mania or depression or a family history of these conditions. The point is made with some vigour by Akiskal and McKinney (1975) who regard melancholia as a final common pathway of various interlocking processes at chemical, experiential and behavioural levels that, in the language of neurophysiology, translate into a functional impairment of the diencephalic centres of reinforcement. They go on to point out how quantitative factors may permit profound changes in biogenic amines and/or electrolytes which may be the outcome of some genetically determined defect in rate-limiting enzymes involved in the biosynthesis and, possibly, inactivation of neurotransmitters. Indeed, faced by a patient with a severe depression in a setting of physical illness, it is exceedingly difficult to decide which, among a number of rival aetiological factors, might be the most important. For example, a hypertensive patient being treated with methyldopa suffers a cerebrovascular accident after which he becomes profoundly depressed. Ten years earlier he suffered an attack of depression from which he recovered with ECT and drugs. He has also recently retired from an active professional life. Which of these factors was the "cause" of his depression? Was it the medication affecting levels of noradrenalin at alpha adrenoreceptors in the brain or damage sustained by a number of relevant structures from a cerebral haemorrhage? Or were his predisposition to depression as manifested by his earlier attack and his recent change in psychosocial status — a loss in psychodynamic terms — the responsible agents?

Nevertheless, as far as symptomatic affective disorders are concerned, it seemed sensible to concentrate on the neuroanatomical and neurochemical factors, which conceivably could be deranged as a consequence of disease or exposure to drugs and toxins. The balance of evidence tends to favour a disturbance of noradrenergic control of the hypothalamic–pituitary axis, which in its turn may be modulated by influences from the limbic area of the brain, with particular emphasis on the orbitofrontal and cingulate areas connecting with the hypothalamus and other limbic structures. Furthermore, there is every reason for thinking that, in neurochemical terms, affective disorder is not an homogeneous condition. Indeed, genetic and clinical evidence suggests this very strongly. Deficiencies of serotonergic mechanisms may be important in some patients but less so in others. They may also play a more vital role in the brain stem than in the hypothalamus. These are important considerations when it comes to treatment and also aid our better understanding of the responses of affective disorders to the administration of a variety of drugs. With respect to the endorphins, it is probably far too soon to reach any conclusions about their possible role in the aetiology of depression. On the evidence so far their euphoriant, but not their analgesic, properties appear more relevant to their action in depression. There are, however, a number of conflicting observations in this area of brain biochemistry which will only be reconciled by further work and more critical experiments designed to test out the action of these and other peptides in the brain.

3

Symptomatic Affective Disorders in Old Age

The incidence of depression and age-related suicide rates increases sharply in the elderly, particularly in men. Ban (1978) considered that 10 per cent of the population aged over 60 suffers from depression and that the disorder afflicts 50 per cent of aged persons with physical illnesses. Among older patients admitted for psychiatric treatment it was found that 50 per cent aged 60–70 were depressed, in half of whom the condition had developed for the first time in their lives. Ferguson Anderson (1978) found that clinically significant anxiety and depression affected 13 per cent of healthy men and 18 per cent of women. For patients with physical disease, however, the frequency of depression increased to 31 per cent of men and 38 per cent of women. Rather lower figures were recorded by Williamson in Edinburgh (1978), who found that 5.4 per cent of the older section of the population was significantly depressed, compared with 14 per cent of those attending a psychiatric clinic. Gibson (1961), commenting on this high incidence of affective disorder in old age, quotes figures obtained from the Registrar-General's statistics for 1952–1958 which show that 27 per cent of patients aged 65 and over admitted for psychiatric treatment were depressed. In his own study of 100 geriatric admissions to a psychiatric hospital in the Newcastle-upon-Tyne region, 45 were suffering from affective disorder, two of whom were manic. Post (1964, p. 178) writes, "The importance of depressive disorders in the elderly is second only to that of the dementias of old age." Later (1978) he quotes figures showing that depression afflicted some 30 per cent of elderly invalids visited by a domiciliary nursing service and that severe depression is essentially a disorder of late life. The high rate of suicide among the elderly, particularly those with hypochondriacal depression (De Alarcón, 1964) has been noted by a number of writers (Sainsbury, 1962; Barraclough, 1971; Whitlock, 1977a) and Spicer *et al.*, (1973) found that the peak incidence for depression in men was between the ages of 55 and 70 and in women between 45 and 70. Mania, on the other hand, increased steadily in males from the age of 45 onwards, whereas in women there was little alteration in incidence rates apart from a small increase between the ages of 40 and 55.

Clearly there is substantial evidence linking severe affective disorder with ageing, but the reasons for this association are complex and in any given patient a number of variables has to be considered. Among these should be included psychosocial stresses, genetic and constitutional factors, coexisting physical and cerebral diseases and biochemical changes taking place in the ageing brain. To these might be added iatrogenic contributions, notably medications known to cause depression in some patients (Ferguson Anderson, 1971; Whitlock, 1977a; Doberauer and Doberauer, 1978).

With respect to the genetic factor, it has been claimed that, compared with younger subjects, elderly depressed patients less frequently have positive family histories of affective disorders (Stendstedt, 1959; Angst, 1966; Mendelewicz, 1976; Hopkinson and Ley, 1969; Post, 1975). Only about half of those becoming depressed after the age of 60 have no past history of affective disorder (Roth and Kay, 1956), although Post (1962) found that only 33 per cent had no such antecedent history. Whitlock and Hopkins (unpublished paper), investigating two groups of 50 patients admitted to hospital with severe depression, found that, compared with younger patients, those aged 60 and over had similar family records, with 30 per cent of each group having first degree relatives with histories of suicide or affective illnesses requiring hospital treatment. Those aged 60 and over suffering from first attacks of depression had positive family histories of affective disorder as frequently as those who had previous histories of depression or manic-depressive psychosis. This finding was similar to that of Jacoby and Levy (1980) who observed that the prevalence of a positive family history of affective disorder was equally distributed between early and late onset cases of depression.

PHYSICAL ILLNESS AND DEPRESSION

Physical illnesses are understandably more common in older than in younger patients, and this very strong association between affective and physical disorders, particularly in older patients, has been commented on in a series of investigations by Roth and Kay (Kay *et al.*, 1955; Roth and Kay, 1956; Kay, 1959; Kay, 1962). Roth and Kay (1956) found that patients with late onset affective disorders had higher rates of physical illness than those who first experienced depression or mania before the age of 60. The major contribution to this difference came from men suffering from chronic physical illnesses, whereas acute illnesses were rather more frequent in male patients with early onset affective disorders. Kay (1962) found that mortality rates were higher in the late onset affective patients and that their periods of survival were shorter than those of elderly patients with previous histories of affective disorder (see also Kay, 1959). Serious illnesses were more often found in the late onset patients who had less frequent positive family histories of affective disorder. This association between physical disease and depression in old age has again been recently disucssed by Roth (1977), who observed how many patients develop depression following viral infections, endocrine disorders or as complications of medication. Among the aged a significant relationship has been shown to exist between affective disorders and physical illnesses, particularly those giving rise to lasting defects or disablement.

Post (1969) quoted figures implying that acute physical illnesses were associated with depression in 34 per cent of elderly patients, and Gibson (1961) found that 62 per cent of 45 patients aged 60 and over had at least one coexisting physical illness. Of these 45 affectively ill patients, 22 became pyschiatrically ill for the first time after the age of 60. Seventeen had associated physical diseases. In the study referred to earlier, Whitlock and Hopkins found that 82 per cent of patients with depression aged 60 and over had one or more physical illness or were taking medication likely to cause depression, compared with 64 per cent of those aged less than 60. In neither group were first attacks of depression more significantly associated with physical illness when compared with those who had suffered previous episodes of affective disorder. How far these disparate findings relate to the exclusion in our study of patients with neurotic depression is unclear, as not all investigations have been limited to patients with typical endogenous depression or the depressive phase of a manic-depressive psychosis.

Although some authors claim that endogenous depression is more common than neurotic depressive reaction in the aged, Kay (1976) doubts whether this is correct. None the less, whatever the facts might be, there is abundant evidence that elderly depressives and elderly suicides have high rates of physical illness (Ferguson Anderson, 1971; Post, 1969; Sainsbury, 1962; Barraclough, 1971). Even then one might conclude that by no means all these patients with depression became ill solely on account of their coexisting physical illnesses. In fact, of our 50 patients aged 60 and over, in only 10 cases could depression be attributed with reasonable certainty solely to drugs or physical illnesses. In the remainder with physical diseases, genetic loading and previous attacks of depression suggest that the drugs and physical disease acted more as precipitants of depression in predisposed subjects rather than as essential causes. Of these 10 patients, three had malignant neoplasms, two were myxoedematous, two had become ill after viral infections, two were taking a number of drugs known to cause depression, and one was severely anaemic.

Cerebrovascular Disease

When one turns to the question of the relationship between affective disorder
and degenerative cerebral conditions — mainly cerebrovascular disease — the
overall impression gained is that patients who suffer from affective disorders
in old age do not develop cerebrovascular disease more often than the general
population, but that in about 12 per cent of patients who become depressed
the affective illness is the presenting symptom of brain damage caused by
cerebral arteriosclerosis.

For example, Kay *et al.* (1955), comparing 175 patients aged 60 and over
suffering from affective illnesses with 14 patients with "organic" depression,
found that in eight of the latter group the emergence of organic features and
affective illness coincided, whereas in the remainder affective symptoms
preceded the organic signs by months or years. They went on to examine the
outcome for patients who had early and late onset affective disorders. After
excluding the 14 patients with organic signs and symptoms, the authors
concluded that cerebral degeneration of the senile and arteriosclerotic kind
was unlikely to be an aetiological factor of importance in affective disorder in
the senium, whether or not it was of early or late onset. On the other hand,
Roth and Kay (1956) found that chronic physical illness in men was a
common accompaniment of affective disorder in old age more often in late
onset than in early onset cases. Kay (1959) found a higher than expected
mortality rate in patients with late onset affective disorder, with cerebrovascular disease being a likely factor in about 10 per cent of cases. There was no
evidence of any genetic association between cerebrovascular disease and
affective disorder. Kay (1962), in a follow-up study of patients with early and
late onset affective disorder, found a significant increase in deaths of patients
with late onset illnesses, with cerebrovascular accidents playing a major role.
In about 9 per cent of the patients cerebrovascular disease could have
contributed to the onset of affective symptoms. Nevertheless, Kay argued that
cerebrovascular disease was not an important cause of late onset depression.
Roth (1971), on the other hand, considers that in a minority of cases there is an
association between cerebrovascular disease but not between senile changes
and depression. He finds that in 16–18 per cent of new cases of cerebrovascular
disease there is an associated affective disorder. This could be a chance
association, an indication of the normal ageing process, but, in Roth's
opinion, depression is commonly observed in the early stages of arteriosclerotic dementia.

Post (1962) found that 12 per cent of his elderly depressives showed signs
of cerebrovascular disease on admission, compared with an expected figure of
4.4 per cent. In all but three of these patients the depression started after a
cerebrovascular accident which Post regarded as a precipitant in a
predisposed subject. Like Kay he did not find a higher incidence of new cases
of cerebrovascular disease during the follow-up period. He concluded (p. 48)

that "the relatively greater frequency with which arteriosclerotic disorder was found in our elderly depressives seemed to indicate an aetiological linkage between affective illness and cerebrovascular disorder". He went on to consider whether the physical changes caused or precipitated depression and felt that, because these patients responded to antidepressant treatment, precipitation was the answer. However, many patients with severe depression for which serious physical illness appears to be the essential cause undoubtedly do recover from their affective illnesses with appropriate treatment even when the underlying physical illness remains unchanged or progresses. Furthermore, in the absence of full details about past history or family history of affective disorder in these patients, the question of predisposition remains an open one. Later, Post (1975) is more emphatic when he writes, "Depressive illnesses occur more commonly in relation to cerebrovascular disease than can be explained in terms of chance association." He goes on to observe that the family histories of affective disorders are about the same in depressed patients with cerebrovascular disease as in those without it and that, although depression may remit with appropriate treatment, relapse and subsequent chronicity are frequent. In contrast, Nielsen *et al.* (1977) could find no association between cerebrovascular disease and affective disorders in their 15 year follow-up of psychogeriatric patients, and Varsamis *et al.* (1972) concluded that the mortality rates of elderly depressives are comparable with those of the general population. On the other hand, it does appear that cerebrovascular disease can precipitate or, possibly, cause depression in older persons, in some instances being the herald of arteriosclerotic dementia which becomes more obvious with the passage of time. There is also good evidence that patients who suffer strokes become depressed (Adams, 1967; L. J. Hurwitz, 1969), but Horenstein (1970) considered that such depressions were more in the nature of grief reactions to loss and disability and that true psychotic endogenous depression was unusual. Blazer (1980) has also drawn attention to the distinction between depression as a syndrome and dysphoric reactions in elderly patients, but it does appear that depressive symptomatology is more common in patients with multi-infarct dementia than in those with senile dementia (Slater and Roth, 1977, p. 594; Brandon, 1979).

The advent of computerized tomography has made it possible to assess the presence of brain damage in elderly depressives thus avoiding use of air encephalography. Employing the more recent technique, Jacoby and Levy (1980) found that a minority of late onset depressives had illnesses which could be related to cerebral atrophy. After taking all the facts into consideration, they concluded that approximately 12 per cent of the patients with depression had evidence of cerebrovascular disease, the same figure obtained by Post (1962). Jacoby and Levy (1980) write, "Thus, the possibility of a structural basis for some types of depression in old age remains open. Clearly, confirmatory and long-term prognostic studies are required."

BIOCHEMICAL FACTORS ASSOCIATED WITH AGEING

Accepting for the moment the probable correctness of the biochemical hypotheses of affective disorder, one might presume that functional losses of catecholamines with associated changes in other neurotransmitters would contribute to the increased frequency of affective disorder in the elderly. Robinson *et al.* (1972) found that levels of monoamine oxidase (MAO) activity in human brains and platelets increase with age. In older subjects there was an associated fall in noradrenalin and a rise in 5-HIAA, the principal metabolite of 5-HT. Lipton (1976) and Grauer (1977) have commented on the association between falling oestrogen levels in the female and increased MAO activity, which appears to reach a peak in the premenopausal depressed woman. Other writers (Gurland, 1976; Gottfries *et al.*, 1979) have considered these findings and their relevance to depression in older subjects. Gottfries *et al.* (1979) found that the brain enzymes involved in the conversion of tyrosine to noradrenalin and of dopa to dopamine showed reduced activity with age leading to falls in levels of dopamine and noradrenalin which were even lower in cases of Alzheimer's disease and senile dementia. MAO activity was also increased in the platelets of patients with Alzheimer's disease. The findings with respect to 5-HT varied depending on which brain site was being studied, with higher levels observed in the hypothalamus and mesencephalon but lower amounts in the hippocampus and globus pallidus. Bowen *et al.* (1974) recorded a decline in L-dopa and glutamic acid decarboxylases in patients with senile dementia and Parkinson's disease, and Bowen and Davison (1978) noted how cerebral noradrenalin levels decline with age, rising MAO activity and reduced levels of synthesizing enzymes. With the amine hypothesis of affective disorders in mind, Cawley *et al.* (1973) found that elderly depressed patients had a lowered tolerance to barbiturates which improved when the patients recovered. Patients with evidence of cerebral disease also had lower barbiturate tolerance thresholds with less improvement when their depressions lifted. The authors considered that this phenomenon was caused by decreased cortical arousability in depression, which, in its turn, might be related to diminished levels of catecholamines secondary to the increase of MAO activity in older patients.

Bowen and Davison comment on the decrease in cholineacetyl-transferase (CAT) activity, which presumably implies reduced formation of acetylcholine. On the other hand, there is also a decrease in receptor binding of acetylcholine since if scopolamine, an acetylcholine receptor blockading drug, is given to younger subjects, psychological defects appear similar to those observed in old age. This reduction in CAT is also found in senile dementia and Alzheimer's disease, whereas in multi-infarct dementia there is reduced cerebral blood-flow leading, possibly, to a decline in the availability of oxygen with consequent falls in dopa and 5-HT. Perry *et al.* (1977) reported on a reduction of CAT in the brains of elderly patients who had been diagnosed as cases of senile dementia, arteriosclerotic dementia and depression, with the greatest falls being found in patients with senile dementia. Davies and Maloney (1976) observed a selective reduction of CAT and choline esterase activity in the brains of patients who had been diagnosed as cases of Alzheimer's disease during life. The falls were most marked in the amygdalae, hippocampus and cortex and in areas where the density of neurofibrillary tangles was greatest.

It is not entirely clear from these studies whether the apparent loss of cholinergic activity is caused by loss of cells leaving the remainder relatively intact. or whether there is a total decline in acetylcholine receptor binding activity If the former possibility is correct, one might consider that a normal level of acetylcholine activity in intact cells, coupled with a loss of catecholamines, could lead to depressed affect in patients with incipient Alzheimer's disease and senile dementia. In fact, Bowen *et al.* (1979) found reduced CAT levels in the temporal lobes of the brains of Alzheimer patients with normal levels in the caudate nucleus implying a selective loss of neocortical cholinergic neurones in this condition. This finding could also be relevant to the development of extrapyramidal symptoms in Alzheimer's disease, given the fact that catecholamine transmitters are reduced in this condition.

PSYCHOSOCIAL STRESS

The commonsense view that depression in old age is caused by deprivation, isolation and losses has been vigorously criticized by Grad de Alarcón (1971). The belief that stresses of this kind are essential and dominating causes of depression is not unequivocally supported by the evidence. Rather, it seems, the prior circumstances and premorbid adjustment of the patients are crucial contributions to the outcome of stresses like retirement, bereavement and loss of social contacts. As Grad de Alarcón writes, "No clear causal effects of social deprivation on mental illness have been found and some social factors thought to be causal are more likely consequences of the illness." Post (1978) also has reconsidered his earlier opinions on this subject. He writes, "The idea that traumatic experiences and stresses of various sorts might be of special importance in precipitating the depression of elderly persons and thus explain the increasing frequency of these disorders with rising age does not seem to hold water." In our own study (Whitlock and Hopkins, unpublished), social factors as the sole apparent cause of depression in the 50 patients aged 60 and over were found in only two cases compared with 10 in those aged less than 60. In nine other patients aged 60 and over, social stresses — mainly bereavement — appeared to contribute to the onset of depression, although in these patients coexisting physical illnesses and genetic and consititutional factors may have rendered them less able to withstand the impact of loss and the adjustments required of them.

PRESENILE DEMENTIA

"It is not uncommon to encounter patients with depression in middle life who respond well to treatment, yet who later merge imperceptibly into the early stages of presenile dementia. It is, therefore, plain that purely depressive symptoms may be the earliest and only features of dementing illnesses" (Pearce and Miller, 1973, p. 41). Miller (1977, p. 6) also comments, "Emotional changes, especially depression, are common in the early stages of a dementing illness and may even be the presenting symptoms . . . the picture can often be confused with an endogenous depression." Such observations leave little doubt that severe depression can be an early feature of Alzheimer's disease, but unless one can ascertain the prior existence of positive family histories and attacks of depression occurring independently of cerebral disease, one cannot say with certainty that the developing dementia was the sole or essential cause of depression in these patients. Furthermore, incorrect diagnoses may augment the apparent association between depression and dementia in patients who are manifesting a pseudo-dementia syndrome (Kiloh, 1961; Post, 1975). Nevertheless, a number of reports specifically mention the presence of severe depression during the early stages of presenile dementia, and my own experience would certainly support this association, which in some cases includes suicidal behaviour or thoughts.

Stengel (1943) commented on the occurrence of depression and suicidal behaviour before the clinical diagnosis of dementia was made in his series of nine cases. Of eight patients with sufficient data one was depressed and suicidal, another depressed and diagnosed as involutional melancholia and a third developed an attack of mania. None of these patients had a previous history of depression or mania, but the manic patient had a positive family history of suicide. Sim and Sussman (1962), reporting on 22 cases of Alzheimer's disease confirmed by biopsy or at autopsy, found that 12 were severely depressed. None appeared to have experienced earlier attacks of depression, but five patients had positive family histories of mental illness whose type was unknown. In 11 patients with other varieties of presenile dementia three were depressed. Of another 13 patients with presenile dementia whose diagnoses were not checked by biopsy, seven were depressed. Carlson (1976) described a 40-year-old woman with no earlier attacks of affective illness who presented with a three-year history of depression. Ultimately she was diagnosed as suffering from presenile dementia with severe memory defect and evidence of ventricular dilatation and cortical atrophy. Liston, in a series of papers (1977, 1978, 1979a, 1979b), has reported his findings on 50 patients with presenile dementia. Thirteen of these patients had symptoms of endogenous depression, but nine had past histories of depressive spectrum disorders. Summarizing the findings in three other reports, Liston found that 16.5 per cent of patients, ultimately diagnosed as cases of presenile dementia, had suffered from depression before a formal diagnosis of dementia was made. On the other hand, Liston reported that 30 per cent of his patients at the onset of their illnesses experienced depression as a discrete, subjective symptom and not as a full-blown syndrome of melancholia. Other symptoms of endogenous depressive disorder, however, were not uncommon (Liston, pers. comm., 1980). Ziegler (1954) found that six of 40 patients with cortical atrophy demonstrated by air encephalogram showed severe depression, but certainly not all were suffering from presenile dementia and details of past personal history and family history were not provided. In summary, therefore, it does appear that a percentage of patients ultimately diagnosed as suffering from presenile dementia experience severe depression at the onset of their illnesses. In those cases one might conclude that the cerebral disease was the essential cause of the affective disorder. In others, however, previous attacks of depression and, possibly, positive family histories of affective disorder seem to indicate a predisposition to recurrence of depression which is now being precipitated by the degenerative process. From the description of symptomatology in these patients it does appear that some had severe depressive symptoms and were not simply reacting with a transient down-turn of mood to psychological difficulties which, in many cases, they were able to appreciate.

The pathogenesis of Alzheimer's disease is unknown, but in recent times (Davies and Maloney, 1976) attention has been focused on a decline in cholinergic activity in the brains of patients with this disorder. In addition, there are falls in catecholamine neurotransmitters (Adolfsson *et al.*, 1979) and reduced activity of dopamine-beta-hydroxylase (Cross *et al.*, 1981) which was thought to reflect degeneration of noradrenergic neurons. Histological evidence shows degenerative changes in the locus coeruleus which could be responsible for this abnormality. One can only speculate whether the decline in noradrenergic activity would be the cause of depression in the early stages of Alzheimer's disease although, in theory, the cholinergic defect should not produce this type of reaction.

The diagnostic problem of presenile dementia has been commented on by a number of authors. Marsden and Harrison (1972) found that in 106 patients given a diagnosis of presenile dementia, 15 were not demented. Eight of these patients were depressed, but the authors considered that about 25 per cent of patients with dementia had evidence of depression. Nott and Fleminger (1975) followed up 35 presenile dementia patients and found that 20 had been misdiagnosed. However, in both groups significant affective symptoms had been present. Seven of the 15 demented patients had been depressed and two had previous histories of affective disorder, whereas 17 of the 20 non-demented patients had shown affective changes. Seven of these patients had previous attacks of depression and one had also been manic. *Moderate* cerebral atrophy was found by neuroradiology in five of the non-demented group compared with six of the demented patients, an additional three of whom showed *gross* changes. Ron *et al.* (1979) followed up 52 patients aged less than 65 who had been given a firm diagnosis of presenile dementia. At follow-up 33 were dead and 16 had been misdiagnosed. Once again the incidence of affective disorder in these misdiagnosed cases was high. One has to conclude that diagnostic accuracy in patients with the apparent features of presenile dementia is difficult to achieve. Unless the diagnosis is supported by comprehensive neuroradiological studies and confirmed at autopsy, one must question the figures some investigators give of the incidence of severe depression in patients who may ultimately require revision of the original diagnoses. However, there is sufficient evidence to support the feeling that some patients with presenile dementia present with serious affective illnesses, the existence of which may be a real barrier to early diagnosis (Liston, 1978).

4

Infectious Diseases and Affective Disorder

VIRUS INFECTIONS

> The second important psychosis (after toxic-confusional psychosis) associated with virus infections is the affective psychosis proper. Characteristically this is a depression of variable severity and appears some weeks after the onset of infection . . . it is well known that an acute virus illness might be followed by sudden, attempted suicide (Gould, 1957).

Curiously, despite the more or less universal acceptance of the occurrence of depression after viral infections, there is an almost total absence of adequate studies. Standard textbooks of medicine have little to say on the subject, while modern psychiatric texts seem content to report the syndrome but say nothing about its pathogenesis. Sim (1974, p. 526), for example, writing on precipitants of depression, states that "infection is the commonest and influenza the most notorious, an epidemic being followed by a spate of cases". Firm evidence for this statement is difficult to find, although Ewald (1928) in a review of 124 cases of influenzal psychosis recorded 40 per cent with depressive and neurasthenic states. Tuke (1892, p. 687), on the other hand, regarded influenza as a prime cause of melancholia. "In no other allied disease," he wrote, "is the nervous system attacked to such a degree." Of 18 patients whom he described, 11 became depressed and four manic. Moran (1969) attempted to relate suicide data in the USA to influenza deaths. However there was little evidence that even the major pandemic in 1918 had any noticeable effect on what might be regarded as an indicator of severe depression in the community. Haig (pers. comm., 1978) has discussed some of the difficulties to be faced when trying to relate a preceding viral infection to a subsequent depressive illness. Four of his 31 subjects became severely depressed and, although none had a past history of depression, one female patient had become moderately depressed when taking an oral contraceptive. The depressive episodes lasted 4–14 days. In two patients infection with influenza B virus was confirmed serologically but in the other two it was not. Presumably some other virus was responsible for their illnesses.

In a general review of the subject (*British Medical Journal*, Editorial, 1976) attention was drawn to depression following a variety of viral infections, and O'Neill (1959), apparently recovering from a bout of post-influenzal depression himself, commented on the quite disproportionate severity of symptoms in some post-viral states which do not occur necessarily in patients with past histories of depression. He asked the following very pertinent questions. Why does depression develop, sometimes a long time after the patient has recovered from the illness? Why does it last so long? And why do only a minority of influenza sufferers develop this condition?

Imboden *et al.* (1961) felt that subjects developing post-influenzal affective disorders were "depression-prone", a conclusion based on the scores recorded by a number of patients tested with the Minnesota Multiphasic Personality Inventory (MMPI). Burr (1918) considered that, although the frequency of psychiatric disorders following influenza was not known, all patients develop some mental symptoms which in most cases are minor, usually in the form of mild depression and "neurasthenia". However, he mentioned three cases of severe post-influenzal depression associated with suicidal thoughts and another patient with classic delusions of guilt and self-blame who tried to jump out of a window. Manic symptoms were also mentioned as rare sequelae to influenza but, in the absence of more detailed clinical data, it is impossible to say whether these cases represented a more than usual frequency of severe affective disorder at the time of a viral epidemic. Menninger (1919a; 1919b) claimed that influenza as a cause of psychiatric disorder was recognized as far back as 1385. He also quoted a study by Petrequin (1837) who wrote of a patient tormented by sad ideas and of four suicides in the course of an influenza epidemic in Paris. Menninger himself described three cases of manic-depressive psychosis, two manic and one depressed, with no past histories of similar illnesses. In this connection should be mentioned the case described by Steinberg *et al.* (1972), a 21-year-old woman who first became depressed and subsequently manic after an attack of viral influenza. Although influenza apparently can cause depression, according to Menninger (1930) these patients generally recover after the viral infection. Nonetheless, in my experience, post-influenzal depression in elderly patients can prove to be singularly resistant to treatment.

It has to be admitted that, in the absence of well-designed studies supported by virological tests, it is impossible to decide just how frequently influenza precipitates or causes depression. Yet all practicing psychiatrists have seen patients, particularly older subjects, who develop severe and sometimes intractable depression after an illness diagnosed as influenza. Burr and Menninger were writing at the end of the First World War when epidemic encephalitis was achieving pandemic proportions throughout the world. Sixty years later it is impossible to verify the precise diagnoses in their cases, and it cannot be assumed that the illnesses preceding attacks of depression at that time were, in fact, influenza and not some other type of viral infection. It is, for example, well known that depression in post-encephalitic Parkinsonism is relatively common with successful suicide being frequently recorded (Slater and Roth, 1977, pp. 383–384).

A recent epidemiological investigation by Sinanan and Hillary (1981), which failed to demonstrate higher levels of influenza antibody titres in depressed patients who claimed to have had the illness when compared with other patients with other psychiatric diagnoses, does not prove that viral influenza cannot cause or precipitate severe depression in some cases. The effect of earlier infections on the levels of antibody titres and the likelihood that re-exposure leading to subclinical infections would increase their states of immunity were not considered by these authors (Whitlock, 1981a).

If all too little is known about the role of influenza, even less seems to have been written about the other major infection commonly cited as a cause of depression, viral hepatitis. Ford (1943) mentioned depression, irritability, drowsiness, loss of appetite, constipation and headache as prodromal symptoms which were said to clear once appetite was restored. On the other hand, Findlay et al. (1944), described profound mental depression continuing for some time after the major symptoms of hepatitis had cleared up. Stokes et al. (1945) stated that "some degree of mental depression is very common . . . [and] any increase . . . should be treated as a danger sign". Leibowitz and Gorman (1952) regarded profound mental depression as the most common and distressing symptom, although in one series it occurred in only 2.8 per cent of cases. One of the two cases they described had a past history of depression. Later writers also appear to consider depression to be a common complication of viral hepatitis. Martini and Strohmeyer (1974) write, "The degree of depression in some persons recovering from hepatitis is remarkable, particularly in those persons who have not experienced this before. We know of 2 persons who committed suicide in this phase." Lowy (1965) felt that true manic-depressive disorder was unusual, whereas depression as a reaction to the discomforts of hepatitis was common.

More recently, attention has been given to another relatively common infection, infectious mononucleosis, as a cause of depression. I have seen cases of severe and protracted depression in young men following proven infections by the E.B. virus. Cadie et al. (1976) found a higher incidence of depression in women following infectious mononucleosis, but as they did not define what symptoms were present, it is impossible to say with certainty whether a depressive syndrome or symptom had developed. None of their patients were severely depressed, and some had been mildly depressed before they developed the infection. Peszke and Mason (1969), in a study of university students, concluded that those who became psychiatrically ill did not show any particular predisposition as judged by their score, when healthy, on the Cornell Medical Index, but Greenfield *et al.* (1959) concluded that weak ego strength causes delayed recovery from infectious mononucleosis which is not, in their opinion, a direct cause of depression. Hendler and Leahy (1978) described two adolescent patients who became depressed and suicidal, one of whom responded to tranylcypromine but not to imipramine. Klaber and Lacey (1968) gave details of five patients who developed acute psychiatric disorders in the course of attacks of infectious mononucleosis. Three were acutely depressed and suicidal.

Unfortunately, none of the authors so far mentioned discusses the presence or absence of positive family histories or previous attacks of affective disorder in their patients. To this the recent study by Goldney and Temme (1980) is a notable exception. This patient, a 23-year-old woman, who developed a manic-depressive psychosis some six weeks after being ill with infectious mononucleosis, had a previous minor depressive episode and, possibly, a mild hypomanic illness in response to the use of diethylpropion. Although there was no clear-cut history of affective disorders in her family (alcoholism was mentioned), one might conclude that in this patient the viral infection acted as a precipitant rather than as the sole essential cause.

As CNS involvement occurs in 0.7–26.5 per cent of patients with glandular fever (Silverstein, 1978) it is hardly surprising that some patients develop psychiatric sequelae. Bernstein and Wolff (1950) reported autopsy evidence of meningitis and generalized cortical involvement in fatal cases, findings which are closely similar to those noted in other types of encephalitis.

Viral encephalitis, particularly the epidemic of encephalitis lethargica following the First World War, carried with it a high incidence of psychiatric disorder. Barton Hall (1929) noted that 92 of 113 patients who had suffered from encephalitis lethargica showed some kind of mental disturbance. Thirteen adults developed psychotic illnesses which included manic-depressive psychoses. Cooper (1936) found depression in 98 of 174 patients, in 60 of whom the mood disturbance was regarded as reactive to their physical and mental disabilities. Seventeen attempted suicide before admission. In all, 45 patients had attempted suicide during the course of their illnesses and another 21 had threatened suicide. Only one case was known to have suffered from manic-depressive psychosis just before the attack of encephalitis. Sobin and Ozer (1966) observed a variety of psychiatric illnesses in their 10 patients with acute encephalitis, one of whom was depressed and suicidal.

Himmelhoch *et al.* (1970) have drawn attention to severe psychiatric illnesses as the presenting symptoms of subacute inclusion-body encephalitis.

Of their eight cases three showed severe depression either early or late in their illnesses but one, a 56-year-old woman, was later found to have a small oat-cell carcinoma of the lung. Subacute encephalitis mainly affecting the limbic area of the brain has been discussed by Brierley *et al.* (1960) and by Glaser and Pincus (1969). Leaving aside until later the possible relationship of this condition to malignant neoplasms, it is noteworthy that severe depression seems to be a frequent feature of this condition. Glaser and Pincus's fifth case, however, became depressed and finally committed suicide after treatment with adrenal corticosteroids, but two of the three patients described by Brierley *et al.* were severely depressed at the start of their illnesses. The relationship of the condition to a latent measles infection or reinfection with a neurotropic strain of the virus is unclear (Lishman, 1978). Indeed there is uncertainty about whether this rare condition is caused by a virus in the first place (Corsellis *et al.*, 1968). The occurrence of severe depression and, later, gross memory impairment could be related to the neuropathological findings in the three cases described by Brierley *et al.* (1960). They commented on the inflammatory changes which were particularly severe in the amygdalae, the hippocampus, the posterior orbital surface of the frontal lobe and the cingulate gyrus. The relevance of these areas to severe affective disorder has been discussed in Chapter 2 (pp. 7–9).

    Related to the issue of epidemic encephalitis is the condition known as epidemic myalgic encephalomyelitis, sometimes called Royal Free disease. Conflicting opinions have been expressed about this disorder which in some quarters (McEvedy and Beard, 1970, 1973) is regarded as a form of epidemic hysteria, but by others as a genuine infection of the central nervous system. Kendell (1967) observed that three patients were so depressed that they required compulsory admission to hospital, while a fourth committed suicide. In his review of one outbreak, he noted a high incidence of depression and went on to describe two depressed patients of his own, both of whom were chronically ill but neither of whom had suffered from previous depression nor histrionic outbursts. A recent brief review (*British Medical Journal*, Editorial, 1978) felt that there was strong evidence in support of an organic aetiology for this condition. This conclusion was disputed by Easton (1978) but Wookey (1978) robustly asserted her belief in the viral origin of this condition and rejected the notion that it was a manifestation of hysteria. In any case, whether or not hysterical symptoms develop in these patients, such a finding does not exclude an infection of the central nervous system as an important precipitating cause.

    Ramsay (1978) has reviewed the findings in 53 cases and commented specifically on evidence of involvement of the central and sympathetic nervous systems. Mental and physical exhaustion can be severe. Some patients recover completely, but others are prone to relapse, while some show no recovery at all. These points have been emphasized by a sufferer from the condition

(Church, 1980; pers. comm., 1980). She writes, "The depression that goes with meningo-encephalomyelitis in some cases can be quite severe and is the greatest threat to life with the illness. That it is endogenous and not reactive was made clear to me through the recoveries and relapses." Undoubtedly this writer has little patience with the hysterical concept of the condition.

Tropical viral infections such as Dengue and sand-fly fevers are associated with severe depression in some patients (Beeson and McDermott, 1971; Adams and Maegrath, 1974). The latter authors say of Dengue fever that "the most severe complication is profound depression which may continue for several weeks" and, in the case of sand-fly fever, they state that "the patient is deeply depressed" and that "the depression is relieved only slowly and convalescence may be a matter of weeks". Another tropical infection, trypanosomiasis, is said to cause depression. Some 80–95 per cent of patients show mental symptoms among which "endogenous depression is a distinctive feature of the early cases" (Lambo, 1966).

In recent years considerable interest has been shown in the alleged causal relationship between herpes simplex infections and depression. A number of studies (Rimon and Halonen, 1969; Rimon *et al.*, 1971; Halonen *et al.*, 1974; Lycke *et al.*, 1974) have claimed to have found higher levels of herpes simplex virus (HSV) complement-fixating antibody in the sera of psychotic, depressed patients than in controls. Patients with neurotic (reactive) depression did not show this phenomenon. In the study by Lycke *et al.* (1974), in addition to HSV, there were higher titres of measles and cytomegalovirus (CMV) antibodies, although Halonen *et al.* (1974) were unable to demonstrate higher titres against rubella and measles in their patients. In contrast Chacon *et al.* (1975), who looked at antibodies to mumps and influenza viruses in addition to HSV, and Pokorny *et al.* (1973) were unable to confirm or replicate the Scandinavian findings. Torrey *et al.* (1978) were likewise unable to detect any elevation of HSV or CMV antibodies in the sera or CSF of patients with functional psychoses including four with manic-depressive psychosis. Crow (1978) considers that the nature of the relationship between HSV and psychiatric illnesses other than herpes encephalitis remains obscure, although some of the studies described suggest the possibility of an association with some kinds of depression.

At this stage, therefore, it would be premature to conclude that HSV infections, latent or overt, cause severe depression, although when taken in conjunction with the known effects of other viruses, one must admit that such a relationship could exist. An alternative explanation might be that severe depression affects the body's immune defences, at least temporarily, thus allowing a latent infection to develop and so cause a secondary rise in antibodies. At the clinical level, both in psychiatry and dermatology, skin lesions of herpes simplex have often been observed following periods of emotional tension, and one might anticipate such lesions in some patients if they should become severely depressed. Interestingly, experimental encephalitis infections of mice have been shown to affect transmitter amines and their metabolities in the central nervous system. Lycke and Roos (1968) found an increase in homovanillic acid and 5-HIAA, suggesting increased turnover of dopamine and 5-HT, a finding confirmed by the same authors (Lycke *et al.*, 1970; Lycke and Roos, 1972). Precisely what this signifies in terms of the biogenic–amine theory of depression is unclear, but the possibility that viral infections of the brain can reduce available transmitter substances is one which needs to be examined.

BACTERIAL INFECTIONS

Compared with the apparent frequency with which viral infections can precipitate or cause depression in some patients, similar illnesses following bacterial infections, whether systemic or cerebral, are uncommon. Pai (1945) has claimed that many patients recovering from meningococcal meningitis have prolonged but mild depression but, in the absence of feelings of guilt, suicidal thoughts and other symptoms, it is doubtful whether a formal diagnosis of depression could be made. Typhoid fever, as its name indicates, causes cerebral disturbances mainly in the shape of delirium and clouded consciousness. Depression has been observed (Gadehold and Madsen, 1963; Muhangi, 1972), but Khosla *et al.* (1977) found no cases of depression and only one case of mania in their 124 patients. One might conclude that the occasional case of severe affective disorder in the course of an enteric infection is more coincidental than indicative of a causal relationship.

Brucellosis, on the other hand, does seem to be associated with depression in a significant number of patients, possibly because of the prolonged and relapsing nature of the infection. Calder (1939) found neurasthenic-depressive symptoms in impressive numbers in his series of 550 patients, and for two of them admission to hospital was necessary as a precaution against suicide. Harris (1950) stated that depression is frequently observed and Dalrymple-Champneys (1960) observed depression in 50 of 1,500 cases but gave few details apart from noting suicidal tendencies in two of them. Alapin (1976) found two cases of chronic depression (one suicidal) in his 122 patients. Masson *et al.* (1976), in a survey of psychiatric patients, found 20 with positive serology for B. Abortus infections. They were depressed and suicidal. However, many of these patients had past histories of unspecified psychiatric disorders and the later illnesses with abortus infections could have been coincidental or, alternatively, the infection could have acted as a precipitant in predisposed subjects. Imboden *et al.* (1959) felt that premorbid personality and current psychosocial problems had more to do with chronic depression in some brucellosis patients than the infection itself, while Mohr and Wilson (1973) considered that psychosis, including manic-depressive psychosis, was a rare complication of brucellosis. On the other hand, Adams and Maegrath (1974) regard depression and fatigue as part of the infective syndrome which is often mistaken for a neurosis. Despite this rather conflicting evidence it does appear that depression, whether it is a reaction to chronic illness in a predisposed subject or an illness directly attributable to the infecting organism, does occur in brucellosis patients sufficiently often to justify appropriate antidepressive treatment as an adjunct to other measures designed to eliminate the infection. Routine serological tests for brucellosis and other infections in depressed patients might be a useful investigation, particularly in younger subjects.

Two other infections require consideration — toxoplasmosis and syphilis. The discussion of GPI presenting as a depressive illness will be deferred to a later chapter, but adult infections with toxoplasmosis — sometimes misdiagnosed as infectious mononucleosis — can undoubtedly be attended by depressive symptoms of a fairly prolonged and severe kind. The following case illustrates some of the clinical features.

A 28-year-old man developed an influenza-like infection in June 1979. Since that time he had felt unwell, his main complaints being lethargy, fatigue and feeling variably depressed. He also mentioned that he had lost weight and had a reduced interest in former social and recreational pursuits. His sleep and appetite appeared to be relatively normal. When seen some eight months after his initial illness he was depressed and mildly retarded. He did not admit to feelings of self-reproach or to suicidal thoughts. Tests revealed positive serological reactions for toxoplasmosis, but the test for infectious mono-nucleosis was negative.

Hafström (1959) described six patients with toxoplasmosis, one of whom was depressed and required ECT. He commented, "The so-called glandular form of toxoplasmosis is associated with pronounced feelings of malaise, marked fatigue and depression." Catel (1957) mentioned psychiatric symptoms without specifying depression but Wahle (1958) noted weakness, fatigue, anorexia and depression in the febrile-lymphadenitis variety of this disease. None of the seven psychotic cases described by Ladee *et al.* (1966) were obviously depressed, although these authors mentioned depression as one of the symptoms of adult toxoplasmosis.

Very few of the papers quoted in this chapter have provided sufficient information on the nature of the affective illnesses or the patient's family or past personal history. In the absence of these data it is impossible to say whether viral infections cause or precipitate depression. However, on the assumption that actual invasion of the brain takes place in some patients, it seems likely that such infections do cause affective illnesses which would not have occurred had the patient not developed the physical disease. Syphilis apart, bacterial and other infections only rarely cause depression severe enough to require psychiatric treatment, but neurasthenic-depressive syndromes can follow abortus fever sufficiently often to warrant blood culture and serology investigations in some cases of depression whose aetiology is obscure.

5

Neurological Disease and Affective Disorder: Part I

INTRODUCTION

One could predict with reasonable assurance that in any major disease of the brain severe depression will be manifested by some patients. In fact, De Paulo and Folstein (1978), using two rating scales, found that 67 per cent of 126 patients with neurological disease showed evidence of cognitive defect, emotional disturbance or both. Patients with cerebral disorders had very much higher rates of psychiatric disturbance than patients with peripheral neurological diseases. Tumours, degenerative changes, cerebrovascular disease, infections and major system diseases such as multiple sclerosis and parkinsonism are all associated, either early or later, with prominent psychiatric symptoms and syndromes whose incidence varies from patient to patient. Moreover, many writers have pointed out how often depression may mask an underlying tumour which is not necessarily malignant, examples being the two cases described by Chambers (1955) who were found to have, respectively, a subdural haematoma and a large cerebellar cyst. Bramwell (1888), who wrote of depression of spirits as a presenting symptom of cerebral neoplasm, speculated on whether preceding emotional distress might conduce to tumour formation, and Adams and Hurwitz (1974) observed how depression may appear at the onset of a stroke and later lead to suicide. Parant (1892) commented at length on melancholia as a complication of paralysis agitans and the serious risk of suicide by some patients.

When one is faced by a mass of conflicting evidence, it is difficult to decide which of the various afflictions of the brain should be regarded as specific

43

causes of depression and which are precipitants in predisposed subjects. What is certain is that depression or mania are by no means the sole, or necessarily the commonest, psychiatric manifestations of neurological disease, and the main task of the clinician is to stay alert to the possibility of such a condition, particularly when well-defined neurological symptoms are slight or absent.

INFECTIONS

Viral and bacterial infections that can affect the brain have already been reviewed. Syphilis in the form of GPI, a common diagnosis in the past but a rare disease today, has been discussed by Dewhurst (1969). The classic picture of an expansive euphoria, although it still occurs, seems more often to be replaced by depression which, in Dewhurst's series, was the most usual presentation, followed by dementia. Two of Steel's (1960) 14 patients were depressed and three were hypomanic, and Storm-Mathieson (1969) observed that 15 per cent of men and 23 per cent of women showed depressive symptoms. Even so, a large number were euphoric and all showed minimal or advanced signs of dementia. None of these authors makes any mention of positive family histories of affective disorder or previous episodes of depression in their patients. Dewhurst emphasized the changing pattern of symptomatology of GPI over the past 100 years and it is unlikely that there would be more patients today with past histories of affective illness than was the case at the beginning of the century. The following patient, who showed both features of dementia and depression, was admitted under the author's care a few years ago.

A.J., male, aged 64. The patient was admitted with a recent history of confusion, inappropriate behaviour, impaired memory and what might have been a suicidal attempt when he jumped out of a window. On examination he showed the classic features of GPI. Serology for syphilis was positive in blood and CSF, as was the colloidal gold test. He appeared to be deeply depressed and retarded, expressing feelings of unworthiness and guilt. He did not manifest any signs of grandiosity or euphoria.

CEREBRAL INJURY

As the psychiatric sequelae of head injury have been fully reviewed by Lishman (1968, 1973, 1978) it would be superfluous to review this topic in detail again. In his investigation of 144 patients with severe psychiatric disability 1–5 years after head injury, Lishman (1968) found that affective symptoms were present in 113 patients of whom 58 were episodically or continuously depressed. Depression was more often associated with right-hemisphere damage, particularly to the frontal lobe. There was a strong association between affective and cognitive disturbances and somatic complaints. Symonds (1937) described two cases of manic-depressive psychosis developing before full recovery from head injury had occurred, but Achté *et al.* (1969) found an incidence of affective psychosis in only one per cent of 3,552 patients who had sustained head injuries in the Finnish–Russian War. There were 29 suicides, 12 of whom had suffered from depression. Of the 317 patients with psychosis 11.7 per cent were psychotically depressed. Lishman (1978) considered that affective psychoses after head trauma often bore little relationship to the degree of damage and that the injury had precipitated the depression in predisposed subjects. On the other hand, specific damage to the hypothalamus may be significant in some cases (Hoheisel and Walch, 1952), and Mock (1950) has described depressive illnesses as the presenting symptoms of subdural haematomas following head injury. The two patients reported by Hambert and Willén (1978) became severely depressed and finally committed suicide. Both, however, had suffered from recurrent bouts of depression before their injuries and in these patients it appears that the cerebral damage had precipitated affective changes in predisposed subjects.

Some of the largest series of patients reported have been based on military casualties, but today the battlefield has moved to the highways where car crashes provide a constant flow of patients with brain damage of all grades of severity. Lewin *et al.* (1979) have given details of 479 survivors, among whom four per cent had developed typical symptoms of endogenous depression during the ensuing 10–24 years. Suicide was responsible for three of the 75 deaths in this series when the cause of death was known.

Minor, as well as major, head injuries are often followed by protracted affective and other symptoms. In one study (Kay *et al.*, 1971) 37 per cent of patients with simple concussion and 23 per cent of those with brain damage were depressed when followed up six months later, but another investigation (Rutherford *et al.*, 1977) reported depression in only 5.5 per cent of their 145 patients with minor head injury reviewed six weeks later. A detailed investigation by Merskey and Woodforde (1972) of 27 patients who sustained minor head injuries found that seven showed typical features of endogenous depression and that another 19 had depression as a symptom. The authors commented, "The depression is sometimes typically endogenous in pattern but more often has mixed features." Interestingly, they concluded that depression after severe head injury comes on after a latent period of some months compared with these milder cases when the onset is more rapid. The aetiology of post-concussional affective disorder seems to have more to do with actual brain damage than, as is often believed, with the issue of compensation. There is evidence of slowing of cerebral blood flow, changes in the permeability of the blood–brain barrier, disturbances of vestibular function and post mortem findings of diffuse capillary haemorrhages, as well as the actual severance of nerve fibres in many parts of the brain (Taylor and Bell, 1966; Taylor, 1967; Oppenheimer, 1968). Findings of this kind might be considered sufficient grounds for assuming that affective and other changes after head injury are based on cerebral pathology and not wholly on personality factors or some special predisposition. The patients described by Merskey and Woodforde had no prior history of psychiatric illness.

CEREBROVASCULAR DISORDERS

An elderly patient, partially incapacitated by a stroke, might justifiably become depressed, but Folstein *et al.* (1977), comparing a group of recovered patients with orthopaedic controls, found that 45 per cent of the former compared with 10 per cent of the latter were depressed, despite similar degrees of disability. Psychological symptoms occurred more often in patients with right-hemisphere lesions. Robins (1976a), on the other hand, concluded that, compared with a group of patients with spinal cord lesions and orthopaedic diseases, the incidence of depression in stroke patients was no greater. Nonetheless, the patients with cerebrovascular disease scored higher on the Hamilton Rating Scale, and patients with non-dominant sided lesions were more depressed. Robins included among his controls patients with rheumatoid arthritis, some of whom might be expected to manifest serious depression. This would augment the control scores considerably. One would also have to take into account the possible depressing effects of anti-inflammatory drugs and steroids in arthritic patients. Both Post (1962) and Corsellis (1962) found a higher incidence of depression in elderly patients with cerebrovascular disease and, often, their responses to treatment were short-lived or minimal.

Maneros and Philipp (1978) found that seven patients with basilar artery insufficiency showed typical endogenous depression. Four were suicidal but none had a past history of affective disorder. In the absence of controls it is impossible to say how specific this finding is as Marshall (1972), in a survey of disorders of the vertebro-basilar arterial system did not mention depression as a prominent symptom.

However, both of the cases recently described by Trimble and Cummings (1981) had prominent affective symptoms following haemorrhage into the upper brain stem. Neither patient had a past history of major depression or mania. The authors considered that the location of these lesions in the upper brain stem would impinge on ascending adrenergic, serotonergic and dopaminergic transmitter pathways originating in brain stem nuclei and projecting to diencephalic and forebrain structures. Disruption of these tracts could have been responsible for their psychiatric, as well as their neurological, symptoms.

Evidence has accumulated showing that cerebrovascular accidents alter catecholamine levels in the blood and cerebro-spinal fluid of patients suffering from recent infarction or haemorrhage (Misra *et al.*, 1967; Meyer *et al.*, 1973; Meyer *et al.*, 1974). Experiments have also demonstrated disturbances of catecholamines when a cerebral infarction is produced in laboratory animals (Robinson *et al.*, 1975; Robinson and Bloom, 1977), but to what extent these changes can contribute to depression in patients who have suffered strokes is not known. One can hardly imagine that alterations in cerebral biochemistry observed during the acute phase of an illness would persist for months, long after recovery from the initial shock and disruption of brain substance had taken place. However, studies of homovanillic acid and 5-HIAA in the CSF of patients recovering from head injuries suggest impairment of dopaminergic and serotonergic metabolism for at least 2–3 months after injury (Vecht *et al.*, 1975).

The psychiatric sequelae of subarachnoid haemorrhage have been examined by Storey (1967, 1970, 1972) who followed 261 patients for six months to six years. Psychiatric morbidity was present in 55 per cent of the patients and was severe or very severe in 13 per cent. Depressive and anxiety states were frequent but unrelated to physical disability or to the degree of brain damage. In fact, whereas patients with brain damage who became depressed had little evidence of past affective illness, those without brain damage were more likely to have exhibited depressive reactions before their subarachnoid haemorrhages occurred. Sixty-nine of the 242 patients were depressed at follow-up, eight per cent being severely affected. Nonetheless, there were only three cases of manic-depressive psychosis. One of these had a previous history of depression and the other two were said to have been cyclothymic. On the evidence, one might conclude that some of Storey's patients were reacting adversely to their illnesses, whereas others had become more severely depressed as a direct consequence of brain damage. The possible involvement of the hypothalamus in patients with aneurysms of the posterior communicating artery might explain the rather larger number of severely depressed patients with this lesion. Logue *et al.* (1968) found alteration in mood in 15 and depression in 10 of 79 patients followed up after a subarachnoid haemorrhage. Three of those with mild hypomania had a past history of depression and, although seven of the depressed patients were thought to be reacting to their illnesses, in three the mood changes were regarded as being directly caused by their cerebral lesions.

In contrast to these findings Okava *et al.* (1980), reporting a follow-up investigation of 95 patients with haemorrhage from aneurysms of the anterior communicating artery, did not find any excess of depressed patients in the survivors.

CEREBRAL TUMOURS

Whereas there is general agreement that psychiatric symptoms are common in patients with cerebral tumours, the number with affective disorders is less easy to ascertain. Lishman (1978) has discussed the factors most likely to influence the development of psychiatric disturbances in patients with cerebral neoplasms. These include the site and type of tumour, its rate of growth, the presence or absence of raised intracranial pressure and the premorbid qualities of the patient. Reviewing the investigations of Keschner *et al.* (1938) and Hécaen and Ajuriaguerra (1956), Lishman records that between 52 and 78 per cent of patients with cerebral tumours suffered from mental symptoms, with 15–18 per cent developing them early in the course of the illness. Supratentorial tumours, particularly those arising in the frontal and temporal lobes, were more likely to cause psychiatric disturbances than those occurring elsewhere. Slowly growing tumours were also more conducive to mental symptoms before neurological signs appeared. With respect to affective disturbances, Keschner *et al.*, and Hécaen and Ajuriaguerra found that these occurred more often in patients with supratentorial neoplasms with, once again, predilection for temporal and frontal lobe sites of origin. Nevertheless, according to Lishman, affective changes rarely occur in isolation but frequently accompany other mental manifestations. He writes (1978, p. 264), "Depression and anxiety are . . . common with cerebral tumours, sometimes as understandable reactions and sometimes pathological in degree." Other patients may show an inappropriate euphoria and both depressive and hypomanic psychoses have been reported.

Soniat (1951) found that 66 (51.5 per cent) of 128 patients with cerebral tumours had psychiatric symptoms and again, predominantly, these occurred in patients with lesions in the frontal and temporal lobes. Assal *et al.* (1957), after reviewing the literature, recorded that 11.7 per cent of patients suffered from affective changes. In their own 35 cases, 19 of whom were psychiatrically assessed, three were depressed.

When one examines the numerous reports on patients with cerebral neoplasms, the frequency with which affective syndromes and symptoms are mentioned seems to some extent to depend on the source of the case material. Neurologists, preoccupied with the precise delineation of motor and sensory disturbances, may mention depression in passing but rarely give much detailed information. On the other hand, psychiatric investigators may emphasize emotional and other symptoms while omitting data on some of the neurological and pathological aspects of the tumours. What does emerge is the relatively high frequency with which cerebral tumours are not diagnosed during the lifetime of some psychiatric patients, only to come to light at autopsy (Jamieson and Henry, 1933; Redlich *et al.*, 1948; Strauss, 1955; Remington and Rupert, 1962; Andersson, 1970; Donald *et al.* 1972). Selecki

(1965) has drawn up a table (Table 5.1) showing the frequency of cerebral neoplasms among mental hospital patients and the percentage of cases where the diagnosis was missed during life. Lishman (1978) also quotes a number of autopsy studies on psychiatric patients which found a greater than expected incidence of undiagnosed cerebral tumours, with meningiomas predominating. Lishman, like other writers, emphasizes the need for the psychiatrist to be "brain-tumour conscious". He goes on to comment (p. 293), "The principal safeguard (against mis-diagnosis) is to be especially cautious in accepting as 'neurotic' someone whose previous adjustment has been good and in whom precipitating causes seem insufficient."

The presence of affective symptoms as reported by neurologists varies considerably. Botez (1974), for example, analysing the findings in five series of frontal lobe tumours amounting to 1,690 patients, has nothing to say about depression as a syndrome and states that he has never observed mania in patients with tumours in this region of the brain. He has more to say about personality change, euphoria and facetiousness as common features of tumours of the frontal lobe. Strobos (1974) mentions depression developing in patients with temporal lobe tumours but gives no details. Similarly, Suchenwirth (1974) comments that depression and euphoria can occur in association with parietal lobe tumours. Mania and depression have been described in patients with callosal tumours (Kretschmer, 1974) and neoplasms involving the thalamus (Payne, 1974). For more detailed information one has to turn to other sources, some of which have been summarized in Table 5.2. This shows data from twenty-nine reports and includes the total number of patients, the number with psychiatric symptoms, the frequency of depression or mania and, when possible, the cases where meningiomas were found at operation or autopsy. The impression of an excess of affective disorders associated with meningiomas may be fortuitous, largely because many of these studies were based on psychiatric patients and, in any case, the patients reported were probably selected because of important features of their illnesses. Furthermore, meningiomas are relatively silent tumours which can grow to a considerable size before detectable neurological symptoms appear. Consequently, patients with functional psychological disorders may be admitted to hospital where only later are the causes of their illnesses correctly diagnosed. The majority of such tumours will be supratentorial in site, although depression can occur when subtentorial meningiomas develop, as the following case illustrates.

A.B., female, aged 55. This patient was admitted suffering from a fairly severe depression which initially was attributed to her worries over a natural disaster three months earlier. There was no family history or past personal history of affective illness. Although she denied any intention of taking her life, she admitted that she felt that she would be better off dead. The only abnormal physical sign noted at the time was nystagmus which could have been caused by her medication. She was treated with tricyclic antidepressants and ECT. After her third ECT she became mildly confused and experienced vertigo. She fell, possibly because of the hypotensive effect of her medication. The antidepressants were stopped and she made a good recovery from her depression.

One year later she developed symptoms of raised intracranial pressure. A large meningioma in the posterior fossa was removed but unfortunately she died shortly after the operation. At the time of her psychiatric illness, apart from the nystagmus and confusion from ECT, she did not manifest any major neurological symptoms sufficient to permit a diagnosis of her tumour to be made.

Turning to individual reports, Minski (1933) found that 14 of his patients had been depressed and seven were described as "excited". From the description, some at least would have been classed as hypomanic, with others showing the more characteristic facetiousness, euphoria and inappropriate jocularity associated with frontal lobe tumours. Minski considered that these changes developed from the premorbid personality features of the patient, but it could also be argued that these qualities were the early presenting signs of slowly growing tumours. Unfortunately, Minski gave no details of the type of tumour in his patients but, of the 21 patients with depression or excitement, 13 of the tumours were on the left side, six on the right, with two others lying in the midline or cerebellum. Jamieson and Henry (1933) estimated the frequency of mental symptoms in patients with cerebral neoplasms to be 40–75 per cent, but possibly present in all patients. Of their 26 patients, seven had psychotic illnesses before their tumours were diagnosed. In 70 per cent of the cases the diagnosis was made at autopsy. Fifty per cent of the patients were consistently depressed, five threatened suicide and one made several attempts. Four of seven cases described in some detail had tumours in the posterior fossa. Another patient, who became depressed after an attack of influenza, also had a positive family history of affective disorder, but died later from a glioblastoma of the right cerebral hemisphere. In two other cases it could be said that severe depression long antedated the development of neoplasms and was probably unrelated to the final cause of death. Keschner *et al.* (1936) reported on 110 patients of whom 21 had various degrees of depression, while a further six were hypomanic. Irritability and depression were more common in patients with left-sided tumours, a fact which they attributed to the development of dysphasia in patients with tumours in the dominant hemisphere. In their later study of 530 cases (Keschner *et al.*, 1938) they found that 46 per cent experienced irritability, depression and anxiety which often preceded the diagnosis of cerebral neoplasm. They considered that, as mental symptoms were less frequent in patients with subtentorial tumours, raised intracranial pressure was not the major cause of such disturbances.

Table 5.1
Cerebral Tumours in Mental Hospitals: Autopsy Material[a]

Author and Year of Publication	Years of Study	Hospital	Number of Autopsies	Number of Tumours	Percentage of Tumours	Percentage of Diagnoses Missed Clinically
Blackburn (1903)	1884 to 1902	St. Elizabeth's Hospital	1642	29	1·7	72·4
Knapp (1906)	1906	Boston City Hospital	5069	101	1·9	?
Morse (1920)	1915 to 1917	Eleven Massachusetts hospitals	?	46	2·6	31·0
Davidoff and Ferraro (1929)	1903 to 1929	New York State Psychiatric Institute and 16 other New York State psychiatric hospitals	1450	75	6·1	?
Rudershausen (1932)	1932	Germany	31,698	546	1·7	?
Hoffman	1923 to 1935	St. Elizabeth's Hospital	2000[b]	69	3·4	33
Larson (1940)	1937 to 1938	Western Washington State Hospital	223	25	11·2	?
			2000	69	3·45	?
Crumpacker and Riese (1945)	1943 to 1944	Eastern State Hospital, Williamsburg, Vancouver	120	8	6·1	37·5
Braetalien and Gallavan (1950)	1938 to 1949	Colorado State Hospital	1168	54	4·6	55·0
Klotz (1957)	1947 to 1954	New York State Hospital No. 5	700	14	2	?
	1943 to 1953	New York State Hospital No. 6	510	5	1	60
	?	New York State Hospital No. 19	200	2	1	100
Patton and Sheppard (1956)	1907 to 1954	New York State Hospital No. 4	6171	99	1·6[c]	83·7
	1938 to 1954	Western State Hospital	2161	78	3·6	?

[a] From Selecki (1965), after Waggoner *et al.* (1954).
[b] These 2000 autopsies represent 99% of all deaths in this hospital from 1923 to 1935.
[c] Of these tumours, 32% were meningiomas.

Table 5.2
Reports of Psychiatric Symptoms in Patients with Cerebral Tumours

No.	Author and Date	No. of Cases	No. with Psychiatric Symptoms	Site of Tumour	No. Depressed	No. Manic or Hypomanic	No. with Meningiomas	Comments
1.	Kolodny (1928)	38	Not stated	T.L.		8	NK	No data on type of tumour given
2	Jamieson & Henry (1933)	26	26	Not stated	13	0	Not stated	Site and type of tumour not given
3	Minski (1933)	58	58	F.L. 26 T.L. 15 Other 17	14	7	Not stated	Type of tumour not given
4	Strauss & Keschner (1935)	85	77	F.L.	13	5	24	Depressed patients included 4 with manic-depressive psychosis
5	Keschner *et al.* (1936)	110	103	T.L.	21	6	13	Affective symptoms not related in paper to type of tumour
6	Frazier (1936)	105	Not stated	F.L.	16	9	40	Relationship between mood disorder and tumour type not discussed
7	Keschner *et al.* (1938)	530	412	F.L. 68 T.L. 56 P.L. 32 O.L. 11	245 with affective symptoms		99	Relationship between type of tumour and psychiatric symptoms not stated
8	Sachs (1950)	8	8	(See comments)	1	0	8	Depressed patient had right parietal lobe parasagittal tumour

No.	Author (year)			Site				Comment
9	Oppler (1950)	1	1	Right para-sagittal	0	0	1	
10	Smith (1954)	3	3	Left frontal	1	1	1	Only one patient had a cerebral neoplasm
11	Waggoner & Bagchi (1954)	6	6	F.L. 3, Other 3	4	0	2	
12	Strauss (1955)	4	4	T.L. 1, F.L. 2, A.N. 1	4	0	1	
13	Netsky & Watson (1956)	6	1	F.L. 5	1	0	1	Depressed case had diffuse lymphoma
14	Assai et al. (1957)	35	Not stated	Diffuse 1, Posterior fossa	3	0	NK	Only 19 psychiatrically examined. 8 of 16 survivors depressed post-operatively
15	Pool & Carroll (1958)	25	25	Varied sites	19	0	7	One patient had acoustic neuroma, another, epidermoid cyst
16	Prout & Epple (1959)	1	1	Right frontal	1	0	1	
17	Remington & Rupert (1962)	34	34	No data	10	0	NK	
18	Malamud (1967)	18	18	T.L. 11, Third ventricle 7	4	1	0	All temporal lobe cases had epilepsy
19	Hunter et al. (1968)	3	3	F.L.	1	1	3	
20	Avery (1971)	7	7	F.L.	5	1	7	
21	Direkze et al. (1971)	25	17	F.L.	5	0	6	
22	Blustein & Seeman (1972)	3	3	F.L. 1, T.L. 1, Other 1	1	1	0	
23	Donald et al. (1972)	12	12	F.L. 4, T.L. 3, Other 5	2?	0	2	Psychiatric data inadequate for accurate diagnosis

Table 5.2 — *continued*

No.	Author and Date	No. of Cases	No. with Psychiatric Symptoms	Site of Tumour	No. Depressed	No. Manic or Hypomanic	No. with Meningiomas	Comments
24	Rieke (1975)	9	9	See Table 5.3	9	0	2	
25	Rieke (1975)	14	14	Midline 6 T.L. 5 Parasagittal 2 Other 1	14	0	6	
26	Kanakaratnam & Direkze (1976)	56	26	F.L.	12	0	16	
27	Carlson (1977)	3	3	F.L.	3	0	1	
28	Burkle & Lipowski (1978)	1	1	Third ventricle	1	0	0	
29	Heath *et al.* (1979)	31	9	Cerebellum	3	0	1	Two cases verified at operation

F.L. = Frontal Lobe   T.L. = Temporal Lobe
P.L. = Parietal Lobe   O.L. = Occipital Lobe
A.N. = Acoustic Neuroma

A valuable report by Pool and Carroll (1958) gives details of 25 patients with cerebral tumours, 11 of whom had been receiving psychotherapy, in two cases for 13 years. Nineteen of these patients had been diagnosed as depression and 14 had been treated with ECT. Of the 25, seven were found to have meningiomas, one an acoustic neuroma and one an epidermoid tumour. All these nine patients with benign, treatable neoplasms were depressed. Of the 19 depressed patients, seven had right-sided and seven left-sided lesions, four had bilateral cerebral involvement, and one was found to have a generalized lymphoma of the meninges. In all except one patient the tumours were situated supratentorially. The editorial comment on this paper is well worth repeating: "There is a pathetic, poignant ineffectiveness about doing psychotherapy in the hope of exorcising an expanding brain tumour. We have become so enchanted with emotional factors in the production of symptoms that we sometimes forget organic components".

Although depression and irritability are the commonest affective disorders in patients with cerebral neoplasms, Oppler (1950) described a 29-year-old man who became manic in association with a right parasagittal meningioma. He made a good recovery when the tumour was removed. Avery (1971) found depression in five of his seven patients, mood swings in four, and episodes of mania or hypomania in four, with a further patient becoming hypomanic post-operatively. Apart from one manic patient with a positive family history of suicide but no past personal history of affective disorder, no details of contributions by genetic factors or premorbid affective episodes to the psychiatric disturbances of the other patients were provided.

In contrast, Hunter *et al.* (1968) found that all three of their patients with mental symptoms associated with frontal meningiomas had negative family histories and past personal histories of affective disorder. Their first patient, a 62-year-old woman, was depressed but made a good recovery after surgery. Similarly, none of the four patients with involutional melancholia associated with a variety of affections of the brain (Smith, 1954) had positive family or past personal histories of depression. One patient, a 56-year-old man, was depressed for about one year before his left parasagittal meningioma was diagnosed and successfully removed. Carlson (1977) gives details of three severely depressed patients with frontal-lobe tumours, one meningioma and two astrocytomas. None had a past personal history or positive family history of affective disorder, but one patient with a frontal parasagittal meningioma had a long history of epilepsy and psychosis. Although not specifically mentioned, one might assume that the depressed and confused patient with a colloid cyst of the third ventricle described by Burkle and Lipowski (1978) had not previously experienced any psychiatric illness.

Unfortunately, few of the other writers listed in Table 5.2 comment on the presence or absence of earlier affective disorders in their patients. Sachs (1950) was more concerned with dementia caused by large meningiomas, although his eighth patient, a 69-year-old woman, was depressed for six months before personality changes and dementia supervened. She had no previous history of psychiatric illness and recovered fully after a right parietal parasagittal meningioma was removed.

Three of the six patients described by Waggoner and Bagchi (1954) were depressed. One of them, with a three-year history of depression treated with ECT, died after the removal of a large meningioma situated below the left cerebellar hemisphere. Another patient with an ependymoma of the fourth ventricle was initially depressed but later became manic. The third patient was severely depressed and suicidal. She was found to have a right hemisphere glioblastoma involving the frontal, temporal and parietal lobes. Chambers (1955) described eight patients with a variety of cerebral lesions, including a 50-year-old woman who became depressed in association with a large cerebellar cyst. Soniat (1951) gave few details of the psychiatric disorders affecting 51.5 per cent of his 128 patients, but among the six more detailed case histories is one depressed patient with a left frontal glioblastoma. Rupert and Remington (1963), in a 30-year survey of patients admitted to a psychiatric hospital covering 17,000 patients, found that in only 0.2 per cent were psychoses associated with cerebral tumours. Eight patients were depressed and three suicidal. Another patient with a right frontal meningioma and depression was reported by Prout and Epple (1959). Strauss (1955) described four depressed patients with cerebral neoplasms whose correct diagnoses emerged as a result of electroencephalographic examinations. The tumours were a glioblastoma of the left temporal lobe, a metastatic carcinoma in the right frontal lobe and a large right frontal parasagittal meningioma whose successful removal terminated three years of depression treated by ECT and psychoanalysis. The fourth patient, who had been recurrently depressed and suicidal for some years, had a right-sided acoustic neuroma. The author considered that this patient's past history of depression was a determining factor with the tumour acting as a precipitant of psychiatric illness.

What might appear to be an unusual and not easily explained cause of psychosis is the presence of lesions of the cerebellum and vermis. Heath *et al.* (1979), using CT scan examinations, found that 31 patients with various functional psychoses showed "pathology of the vermis". Three of these patients were depressed. Of two who were treated surgically, one had a tentorial meningioma and the other a cystic tumour of the vermis and lateral lobe of the cerebellum.

Malamud (1967) reviewed the findings in 18 patients with temporal lobe tumours. Four were recurrently depressed and suffered epileptic attacks which, the author felt, were significant causes of their affective disorders. Five of the 25 patients with frontal lobe tumours described by Direkze *et al.* (1971) had been treated unsuccessfully for depression and 26 of 56 patients with frontal lobe tumours (Kanakaratnam and Direkze, 1976) presented with pyschiatric symptoms. In 12 the initial diagnosis was depression. Sixteen of

Table 5.3
Depressed Patients with Cerebral Tumours[a]

Case No.	Sex	Age	Duration of Symptoms	Type of Tumour	Site of Tumour	Past History of Affective Disorder	Comments
1	F	50	20 years	Meningioma	Right parasagittal	Positive	Also epileptic
2	F	30	Post-operative	Sarcoma	Fronto-parietal	Negative	
3	F	59	7½ years	Glioblastoma	Right lateral ventricle	Positive	
4	F	59	3 years	Glioblastoma	Right temporo-parieto-occipital	Negative	Suicide attempt made
5	F	60	2 years	Meningioma	Left tentorium cerebelli	Negative	Suicide attempt made
6	M	31	8 months	Angioreticuloma	Brain stem/pulvinar	Negative	Epileptic after head injury
7	M	48	1 year	Oligodendroglioma	Left frontal	Negative	
8	M	58	3 years	Astrocytoma	Right fronto-parietal	Negative	
9	M	35	5 years	Glioblastoma	Left temporo-parietal	Negative	

[a]Rieke (1975)

the 56 tumours were meningiomas, but how many of these were associated with depression is not stated. Assai *et al.* (1957) have also commented on how depression can occur well before the emergence of neurological symptoms in some patients with cerebral tumours.

Finally, Rieke (1975), after surveying the German literature, reported on 23 patients with depression associated with cerebral tumours, including nine of his own. The principal findings on these nine are shown in Table 5.3. Two had experienced brief neurotic depressive reactions many years before the final onset of endogenous depression, which developed a relatively short time before their brain tumours were diagnosed. Three had suffered from epileptic attacks, and two had made suicidal attempts. The first patient had been treated for recurrent depression since the age of 30 and, in all probability, his relapse at the age of 47 could have been precipitated by his developing meningioma. Six of the other 14 patients described by Rieke had meningiomas. He comments that, although a depressive psychosis can be the presenting feature of a cerebral tumour, it has little value as a pointer to the site and type of neoplasm.

Many of the authors quoted have mentioned specifically the frequency with which cerebral tumours are missed in patients presenting with psychiatric disorders. In this context affective disturbances are no exception, and the main task of the physician is to examine his patient with meticulous care in order to detect minor neurological disabilities which could be present well before the correct diagnosis becomes obvious. It would be unreasonable to subject all psychiatric patients to extensive neuroradiological examinations, but with the advent of the CT scanner, greater use of this technique would probably permit the diagnosis of far more psychiatric patients with treatable brain lesions than the studies that have been quoted have revealed.

BASAL GANGLIA SYNDROMES

Parkinson's Disease

"An association between parkinsonism and depression is now well established." So writes Lishman (1978, p. 757), who also mentions that the commonest psychotic disorders in parkinsonism are affective in nature. Furthermore, although in some patients the depression is reactive, in others it can be directly caused by the disease process. Although the discovery of a biochemical basis for idiopathic and post-encephalitic parkinsonism gives us a better understanding of the aetiology of depression in these conditions, it is still important to assess the relative contributions of genetic endowment, past personal history of affective disorder and, most relevant today, the effects of treatment, particularly those of L-dopa.

It is known that in idiopathic and post-encephalitic parkinsonism there is a reduction in catecholamines and 5-HT, particularly in the striatum (Hornykiewicz, 1971). The loss of dopamine results in a relative preponderance of cholinergic activity; hence the value of anticholinergic drugs in the treatment of the disease. However, it is not only the nigrostriatal tract which is affected but, from the point of view of episodes of depression, the fall of noradrenalin in limbic forebrain structures (Hornykiewicz, 1977) and in the nucleus accumbens and para-olfactory gyrus (Farley *et al.* 1977) is probably relevant. The nucleus accumbens is part of the dopamine-rich limbic forebrain, an area which is of importance for the experience and expression of emotion. However, the role of reduced dopamine as a cause of depression is probably slight in comparison with the loss of noradrenalin and 5-HT. Puite *et al.* (1973) treated 11 depressed patients suffering from Parkinson's disease with L-dopa and a decarboxylase inhibitor and found that, although physical symptoms improved, the patients' moods did not, indicating that depression in Parkinson's disease is relatively independent of the pathogenesis of the physical disorder. Furthermore, the occurrence in paralysis agitans of degenerative changes in the locus coeruleus (Greenfield and Bosanquet, 1953), the main source of adrenergic efferent tracts to the limbic and other parts of the forebrain, seems to provide a possible biochemical and structural basis for affective disorders in this condition.

Warburton (1967), who compared parkinsonian patients with controls, found a higher degree of depression, particularly in female patients, and Robins (1976b), matching 45 such cases with other severely disabled patients, also found that depression occurred more often in the former group. Both parkinsonian and control patients had similar degrees of disability, and it was noted how the affective disorders responded to treatment, although the disabilities did not change. Celesia and Wanamaker (1972) reported that 37 per cent of their patients were depressed on admission or during the preceding year and felt that their mood changes were unrelated to their ages or the duration of the disease.

Horn (1974), who compared parkinsonian patients with a number of paraplegic cases and normal subjects, found similar degrees of depression in the first two groups, both of whom were more depressed than the controls. Age, sex and the degree and duration of the disability had little bearing on the severity of depression shown by these patients. In contrast with these observations, Mjönes (1949) did not detect much in the way of depression in his subjects, although he noted now other writers had stressed the affective disturbances which often antedated the neurological syndrome. Mindham (1970), in a study of 89 patients with symptoms of parkinsonism admitted to the Bethlem-Maudsley Hospitals (London), found that 55 had been diagnosed as depressed and that depression appeared as a major symptom in 90 per cent of the whole sample. Twelve per cent of the patients had a previous history of depression and early dementia was present in about one-third of the group. In many patients, depression improved with appropriate treatment despite the lack of any amelioration of physical symptoms. Although the author considers that depression is linked with the degree of disability, one might rather conclude that it is independent of the neurological symptomatology, although a common pathogenesis might be inferred in the light of the biochemical changes mentioned earlier.

Marsh and Markham (1973) also found that depression in patients with Parkinson's disease did not necessarily improve when the physical symptoms responded well to appropriate treatment. In a later study of psychiatric symptoms in 40 parkinsonian patients treated with L-dopa (Mindham *et al.* 1976), 22 developed depression in the course of treatment, but more than half of these had suffered from earlier depressive episodes. Before treatment was started 24 of 50 patients showed evidence of affective disturbance, indicating a high incidence of psychiatric disorder in association with Parkinson's disease. The authors considered that there was an association between physical disability and the appearance of affective symptoms, and that the association was causal in nature.

The exact relationship between depression and the degree of physical disability in parkinsonian patients remains uncertain. Whereas some writers have found that depressive symptoms respond well to tricyclic antidepressant drugs without a corresponding improvement in their physical status, Mindham (1974), reviewing some of the findings, including his own, asserts that depression correlates well with the degree of physical disability. No doubt there is considerable variation in individual response to treatment, which could account for these discrepant observations.

Svanborg (1973) and Brown *et al.* (1973) also found a high incidence of depression in their patients. Brown *et al.* compared two groups, one attending between 1954 and 1969 — the pre-L-dopa period — the other diagnosed between 1970 and 1972. In the former cohort, depression occurred in 52 per cent of the patients compared with 41 per cent in the latter. Asnis (1977), who reviewed some of the literature on this topic, considered that only 10–12 per cent of parkinsonian patients had suffered from depression before the onset of neurological symptoms. Consequently he argues that the psychiatric disorder is probably reactive. Nonetheless, it can appear in classic endogenous form early in the disease when physical symptoms are not severe and occasionally can be the presenting symptom of the basal ganglia disturbance (Jackson *et al.* 1923; Kearney, 1964).

The question of genetic predisposition and other factors in Parkinson's disease have been discussed by Strang (1970), who recorded a high incidence of the condition in patients exposed to a particular strain of influenza. Stern *et al.* (1977) felt that a genetic factor contributed to depression in Parkinson patients, but Winokur *et al* . (1978) concluded that the lifetime expectancy of depression in the relatives of Parkinson patients was no different from the general population. This suggests that, when depression does occur in the course of Parkinson's disease, it has more to do with biochemical changes in cerebral structures concerned with affect than with any predisposition. Heston (1980) likewise found no evidence of increased affective disorders in first degree relatives of parkinsonian patients.

On the other hand, an unusual familial variety of fatal parkinsonism associated with severe depression has been described (Perry *et al.*, 1975; Purdy *et al.*, 1979). All the patients so far reported have been in their fifth decade of life, with death occurring from respiratory failure some 4–6 years later. The initial presentation is a picture of severe and intractable depression, with the later development of parkinsonian symptoms equally unresponsive to treatment. Although the earlier report considered that a deficiency of taurine was responsible for this disorder, the later study of twin brothers found that the brain content of taurine was within normal limits. In contrast, there was a marked reduction in tyrosine hydroxylase, dopamine, homovanillic acid and L-dopa decarboxylase in the many samples of brain tissue that were examined. As might be expected, severe degenerative changes were observed in the substantia nigra and basal ganglia, as well as focal gliosis in the medulla, with mild depigmentation of the locus coeruleus. The severe depression at the onset of this condition seems to imply a profound disturbance of catecholamine metabolism, which only later causes neurolgical symptoms.

Effects of Treatment

Although the relationship of drugs to affective disorder will be discussed in a later chapter, the psychiatric complications of L-dopa therapy need to be examined here. A number of authors have reported conflicting findings on the psychiatric side-effects of L-dopa, but Goodwin (1972), reviewing the cumulative results of 20 studies involving 908 patients, found that 4.2 per cent became depressed and 1.5 per cent manic or hypomanic. The best predictor of the depressive response to treatment was a previous history of affective disorder, as is the case when hypomanic reactions occur (Ryback and Schwab, 1971; Pearlman, 1971). In fact, if patients with previous attacks of psychiatric illness are excluded, these unwanted effects of L-dopa are relatively low, a finding which suggests that the drug acts as a precipitant rather than as an essential cause of psychiatric disturbances. This greater frequency of previous affective illness in patients who became severely depressed when treated with L-dopa was also observed by Mindham *et al.* (1976). Nonetheless, not all patients who become depressed following the administration of L-dopa have past histories of affective disorders. For example, only one of the two patients described by Wagshul and Daroff (1969) had suffered from earlier episodes of depression. Jenkins and Groh (1970) describe moderate to severe depression in 14 of 90 patients treated with L-dopa, and another patient became manic and grandiose. Neither he nor eight of the other 14 patients had suffered from depression in the past. Four of the patients were suicidal and practically all the depressed patients responded well to treatment with imipramine. These authors considered that Parkinson's disease may predispose patients to severe psychotic, depressive reactions which will be aggravated by L-dopa.

In contrast with those who have found a high incidence of depression in patients treated with L-dopa, others have claimed that depression in parkinsonian patients improves with L-dopa (Svanborg, 1973; Brown *et al.*, 1973). However, there is no satisfactory evidence that L-dopa is an effective antidepressant (Mindham *et al.*, 1976), although it may well improve motor retardation which appears to be associated with a low turnover of dopamine (Van Praag *et al.*, 1975). Hence, in retarded depression, L-dopa may improve motility but will have no beneficial effect on the patient's mental state. Although Riklan *et al.* (1973) observed improvement in depression in patients treated with L-dopa, this was not maintained over the subsequent two years, during which time these patients relapsed.

Of further relevance to the problem of affective disorder in Parkinson's disease are a number of reports on the results of ECT for depression in this condition (Lebensohn and Jenkins, 1975; Asnis, 1977; Klee *et al.*, 1979; Yudofsky, 1979). These investigators found that ECT for depression in Parkinson's disease resistant to drug treatment will bring about a good remission of symptoms with a concomitant improvement in physical disability. Unfortunately, the improvements in physical and psychological health were not sustained in all cases. This response to ECT suggests that increased synthesis of catecholamines brought about by the treatment is the cause of both physical and mental changes and that the pathogenesis of depression is intimately linked with the biochemical changes that have been discovered in the brains of parkinsonian patients. In this context Modigh (1976) found that, whereas ECT caused a sustained increase in noradrenalin neuronal activity, changes in dopaminergic and serotonergic neurons were relatively brief.

Also relevant to this topic are the changes observed after stereotactic surgery to the thalamic nuclei. Hays *et al.* (1966) reported on 27 patients in whom lesions were placed in the ventrolateral nucleus. Most of the patients were mildly or moderately depressed pre-operatively, but on recovering from the treatment there was a decided elevation of mood with loss of early morning waking and feelings of hopelessness, together with an increase in weight and regained interest in normal activities. Not all the patients showed a corresponding improvement in physical symptoms, but they too were mildly euphoric. The authors considered the outcome to be a specific result of the treatment and not equivalent to the behaviour which used to follow prefrontal leucotomy. McFie (1960) also commented on euphoria in seven patients and depression in another treated with stereotactic surgery. Affective changes were more often seen in patients in whom surgery had been performed on the right-sided rather than on the left-sided thalamus.

Post-Encephalitic Parkinsonism

Although most of the papers quoted have been based mainly on patients with idiopathic or "arteriosclerotic" parkinsonism, there is little evidence that patients whose symptoms are post-encephalitic in origin suffer any less from affective disturbances. Lishman (1978) commented that in the early stages of the disease both depression and suicide were common and that affective psychoses were relatively frequent. In some patients with such prolonged, crippling symptoms, depression could justifiably be regarded as a reaction to the illness, although one might conjecture that compulsive elements could contribute to sudden episodes of suicidal behaviour. A most remarkable account of the response of some of these long-term post-encephalitic patients to treatment with L-dopa has been given by Sacks (1973). Patients who had been locked into states of immobility and distorted posture suddenly regained freedom of movement. States of manic excitement and ecstasy developed but improvement, unfortunately, was short-lived and finally depression returned with a recurrence of physical symptoms.

In summary, there is clear evidence that severe endogenous depression is a frequent accompaniment of Parkinson's disease, sometimes leading to suicidal behaviour. Although in a percentage of patients this may be considered as a reaction to increasing disability, in others it is likely that biochemical changes in the nigrostriatal and meso-limbic systems will be responsible for affective disorders. On the other hand, patients who become depressed in response to treatment with L-dopa frequently have suffered from previous depressive episodes, a finding which seems to imply that in these cases the drug is acting more as a precipitant than as an essential cause of affective disturbance.

Huntington's Chorea

Huntington (1872) considered that one of the cardinal features of the disease which bears his name was "a tendency to insanity and suicide", and patients developing the illness may become depressed or psychotic well before the onset of dementia or abnormal movements. Oltman and Friedman (1961), describing their findings in 57 patients, found depression with or without suicidal threats and acts occurring early in the development of the disease in 21 cases. There were six suicidal attempts. Frank manic-depressive psychosis was unusual, although Lishman (1978) mentions that recurrent depressive psychosis, responsive to treatment with drugs or ECT, is common. Oliver (1970) recorded a high incidence of suicide and attempted suicide and of melancholia as the presenting syndrome among Huntington's chorea cases in Northamptonshire. However, among the siblings there was also considerable evidence of psychopathology including psychotic depression and suicidal behaviour. In contrast, James *et al.* (1969) did not specifically mention depression amongst the early signs of Huntington's chorea in patients presenting with psychiatric illness. Dewhurst *et al.* (1969) observed prodromal symptoms of depression in seven of 80 patients, 15 of whom were admitted with depression, suicidal attempts or self-starvation. Mood was characteristically labile, but depressed states appeared to predominate.

In a further study of 102 patients (Dewhurst *et al.*, 1970), there was one suicide and 10 attempted suicides. Of 57 patients presenting psychiatrically, 10 were given an initial diagnosis of affective disorder. McHugh and Folstein (1975), in a report on eight patients, considered that the disturbance of mood resembled more the depressed phase of manic-depressive psychosis than a reactive depression. At times depression could be of delusional intensity resulting in suicide, which was the cause of death in seven per cent of patients in another series. They argued against the affective disturbance being a simple reaction to a progressive and incurable disease but, in any case, in some patients episodes of manic-like behaviour may occur as part of the dementing process. Such a phenomenon may have some resemblance to the inappropriate euphoria observed in some multiple sclerosis patients showing signs of cognitive impairment. Mayer-Gross *et al.* (1969, p. 624) stated that the commonest psychosis seen in Huntington's chorea was a shallow ill-sustained depression which often resulted in suicidal attempts.

The biochemical findings in the brains of patients dying from Huntington's chorea shed little light on the pathogenesis of affective disorder in these patients. Bird (1978) has reviewed work which has found a reduction of GABA in basal ganglia and substantia nigra (Perry *et al.*, 1973). In addition, there is a decline in choline-acetyltransferase activity with consequent falls in acetylcholine. The abnormal movements in Huntington's chorea, which resemble those shown by patients suffering from drug-induced tardive dyskinesia, appear to be caused by sensitivity of degenerating basal ganglia neurons to dopaminergic stimulation. Consequently, administering L-dopa to Huntington's chorea patients will aggravate their neurological symptoms, whereas depleting dopamine levels in the brain with drugs like reserpine and tetrabenazine will often reduce the severity of the chorea. Unfortunately both drugs will precipitate profound depression in some patients (Swash *et al.*, 1972; McLellan *et al.*, 1974). Whether the increase in platelet MAO activity in Huntington's chorea patients (Mann and Chiu,

1978) is a reflection of similar changes in the brain is unknown. If this did occur one might speculate that such an increase could well have a bearing on the frequency of depression in these patients.

In summary, there is evidence of an association of depression and suicidal behaviour in patients who ultimately develop the syndrome of Huntington's chorea. An individual with a positive family history of Huntington's chorea who becomes depressed might be showing the first manifestations of this progressive neuropsychiatric illness but, considering the frequency of psychopathology among non-affected relatives (Oliver, 1970), such a conclusion could be incorrect.

Miscellaneous Basal Ganglia Syndromes

A number of conditions regarded as being secondary to basal ganglia dysfunction may, from time to time, be associated with depression. For example, generalized torsion dystonia, a rare genetic disorder largely confined to Ashkenazi Jews, although often erroneously diagnosed initially as hysteria, can be associated with affective disorder. Lesser and Fahn (1978) mention that three of 84 patients with psychiatric disorders, including 37 so-called hysterics, suffered from manic-depressive psychosis, and a fourth patient was depressed. Patients affected with spasmodic torticollis undoubtedly can experience depression partly, one supposes, on account of the disability, which can be severe in some cases. Most patients with Gilles de la Tourette's syndrome appear to adjust well despite the social embarrassment occasioned by their symptoms (Shapiro *et al.*, 1973). Depression as a complication is rarely mentioned, an exception being the patient described by Carney (1977). This patient, a 29-year-old woman, developed the syndrome at the age of five but recovered at the age of 11. Recently, in the face of a number of domestic stresses, she became depressed and the Tourette symptoms recurred. Both physical and psychological symptoms responded well to 100 mg daily of a tricyclic antidepressant drug.

Striato-Nigral Degeneration

Two rare conditions, striato-nigral degeneration and the Shy–Drager syndrome, both of which show prominent parkinsonian features, warrant further mention. The former condition, originally described by Adams *et al.* (1964), is characterized by progressive physical disability developing in middle life caused by major atrophic changes in the striatum and substantia nigra. Although little was said about mental symptoms, Adams (1968) mentions episodes of confusion occurring before the onset of physical symptoms in one patient and mild personality changes associated with unstable mood and apparent early dementia in another. A third patient had a past history of a suicidal attempt with an overdose of barbiturates.

The Shy–Drager Syndrome

Patients with Shy–Drager syndrome, sometimes known as idiopathic orthostatic hypotension, may develop severe basal ganglia symptoms. One of the patients described by Brown *et al.* (1973) who deteriorated when treated with L-dopa was an example of this condition. However, psychiatric disorders, in contrast with neurological and autonomic disturbances, have not been considered in detail. Barr (1979), for example, who has given an extensive reivew of the condition, does not comment on any abnormal mental states. Bannister and Oppenheimer (1972) report that one of their three cases, a 67-year-old man, was depressed and being treated with imipramine. He developed fairly severe parkinsonian symptoms and died from a carcinoma of the lung.

Depression in this condition could possibly be the consequence of loss of cerebral catecholamines. Black and Petito (1976) demonstrated loss of tyrosine hydroxylase, the rate-limiting enzyme for the formation of adrenalin and dopamine, in the brains of patients who had been diagnosed as examples of the Shy–Drager syndrome during life. There was also evidence of degenerative changes in the nigro-striatal system and locus coeruleus in the brain stem.

6

Neurological Disease and Affective Disorder: Part II

MULTIPLE SCLEROSIS

"Suffering from depression . . . the melancholy fit fell very suddenly, all the colour went out of my life and the world was dirty grey." Thus wrote Barbellion (1919, p. 89); and, later (p. 93), "Back at work — a terrible day — thoughts of suicide — a pistol. Returned to London very depressed. Am not so well as I was three weeks ago. The sight of my eye is affected . . . I have a numb feeling on one side of my face and my right arm is less mobile."

Although Barbellion was describing severe depression which, for the most part, came on before neurological disability had become the dominant feature, most textbooks emphasize the occurrence of unexpected cheerfulness as the commonest affective disturbance in patients with multiple sclerosis. This is largely the result of the paper by Cottrell and Wilson (1926) who reported that 63 per cent of their patients showed an inappropriate euphoria, whereas only 10 per cent were depressed. Despite the presence of major neurological disability, 84 per cent of their patients experienced a sense of physical well-being, while 97 per cent showed some degree of emotional lability. Runge (1928), on the other hand, considered that euphoria was a consequence of intellectual deterioration coming on later in the course of the disease, with depression being more common during the early stages. Among psychiatric writers, at least, Runge's views seem to have been more generally accepted (Braceland and Giffin, 1950; Canter, 1951; Pratt, 1951; Surridge, 1969), but no satisfactory explanation for the discordant findings of Cottrell and Wilson has ever been given. In contrast to their observations that 63 per cent of their patients were euphoric, later observers have found evidence for this in far fewer cases. Braceland and Giffin (1950) considered that only 10 per cent of their patients were euphoric in contrast with 20 per cent who were depressed. Surridge (1969) found that 26 per cent of his patients were euphoric but a further 27 per cent were depressed. Kahana *et al.* (1971), in a study of patients in Israel, recorded euphoria in only five per cent and depression in six per cent of their patients, three per cent of whom committed suicide, a rate that was 14 times greater than in the general Israel population. Pratt (1951) commented more particularly on emotional lability (35 per cent), but only six per cent of his patients admitted to a sense of increased physical well-being. It is important to distinguish between the outward manifestations of mood from the patient's real sentiments least an apparent labile cheerfulness be taken as the patient's true feelings when a far different affective state prevails (Burnfield and Burnfield, 1978). Pratt (1951) also commented on Barbellion's awareness of the disparity between his outward appearance of normality and gaiety and his inner feelings of clouded depression and foreboding. Surridge found that eight of 28 euphoric patients were, in fact, feeling depressed and he considered that euphoria, which was associated with intellectual deterioration in all but two examples, was a pathological phenomenon, the direct result of damage to the central nervous system.

On commonsense grounds it might be expected that patients with a progressively incapacitating disease with repeated remissions and relapses would be depressed. The belief that depression is an understandable response to the illness is held by a number of writers (Gallinek and Kalinowsky, 1958; Surridge, 1969; Kurtzke, 1970; Lurati *et al.*, 1976). Lishman (1978) states, "Depression appears to be reactive in origin in the majority of cases and there is little reason to suspect that it is founded in cerebral pathology." Surridge similarly asserts that "depressive states occur in multiple sclerosis with far greater frequency than has been considered hitherto" and that "they are psychogenic or reactive in nature". Lurati *et al.* (1976), on the other hand, commented that the depth of depression was associated with increasing severity of neurological symptoms, a finding which suggests that, in some patients at least, cerebral damage could have been a possible cause. Similarly, Braceland and Giffin (1950) observed both euphoria and depression in patients with evidence of organic deterioration. Consequently, one might argue that in some patients depression is as likely as euphoria to be the result of brain damage and that the former response is no more a psychogenic reaction than the inappropriate cheerfulness. In short, there is evidence that in some cases manic-depressive or purely depressive symptoms will occur as a result of cerebral impairment.

A number of authors have reported depression before neurological symptoms appear. Pommé *et al.* (1963), for example, described six cases of multiple sclerosis starting with depression whose cause was only diagnosed when neurological signs suddenly developed. Similarly, Mûr *et al.* (1966) recorded how psychiatric illness sometimes precedes the onset of physical symptoms. All three of their patients showed evidence of dementia and one was depressed. An important example was provided by Bignami *et al.* (1961) who described the onset of severe depression in a 22-year-old man one month before symptoms of neurological disease appeared. There was no past history of depression in this patient, who deteriorated rapidly and died. At autopsy he was found to have plaques of demyelination in the hypothalamus, cerebral peduncles and pons. The hypothalamic lesions were thought to be responsible for his severe mood change and one might, on anatomical grounds, assume that in other patients lesions in various parts of the limbic brain would cause affective changes of sufficient severity to justify a diagnosis of endogenous depression or mania. Young *et al.* (1976) stated that mental changes could be early features of multiple sclerosis before physical signs of the disease appear. Two of their five patients were depressed and successfully treated. These authors related the affective symptoms to brain-stem lesions and widespread cerebral demyelination and considered that the frequency of early psychiatric symptoms in multiple sclerosis had been under-estimated. Crémieux *et al.* (1959) described a 47-year-old man who, for a year, had suffered from neurological symptoms of moderate severity but who developed a manic-depressive psychosis. There was no past history or family history of affective disorder. At autopsy plaques of demyelination in both temporal lobes and the thalamus were regarded as the causes of his affective symptoms. Goodstein and Ferrell (1977), who surveyed 200 reports on multiple sclerosis, found only 15 which mentioned emotional difficulties before the onset of physical symptoms. Only five suggested a common pathogenic process for both physical and psychological symptoms. This apparent absence of interest in the psychological status of their patients on the part of neurologists is disconcerting but by no means unusual. For example, a monograph on multiple sclerosis based on 1062 patients seen by McAlpine *et al.* (1955) is quite remarkably uninformative about the mental states of the patients, some of whom are described in considerable neurological detail. Goodstein and Ferrell failed to find any paper in which depression was the presenting feature of multiple sclerosis, but went on to record it in three patients of their own. One of these, a 33-year-old woman with diffuse cortical impairment and severe depressive illness of three months duration, failed to respond to antidepressant treatment. She had shown signs of remitting and relapsing neurological symptoms for some years before her present admission. In addition, she had suffered from recurrent psychiatric illnesses described as "depression" and "nervousness". O'Malley (1966), in his review of the older literature, was manifestly concerned with the relative lack of information on the mental state of multiple sclerosis patients either before or after the onset of the disease. Charcot (1877), an exception, commented on intellectual impairment, euphoria, depression and psychosis occurring in some patients.

Other writers emphasized hysteria as a common feature of this condition and in some instances suicide is mentioned as the consequence of severe mental disorder. O'Malley described three patients with mental changes one of whom, a 35-year-old man, suffered from two attacks of depression before the onset of multiple sclerosis symptoms. He had suicidal ideas during the second attack from which he did not make a complete recovery. Ultimately he became demented and died. Plaques and demyelination were observed throughout the cerebral cortex and basal ganglia.

Caplan and Nadelson (1980) described a 40-year-old female patient who first developed neurological symptoms at the age of 25 with recurrence at the age of 33. Three years later she became severely depressed. Matthews (1979) has given details of three patients with remitting psychoses preceding the onset of physical symptoms of multiple sclerosis. Although diagnosed as schizophrenic, one might consider that the second patient was severely depressed. She recovered completely and later developed neurological signs of multiple sclerosis. Mehta (1976) described a 61-year-old woman who was grossly psychotic and neglected in association with multiple sclerosis. She had a past history of recurrent depression extending over a period of 36 years. Despite her severe psychosis she responded well to lithium therapy and no longer manifested a state of gross degradation and self-neglect. In this patient the later development of multiple sclerosis appears to have precipitated an affective disorder in someone predisposed to this reaction by earlier attacks of depression.

Although the papers so far mentioned have emphasized severe depression as the presenting feature of multiple sclerosis, it is evident that mania can also occur as in the case of Crémieux *et al.* (1979). A patient described by Targowla (1927) became manic in association with predominantly brain-stem signs of multiple sclerosis. Kemp *et al.* (1977) report the case of a 35-year-old woman with a 10-year history of neurological disease. She became severely depressed and, later, manic in response to treatment with ACTH. Her past history of cyclothymia appears to have been the crucial factor determining her response to treatment, although conceivably her predisposition to mood change could have been caused by the effects of multiple sclerosis.

From these reports it is clear that by no means all multiple sclerosis patients with severe affective disturbances are examples of reactive depression. In some cases recurrent depression of a typically endogenous kind has been experienced for some years before the onset of multiple sclerosis symptoms. In such cases a relapse of psychiatric symptoms in association with neurological disease could be regarded as coincidental. Alternatively, the psychosis may have been precipitated by brain damage in predisposed patients. On the other hand, some patients develop severe affective disturbances shortly before the onset of neurological symptoms, and in such cases it is likely that the psychiatric disorder was the presenting symptom of a disease process which had not yet manifested the characteristic neurological features of multiple sclerosis. Once the condition is established, it is very difficult to decide whether the depression is endogenous or reactive, and in all probability no single explanation will cover all cases. With some of these complexities in mind Whitlock and Siskind (1980) compared 30 patients suffering from multiple sclerosis with 30 matched control patients suffering from a variety of neurological disorders of a chronic disabling kind.

The multiple sclerosis cases and controls were well matched for the degree of disability. All patients were assessed for evidence of past and present affective disorder and all completed the Beck Depressive Inventory. The multiple sclerosis patients scored significantly higher on this rating scale than the controls, although their scores correlated to some extent with the degree of disability being experienced. Fourteen of the multiple sclerosis patients were depressed at the time of interview compared with two controls. Eight of the multiple sclerosis patients had suffered from depression before the onset of neurological symptoms and two of these had experienced transitory neurological symptoms which had not been diagnosed at the time. Sixteen of the multiple sclerosis patients and five controls had had episodes of endogenous depression since the onset of their neurological illnesses. Because patients showing clear signs of dementia were excluded, euphoria was not observed, but five showed marked fluctuation of mood with depression predominating. On the other hand, a few patients did show evidence of cerebral or brain-stem involvement characterized by impaired memory, epilepsy and severe dysarthria. At least one patient attempted suicide and others had contemplated taking their lives. One patient, not included in the series of 30, developed manic-depressive psychosis after the onset of multiple sclerosis and finally committed suicide in the depressive phase of his illness. Although many patients had been and were still receiving steroids and/or Baclofen, it did not appear that these drugs were contributing to their affective states. Nevertheless, the role of steroids as potential causes of affective disturbances in multiple sclerosis patients has been discussed by Cass *et al.* (1966). Baclofen, used to reduce muscle spasm, can also induce depression in some patients (Pinto *et al.* 1972; Korsgaard, 1976). The following short case history illustrates some of the features shown by these patients.

A.P., female, aged 28. This patient first developed neurological symptoms at the age of 23 with recurrence three years later. At the age of 27 she became severely depressed with delusions of guilt and the belief that Satan was inhabiting her body. She made a serious suicidal attempt from which she was resuscitated, but she continued to be severely depressed and potentially suicidal. In the meanwhile, her neurological symptoms had progressed considerably to the extent that she was confined to a wheelchair.

Symptoms and signs of affective disorder in most of these patients were characteristically those of the depressive phase of manic-depressive psychosis, confirmed by their responses on the Beck Depressive Inventory. Although a number of environmental factors could well have aggravated their symptoms, it could hardly be said that these patients were suffering from psychogenic reactive disorders. On the other hand, some patients who were manifestly depressed at the time of interview and scored highly on the Beck Depressive Inventory were more clearly examples of a neurotic depressive reaction.

Treatment of Multiple Sclerosis

Apart from the general support, both social and psychotherapeutic which is essential for the management of patients with multiple sclerosis, it is apparent that patients with severe affective disorders may need more specific treatment. A number of writers have observed how severe depression coming on in the course of the disease or preceding its onset responds well to tranylcypromine, tricyclic antidepressants or ECT (Lance *et al.*, 1965; Pommé *et al.*, 1963; Můr *et al.*, 1966; Young *et al.*, 1976). In this respect, these patients do not differ from others with depression following brain damage, and one might consider that this therapeutic response gives some support to the belief that affective changes can be precipitated by brain damage in the course of multiple sclerosis. Kemp *et al.* (1977) used lithium to treat their cyclothymic patient suffering from multiple sclerosis and agitated depression. Later, in response to steroid treatment, she became manic. Mehta (1976) found that a patient with multiple sclerosis and recurrent depression did not respond to tricyclic antidepressants but finally recovered with the administration of lithium. In contrast to these reports, none of the three patients described by Goodstein and Ferrell (1977) responded to antidepressant treatment. It is interesting to note that Matthews' (1979) second patient, who appeared to be psychotic and depressed, finally settled with steroid treatment which also ameliorated her physical symptoms. Earlier she had been treated with chlorpromazine without improvement. Finally, as indicated by Burnfield (1977), the experience of sufferers from multiple sclerosis can provide valuable information about how severe depression in the course of the illness can respond to tricyclic antidepressants. Burnfield also emphasizes the need to continue with counselling and intensive psychotherapy in conjunction with drugs or ECT.

In summary, it has been shown that, although many patients with multiple sclerosis will develop depression as an understandable reaction to their illnesses, others more clearly suffer from endogenous depression which could be the direct consequence of cerebral damage. Pathological evidence implicates areas of the brain such as the frontal lobes and other parts of the limbic system whose impairment through disease or injury often results in serious depression or, less frequently, mania. The very widespread lesions in the brains of multiple sclerosis patients will almost certainly damage these areas, whose functions are of prime importance for the experience and expression of emotion. In such cases, severe depression is an understandable development in the course of, or as the presenting symptom of, a progressive neurological disease.

EPILEPSY

As Lishman comments (1978), affective psychoses have been given less consideration than schizophrenic-like illnesses occurring in epileptic patients. However, there can be little doubt that manic-depressive psychoses, often of relatively short duration, can occur, particularly in patients with temporal lobe foci. Pond (1957), for example, considers that some patients with brief episodes of depression or hypomania are in fact epileptics who exhibit these symptoms as part of a post-ictal confusional or automatic state. This phenomenon has been discussed in considerable detail by Monroe (1970, 1979) under the heading of episodic behaviour disorder or episodic psychosis. He describes patients with brief intense episodes of depression or mania in which the patient complains of a feeling of being engulfed by waves with little elaboration of feelings of guilt, sin or unworthiness characteristic of the more typical depressive syndrome. Nonetheless, such patients are liable to be diagnosed as manic-depressive or as cases of unipolar depression. One such patient with a negative family history for affective disorder, after a prolonged period of psychotherapy, was found to have bilateral discharging foci in the anterior temporal lobes.

Estimates of the frequency of affective disorder in epileptic patients vary considerably. Dongier (1959), in a study of 516 patients, recorded transient affective disturbances in 153 (28.6 per cent) which predominantly occurred in patients with focal, particularly temporal lobe, discharges. Mulder and Daly (1952), on the other hand, in an investigation of 100 patients with temporal lobe epilepsy, found inter-ictal depression in only 16 cases. Flor-Henry (1969a) studied 50 patients with psychotic illnesses in association with temporal lobe epilepsy. Nine had been diagnosed as manic-depressive, with a further 11 classed as schizo-affective. Compared with patients with schizophrenia-like psychoses, those with affective disturbances had illnesses of shorter duration. Taylor (1972) examined 100 patients with temporal lobe epilepsy treated surgically and found that four had suffered from depressive psychoses and a further 17 from depressive neuroses pre-operatively. Betts (1974) in a report on 72 patients, observed that 11 (15 per cent) were depressed and three suicidal. Following admission to hospital 12 (17 per cent) had been diagnosed as endogenous depressions and a further 10 (14 per cent) as neurotic or reactive depressions. Finally, Jensen and Larsen (1979) studied 74 patients with drug resistant temporal lobe epilepsy. Twenty were described as psychotic, of whom six (30 per cent) manifested depression with paranoid delusions and had been treated as cases of manic-depressive or schizo-affective disorder.

In summary, the frequency of severe affective disorder of psychotic intensity in patients with temporal lobe epilepsy ranges from 15–40 per cent if those with schizo-affective syndromes are included with patients showing more typical features of manic-depressive psychosis.

Apart from patients with episodes of inter-ictal depression, there are those who exhibit severe affective disturbances as auras or post-ictal states. A sudden feeling of severe depression sometimes associated with an almost overwhelming wish to commit suicide as precursors to a fit were described long ago. Griesinger (1867) and Maudsley (1874) recorded episodes of intense melancholia and referred to short-lived attacks of suicidal insanity, but it is unclear whether they recognized the epileptic basis for these conditions. On the other hand, Reynolds (1861) mentions sudden depression of spirits as the epileptic aura, and more recently similar disturbances have been recorded by Anasstassopoulos and Kokkini (1969) and by Hancock and Bevilacqua (1971). The former authors described three such cases, one of whom, a 53-year-old woman, "cried and begged to be tied up lest she kill herself". The four patients discussed by Hancock and Bevilacqua manifested suicidal behaviour in a setting of temporal lobe epilepsy. Daly (1958) considered that ictal depression was a relatively rare phenomenon compared with feelings of intense fear, although five of his 52 patients experienced severe depression of brief duration or lasting for a number of days. Williams (1956) studied ictal emotion in 100 patients and recorded depression lasting for less than one hour to three days in 21 cases. One patient with no previous history of depression described feelings of sadness of sudden onset, and another experienced depression and attempted to take her life. A third woman, described as a robust person, gave an account of depression associated with autoscopy ending with a fit. In her case the mood change lasted 2–3 days. Weil (1956) also investigated ictal emotions in seven patients with temporal lobe epilepsy. One patient who experienced olfactory hallucinations was suicidal at times, and in another case the depressed mood lasted for as long as 14 days. Wells (1975) describes two patients with ictal depression who throw some light on the likely mechanism of the phenomenon. Both had EEG recordings carried out during their episodes of depression and both showed features of epileptic status. They recovered with appropriate anticonvulsant medication. Although precise localization of the site of discharge could not be determined, one might presume the existence of foci in some part of the limbic brain, possibly in the neighbourhood of the amygdaloid nucleus. The case described by Fenton and Udwin (1965) who was both homicidal and suicidal certainly suggests that this part of the temporal lobe might be involved in some patients who experience ictal depression with suicidal impulses.

In his careful study of 90 patients with verified temporal lobe epilepsy, Bingley (1958) recorded that seven patients (8 per cent) experienced ictal affective states, but that only three cases had such symptoms as inter-ictal phenomena.

To what extent affective psychoses and ictal mood changes are dependent on the patient's premorbid personality, genetic loading or prior attacks of depression or mania is not always considered in accounts of patients with temporal lobe epilepsy. Serafetinides and Falconer (1962), reporting on 12 patients treated by temporal lobectomy, found that seven had suffered from episodes of paranoid-affective psychosis. Although some had positive family histories of alcoholism and/or psychopathy, in no case had a first degree relative suffered from a major affective disorder. Although the two patients with temporal lobe epilepsy and severe depression described by Taylor (1972) had positive family histories of affective disorder, neither had suffered from similar illnesses themselves before the onset of epilepsy. Dominian *et al.* (1963), in a follow-up study of 51 patients with late onset epilepsy, found that of four patients with psychotic depression two had past histories of similar illnesses. Thirteen of 43 patients who showed psychiatric disturbances were depressed. Eight of 28 patients with psychiatric illnesses before the onset of epilepsy had past histories of depression. The contribution of head injury, which had been sustained by 17 patients, to the onset of depression in these cases is difficult to ascertain but, in view of the high incidence of signs of organic brain disease, one might presume that the earlier history of brain damage was an important factor in the aetiology of depression and other psychiatric disturbances. The question of genetic loading for affective disorder was not examined. Neither of Wells's two patients had past histories of affective illnesses but the family histories of these patients were not mentioned. Jensen and Larsen (1979) found that there was a higher incidence of major psychiatric disorders in the relatives of their patients than in the general Danish population, but they do not provide data on the frequency of affective illnesses. One of the two patients discussed by Hambert and Willén (1978) had a positive family history for affective illness and suicide, and the other had suffered from affective disturbances during the puerperium. Both cases had temporal lobe lesions confirmed at autopsy after death by suicide, but epilepsy had not apparently developed. In these two patients the brain injury could not be held wholly responsible for their subsequent affective disorders.

At this stage one clearly needs a careful assessment of the contribution of genetic loading before the onset of affective psychosis in patients with temporal lobe epilepsy similar to the study by Slater and Gilthero (1963) which examined the genetics of schizophrenic-like psychosis in epileptics.

However, regardless of genetic and constitutional contributions, psychosocial difficulties will be important. Pond (1974) considered that although depression was common it was largely reactive. Bruens (1974) also regarded depressive states as reactive to the epilepsy and society's attitudes to the condition. Episodic manic states are rare, although Dongier (1959) found that they occurred in 4.7 per cent of patients with epileptic psychosis. Bruens, on the other hand, commented on the high rate of suicide as a cause of death — seven per cent in one German investigation — but nonetheless, stated that prolonged psychotic depression was rare. He felt that there was no clear evidence for a genetic predisposition to either schizophrenia or depression in epileptic patients.

Suicide and Attempted Suicide in Epilepsy

As further evidence of severe affective disturbances in epileptic patients, many writers, some of whose investigations have been reviewed elsewhere (Whitlock, 1977), have commented on the high incidence of suicide and attempted suicide. Prudhomme (1941), in a statistical study of in-stitutionalized epileptics in the USA, considered that this mode of death was five times more common than in the general population. Estimates of the frequency of suicide as a percentage of all epileptic deaths varies considerably. Jantz, quoted by Bruens, gave a figure of seven per cent, whereas Zieliński (1974), summarizing three studies, found a rate of 10–22 per cent. Similarly high figures have been reported from Denmark (Henriksen *et al.*, 1970). Considering the liability of epileptic patients to sudden severe bouts of depression with suicidal impulses, these high figures are not entirely surprising. The association between suicidal and aggressive behaviour was commented on by Mark and Ervin (1970) who found that half of their patients with the episodic discontrol syndrome had made suicide attempts.

Attempted as opposed to accomplished suicide is also frequent. Betts *et al.* (1976) found that four per cent of epileptic patients were admitted to a psychiatric hospital on account of suicidal behaviour, and Hawton *et al.* (1980) reported high rates of suicidal behaviour by epileptics, among whom male exceeded female numbers in contrast with the usual preponderance of young women. However, both male and female epileptic suicide attempters were in the same age group (less than 30) as non-epileptic patients. The past histories of these patients revealed a higher than expected number of previous attempts. Anticonvulsant drugs and barbiturates, often combined with alcohol, were the commonest methods used. Similar findings have been reported by Mackay (1979) who found that, among a large sample of attempted suicide patients in Glasgow, epileptics were represented seven times more frequently than other members of the population. Attempts by epileptic patients comprised 1.3–4.7 per cent of all attempted suicide cases. In Mackay's study the figure was 3.5 per cent, the same as that given by Hawton *et al.* from Oxford. The precipitants of suicidal behaviour in epileptic patients appear to be similar to those mentioned by non-epileptic cases with only a minority offering reasons clearly related to their epilepsy.

Gunn (1973) compared 158 epileptic prisoners with 180 non-epileptic subjects also in prison. The epileptics more often admitted to suicidal ideation and considerably more had made suicide attempts in the past. Such actions were more common in patients with temporal lobe epilepsy than in those with epilepsy of unspecified or undiagnosed origin. Delay *et al.* (1957) in France found that about one-third of epileptics admitted to hospital or imprisoned had made suicide attempts. As already mentioned, most attempts are probably impulsive acts in disturbed personalities in response to situational crises, and Lishman (1978) comments that the extent to which such behaviour occurs in the course of psychosis or a psychomotor attack is unknown.

SUICIDAL BEHAVIOUR IN OTHER NEUROLOGICAL CONDITIONS

With the notable exception of Huntington's chorea, suicidal behaviour in the course of other neurological disorders is relatively uncommon. If suicide in epilepsy is the consequence of acute or prolonged mood changes causing severe depression, one might anticipate that other conditions complicated by epileptic discharges would have similar effects.

An investigation of 1052 suicides in England and Wales (Whitlock, 1977) based on coroners' reports, found 66 cases with evidence of CNS disease. In all probability this is an underestimate, as essential data might have been omitted or overlooked. The finding that 6.5 per cent of the total sample were suffering from or had sustained some kind of cerebral disorder before their deaths has to be compared with rates of 7.4 per cent in 135 suicides studied in greater detail in Brisbane (Chynoweth *et al.*, 1980) and of 3.6 per cent among 390 suicides in London reported by Sainsbury (1955), basing his observations on coroners' reports. Sainsbury, however, did not mention epilepsy in his list of disorders and excluded cases with degenerative diseases of the brain associated with old age. As Table 6.1 shows, in England and Wales and in Brisbane, epilepsy and cerebrovascular accidents accounted for the greater part of the suicides with brain disorders.

A surprising finding in the London series was the four patients who died with parkinsonism, a figure estimated by Sainsbury to be 200 times greater than the rate in general mortality statistics. However, suicide is not common in this condition, and in one investigation of 340 deaths among patients suffering from paralysis agitans, only three were caused by suicide (Hoehn and Yahr, 1967). In contrast, although actual suicide is unusual, suicidal rumination associated with depression appears to occur frequently (Warburton, 1967;

Table 6.1
Neurological Disease in Victims of Suicide

	England and Wales[a]	Brisbane[b]	London[c]
Total Suicides	1052	135	390
Total with Neurological Disease	69 (6.5%)	10 (7.4%)	14 (3.6%)
Epilepsy	19	3	—
Cerebrovascular Disease	18	3	4
Cerebral Tumour	3	2	2
Head Injury	5	—	2
Cerebral Degeneration	11	2	—
Parkinsonism	—	—	4
Multiple Sclerosis	6	—	—
Other Diseases	7	—	2

[a]Whitlock (1977)
[b]Chynoweth *et al.* (1980)
[c]Sainsbury (1955)

Robins, 1976b; Celesia and Wanamaker, 1972; Asnis, 1977), but Parant, writing in 1892, commented on the frequency of melancholia in paralysis agitans and the severe risk of suicide entailed by this complication. As epilepsy is a most infrequent complication of Parkinson's disease, the impulsive type of suicides associated with ictal or inter-ictal behaviour would not occur, but suicidal rumination as part of a depressive syndrome is an understandable phenomenon.

Most writers state that suicide by multiple sclerosis patients is exceptional (McAlpine *et al.*, 1965; Kurtzke, 1970), but in a series of 30 patients (Whitlock and Siskind, 1980) there was one known suicidal attempt and 13 other patients admitted to suicidal thoughts. Another patient with manic-depressive psychosis eventually took his life. Epilepsy as a complication of multiple sclerosis can occur in about two per cent of patients (McAlpine *et al.*, 1965), although a figure of eight per cent was given by Trouillas and Courgon (1972). One of the three patients with epilepsy and multiple sclerosis described by Feldman (1957) developed manic-depressive episodes but did not become suicidal in the depressed phases of her illness. Matthews (1962) is critical of some assumptions that have been made about multiple sclerosis as a cause of epilepsy. In some instances the association is coincidental as a result of more than one type of cerebral lesion and other patients may have falls or tonic seizures which are not epileptic in origin. If epilepsy contributes to suicidal behaviour, one might expect that patients with both epilepsy and multiple sclerosis would be more at risk. In one series of 27 patients with grand mal or focal seizures there were six instances of suicide attempts and one fatal suicide (Elian and Dean, 1977).

At present, insufficient is known about the association of epilepsy, cerebral disease and suicidal behaviour to permit more than a tentative hypothesis. On the available evidence, it appears that suicide or suicide attempts occur more commonly in patients with epilepsy alone or when both epilepsy and depression complicate the course of neurological disease. Suicidal thoughts as part of a depressive syndrome do not necessarily entail a higher risk of attempted or fatal suicide.

HEMISPHERIC DIFFERENCES: LATERALIZATION OF CEREBRAL FUNCTION AND AFFECTIVE DISORDER

Earlier mention has been made of the side of the brain showing damage or epileptic discharges in patients with symptomatic affective disorders. This question of hemispheric laterality has been given some prominence by Flor-Henry who, in a series of papers and reviews (1969a, 1969b, 1974, 1976), has claimed to have demonstrated that patients with temporal lobe epilepsy are more likely to develop paranoid and schizophrenic-like psychoses if their lesions are situated on the left (dominant) side of the brain, and manic-depressive psychoses and dysphoric emotional instability if they are on the right (non-dominant) side.

This formulation has recently been citicized by Kiloh (1980), who considered the evidence on which it was based to be statistically weak. He rightly points out that the risk of developing "psychoses" was greatest in patients with bilateral foci and goes on to quote a number of psycho-physiological studies which do not entirely support the original hypothesis. Furthermore, although a case could be made out for schizophrenic-like psychoses occurring more often in patients with dominant hemisphere temporal lobe epilepsy, the evidence for the opposite side being involved more frequently in patients with affective or schizo-affective disorders is far less convincing. Matarazzo's two patients (1976), for example, both severely depressed, showed bilateral temporal lobe foci. Of the depressed patients mentioned by Dominian *et al.* (1963), seven had left-sided, two right-sided and one bilateral temporal lobe foci. Weil (1956) has provided details of two patients with recurrent depression. In one the left temporal lobe appeared to be most involved, in the other the focus was on the right side of the brain. Bingley (1958), in his report on 90 patients with temporal lobe epilepsy, found remarkably few with ictal or inter-ictal affective disturbances. There did not appear to be any preference for one hemisphere over the other as sources of these symptoms, but in his review of the literature Bingley quotes a number of investigations which showed either no evidence of lateralization or a predominance of left-sided lesions in patients with affective disorders.

In contrast, Betts *et al.* (1976) recorded a higher risk of suicide among patients with affective disorders and non-dominant hemisphere epilepsy, and

Sigal (1976) has given the findings in three manic-depressive patients with temporal lobe epilepsy. One had bilateral foci and the other two had epileptic discharges arising from the non-dominant side. Williams (1956) observed that, of 21 patients with ictal depression, four had right-sided and six left-sided foci and that in 11 the sites were bilateral or unlateralized. He concluded that depression as an ictal experience could not be related to any one part of the brain. Ictal fear occurred twice as commonly in patients with left-sided foci as in those with discharges originating from the right side, with the active focus being in the anterior part of the temporal lobe in most cases. Dongier (1959) observed mood swings, depression and mania in 143 patients, 70 of whom had temporal lobe foci. In patients with temporal lobe and psychomotor epilepsy, 66 had foci on the right side and 72 on the left, with 59 occurring bitemporally. It is not clear how many of these 197 patients manifested affective disorders. Jensen and Larsen (1979), after reviewing the findings in their 20 psychotic patients, considered that with respect to Flor-Henry's hypothesis their own findings neither disproved nor confirmed it. Bear and Fedio (1977), in a study of inter-ictal behaviour in temporal lobe epilepsy, found that patients with right-sided lesions displayed more emotional tendencies in contrast with those with dominant sided epilepsy who had more ideational traits. Nonetheless, a slightly larger percentage of left temporal lobe epileptics had been admitted to hospital with a diagnosis of affective disorder or following suicidal attempts. Kiloh (1980) has commented critically on this contradictory evidence and clearly has difficulty in accepting Flor-Henry's claims. In any case, in Flor-Henry's original series of 50 patients, there were only nine with manic-depressive psychoses, four of whom had right-sided, two left-sided and three bilateral lesions. It would be difficult to argue the case for hemispheric preference on figures of this kind.

Equally conflicting findings are reported with respect to the laterality of lesions in patients with affective disorders who have cerebral tumours or following cerebrovascular accidents or head injuries. In the examples of affective disorder associated with temporal lobe tumours described by Minski (1933), the numbers were equally divided between the two sides. There were more patients with frontal lobe tumours exhibiting euphoria, anxiety or depression. In their report on 110 patients with temporal lobe tumours Keschner *et al.* (1936) observed that more of those with left-sided lesions were depressed and irritable. Again, in Malamud's series (1967), all of whom had epileptic discharges, there was no difference in laterality in those depressed patients who had lesions on one side of the brain rather than midline limbic tumours. Of the 19 depressed patients described by Pool and Carroll (1958) seven had right-sided and seven left-sided lesions, with five others having bilateral or generalized neoplasms. Folstein *et al.* (1977), who have given details of 10 patients with right-sided and 10 with left-sided cerebral haemorrhages, found that approximately equal numbers were depressed with no significant differences being found on two depressive rating scales. On the other hand, the patients with left-sided lesions were considerably more irritable. These patients, of course, did not have lesions exclusively situated in the temporal lobes. Lishman (1968) found that patients with penetrating wounds of the head were more likely to exhibit affective symptoms if the lesions involved the right hemisphere. However, it was patients with frontal lobe rather than temporal lobe injuries who showed this preference, as those with temporal lobe damage more often developed cognitive impairment. Achté *et al.* (1967) could not relate affective psychoses following brain injuries to any particular site or severity of damage.

These discrepancies between the effects of lesions in one hemisphere or the other in patients with epilepsy, tumours or other causes of brain damage might be due to differences arising from irritative or destructive processes. It has been suggested that depression following a left-sided haemorrhage or in association with a tumour is caused largely by the disturbances of speech brought about by such lesions. In such cases the depression is seen as secondary to the difficulties experienced by the patient in his struggles to overcome a major disability. This, however, will hardly explain those cases with severe symptoms of melancholia developing well before dysphasia or other impairments have risen. Clearly, this subject requires a further investigation involving large numbers of psychotic patients with well-defined lesions, including those with epileptic foci, tumours or suffering from the sequelae of brain injury.

SLEEP DISORDERS

Gallinek (1954) described three patients suffering from a condition later known as the Kline–Levin–Critchley syndrome, all of whom had episodes of hypersomnia, bulimia and severe melancholia. The first and second cases were suicidal at times but Critchley (1962) considered that Gallinek's first and third patients were not true examples of the syndrome which typically starts in adolescence. Two of Critchley's 11 patients were depressed after attacks of excessive sleepiness and over-eating and one was euphoric. Although the great majority of recorded cases have been male, Duffy and Davison (1968) gave details of a female patient who became depressed and deluded four weeks after admission to hospital. When readmitted later she appeared to be manic. The patient described by Jeffries and Lefebvre (1973) was also a female who had episodes of depression and mania and was suicidal on at least one occasion. In their review of 40 known cases these authors found that, of 37 for whom adequate data were available, seven had attacks of depression, nine had episodes of mania, and three had both mania and depression.

The pathogenesis of this uncommon syndrome is quite obscure, as is the relationship of the affective to the physical symptoms. There are insufficient details on any genetic contribution to the development of affective disorder, although Jeffries and Lefebvre's patient had an uncle who once received psychiatric treatment for depression. Neither of her parents had suffered from affective illnesses.

Another condition with characteristic disturbances of sleep, narcolepsy, seems to have a relatively high incidence of depression, although Daniels (1934) considered that "real" attacks of depression were rare. Nonetheless, seven of the 30 patients described by Heyck and Hess (1954) were depressed, with four showing endogenous features and another suicidal. Roth and Neusimilova (1975) reported on 100 patients with narcolepsy and 30 with other types of hypersomnia. Seventeen of 85 patients with idiopathic narcolepsy were depressed, 11 with characteristic symptoms of endogenous depression. Six of the 23 patients with idiopathic hypersomnia were also depressed, but none of the patients with symptomatic narcolepsy or hypersomnia experienced affective disturbances. There was a strong family history of depression in association with hypersomnia and narcolepsy in these patients. The pathogenesis of narcolepsy is unknown but the authors noted changes in sleep pattern, particularly the increase in rapid eye movement sleep in depressed patients and considered the possibility of some fundamental biological disturbance in these cases.

Sours (1963), in a report on 75 patients with primary narcolepsy found that 15 had at one time been given a diagnosis of depression. No details of family history or past personal history were provided. Roy (1976) comments on the variable opinions offered on the coexistence of mental disturbance and narcolepsy. Ten of his 20 patients had past histories of psychiatric illnesses including four who had suffered from depressive neuroses. Roy considered a genetic factor for psychiatric illness overlapping with narcolepsy to be unlikely and that affective disturbances are reactive to the difficulties created by the condition.

OTHER NEUROLOGICAL DISORDERS

Depression has been described in a number of other conditions affecting the central nervous system, but there is little reason for regarding these as more than chance coincidences or understandable responses to progressive crippling disorders. These comments apply to amyotrophic lateral sclerosis (Brown and Mueller, 1970), myasthenia gravis (McKenzie *et al.* 1969) and Friedreich's ataxia (Davies, 1949). Among the cases of Friedreich's ataxia used as controls in a study of multiple sclerosis (Whitlock and Siskind, 1980) depression was conspicuously absent.

Hyperostosis Frontalis Interna

In the case of hyperostosis frontalis interna the evidence is far from being conclusive (Eldridge and Holm, 1940; Hawkins and Martin, 1965; Wälinder, 1977) for, although the condition, predominantly found in middle-aged to elderly women, is associated with depressive illnesses in some cases, this seems to be a coincidental relationship. As these studies were based on psychiatric hospital admissions, a possible association between hyperostosis frontalis interna and mental illness in general is by no means established, although Eldridge and Holm claimed that the condition was twenty times greater in psychiatric patients than in the general population. Both depression and dementia commonly occur in these women.

Normal Pressure Hydrocephalus

Another condition, normal pressure hydrocephalus, has attracted a good deal of attention in recent years particularly as a treatable cause of dementia in older patients. Some of these patients also appear to be depressed (Rice and Gendelman, 1973; Rosen and Swigar, 1976). One of the patients described by Rosen and Swigar (1976) became depressed and suicidal in association with her progressive dementia, which was aggravated by ECT. She had not suffered from affective illness previously. All five patients discussed by Rice and Gendelman had depressive symptoms and one attempted suicide. In some of their patients the signs of apathy, retardation, loss of interest and poor concentration were more in keeping with a diagnosis of pseudo-depression which was secondary to a progressive deterioration in their mental powers. Both the patients described by Lying-Tunell (1979) had suffered from previous episodes of affective disorder, but in the first case treatment of her normal pressure hydrocephalus appears to have brought her recurrent psychiatric breakdowns to an end. The patient reported by Tsuang *et al.* (1979) also had a past history of depression and a suicidal attempt. In her case one might conclude that her organic brain disease and diabetes had precipitated depression in one already predisposed to this type of illness.

Migraine

Migraine is another condition which appears to be associated with affective disturbances. Klee (1968), for example, reported severe depression during attacks in some cases, and Sachs (1971) described sudden mood changes of relatively brief duration which could be regarded as migrainous affective disorders occurring without headache or other neurological symptoms.

Lishman (1978) mentions how some patients may experience manifest euphoria, hyperactivity and pressure of speech before the onset of attacks, but he is uncertain about the extent to which emotional disturbance and migraine derive from a common pathophysiological process. Bruyn (1968) regarded "dysphoria" in migraine victims as a response to the illness, but he also noted how some patients suffered from interparoxysmal attacks of depression. Selby and Lance (1960), who investigated 500 patients with migraine, state that "a feeling of depression is not unusual after the migraine attack and 19 of the patients with anxiety states confessed to more prolonged episodes of depression in connection with their headaches". Couch *et al.* (1975) recorded a positive correlation between scores on a depressive rating scale and frank neurological symptoms associated with migraine in their patients. Such a finding would be compatible with a general hypothesis that disease causing brain damage would be more productive of affective disorders than more transitory conditions leaving no permanent imprint. One must also remember that on occasions treatment of the condition can precipitate depression in susceptible patients. One of the author's patients, a 22-year-old woman who had already suffered from one attack of endogenous depression, suffered a relapse when she was placed on clonidine as treatment for her migraine. In her case it was considered the recurrence of her depression was precipitated by the drug and unrelated to her migraine.

Pseudo-Dementia and Pseudo-Depression

This is not the place to review the clinical aspects of depressive pseudo-dementia (Kiloh, 1961; Post, 1965, 1975) which have been adequately discussed by Lishman (1978). Nonetheless, particularly in elderly patients, this is a differential diagnosis as important as pseudo-depression mistakenly diagnosed as endogenous depression when a treatable disorder of brain function may be the true underlying cause. Hall *et al.* (1980) have given details of patients presenting in hospital with major or minor depressive illnesses or with manic-depressive psychosis which were caused or aggravated by a number of physical disorders. Predominately these were endocrine, central nervous system or haematological in origin. Lack of organic signs and symptoms up to the time of onset of depressive pseudo-dementia and a relative absence of feelings of guilt, hopelessness and suicidal thoughts in pseudo-depression should enable the correct diagnoses to be made.

7

Endocrine Disorders

Many recent reviews have dealt generally or specifically with psychiatric aspects of endocrine disease or endocrine disturbances in the course of psychiatric illnesses (Granville-Grossman, 1971; Beumont, 1972, 1979; Sachar, 1975a, 1975b; Smith, 1975; Carroll, 1976b; Franz, 1978; Van Praag, 1978; Lishman, 1978). Such complete coverage sets limits to the need for yet a further review of a large and complex aspect of psychiatry. As Williams (1970) has pointed out, "All abnormalities in mentation are associated with altered metabolism. Metabolic changes lead to psychiatric alterations and vice versa."

The very close relationship between the endocrine and central nervous systems, in addition to the alterations in endocrine functions observed in many patients with affective disorders (Chapter 2), make it almost inevitable that any major disease of the glands of internal secretion will cause a variety of psychiatric disorders among which severe emotional disorders will be prominent. Diseases of the thyroid, pituitary, adrenal glands and gonads are all associated with disturbances of mood. Disorders of pancreatic endocrine function can also cause psychological changes, although these rarely take the form of sustained affective illnesses. Furthermore, it is not always easy to say just how much has been contributed to the onset by altered carbohydrate metabolism and how much by cerebrovascular disease which is common in elderly diabetics.

THYROID GLAND

Thyrotoxicosis

Thyrotoxicosis is most commonly associated with anxiety and, in the past, with states of intense agitation known as thyrotoxic mania. Thyroid hormones increase the sensitivity of catecholamine receptors and bring about a fall in monoamine oxidase activity (Sachar, 1975a). However, depression can develop in thyrotoxicosis, and Whybrow *et al.* (1969) recorded this in two of their 10 hyperthyroid patients but observed that depression was more profound in patients who were hypothyroid. Taylor (1975) has given details of a patient with a positive family history of affective disorder who also had suffered from recurrent bouts of depression. In one of these he was found to be thyrotoxic and both disorders cleared when he was treated with propranolol and carbimazole. No doubt in this case constitutional and genetic factors contributed, but the author considered the possibility of his depression being secondary to a fall in thyrotropin releasing hormone (TRH). Kleinschmidt *et al.* (1956) commented on the frequency of depression and anxiety in their patients. Depression, they stated, often preceded the endocrine disorder and became worse with marked agitation as the patient became toxic. Effective treatment led to a state of euphoria which changed to depression if the patient became hypothyroid. Clower *et al.* (1969) described agitated depression in a 50-year-old woman with a past history of depression, and Checkley (1978) has given details of five patients with episodes of affective illness who had also suffered from thyrotoxicosis. On the balance of evidence, Checkley concludes that the attacks of affective disorder and thyrotoxicosis were coincidental and not causally related. All five patients were regarded as constitutional manic-depressives, but in two cases one might speculate that the changes in thyroid function could have precipitated psychiatric breakdowns. In Lishman's opinion (1978) thyrotoxic mania is more common than depression, and the clinical picture of psychosis in the course of the disease often shows a mixture of schizophrenic and affective symptoms.

In an investigation of the incidence of psychosis in hypothyroid patients treated with thyroxine, Josephson and Mackenzie (1980) found 18 examples in the literature for whom adequate details had been provided. Five (three of whom were suicidal) had suffered from depression before treatment and 13 developed short-lived attacks of mania afterwards. These episodes appeared to coincide with peak activity of thyroxine, and the authors considered that the hormone augments catecholamine receptor sensitivity resulting in a hypercatecholaminergic state which was regarded as the basis for their manic illnesses. The authors recorded that 10 of the patients had suffered earlier psychiatric illnesses and that seven had positive family histories of mental disorder. The nature of these illnesses was not specified but, presumably, they would have been mainly affective in nature.

Although unrelated to excess or deficiency of thyroid hormone as causes of mental disorder, the report by Jackson *et al.* (1978) of severe depression in patients with familial medullary thyroid cancer is of considerable interest. This condition has been reviewed by Williams (1979) who did not mention any mental disturbances. The carcinoma develops from parafollicular or C cells of the thyroid gland and gives rise to a very marked increase in secretion of calcitonin. In addition, the C cells have a high content of 5-HT and patients with medullary thyroid cancer excrete large quantities of 5-HIAA in their urines. Raised blood levels of dopa-decarboxylase, and histaminase and prostaglandins have also been recorded. About 20 per cent of patients have associated phaeochromocytomas, and others develop Cushing's syndrome in response to ectopic ACTH production.

Jackson *et al.* studied 64 affected individuals in 11 families and found that 16 patients suffered from depressive illnesses. Three cases remitted when the thyroid cancer was resected and six, whose tumours could not be removed, improved with tricyclic anti-depressants. Eleven of the 16 patients became mentally ill before their thyroid abnormalities were detected. The depressive symptoms were not correlated with calcitonin levels. The authors could not explain the origin of severe depression in these patients but suggested the possibility of a false neurotransmitter biogenic amine being secreted by the tumour cells as a cause.

A number of authors (Arnold *et al.*, 1974; Brenner, 1978; Thomas *et al.*, 1970) have described what is termed apathetic thyrotoxicosis. Most of the patients, who are elderly, are clinically apathetic, depressed and retarded. The typical signs of thyroid over-activity are absent, the patients look particularly aged and may show ptosis rather than widely dilated eyes and exophthalmos. The diagnosis is often overlooked until thyroid function tests reveal the true state of affairs. The patient described by Brenner (1978) was a 74-year-old woman who had been diagnosed as senile dementia and melancholia. She was suicidal but recovered when her thyrotoxicosis was treated. There was no previous or family history of affective disorder in this patient. The author considered that the condition was the result of depletion of catecholamines or loss of endorgan sensitivity.

On balance, the evidence indicates that most patients who become manic or depressed if they develop thyrotoxicosis do so because of genetic or constitutional predisposition. In aged patients, biological and biochemical changes may be responsible for the appearance of depression and apathy, which clearly is not equivalent to the usual picture of endogenous depression in most instances.

Hypothyroidism

Sachar (1975a) says that, although depressed mood in myxoedema is typical, clinical depression is not, but Pitts and Guze (1961) described three depressed patients with hypothyroidism, one of whom had a past history of manic-depressive psychosis. A myxoedematous patient of Clower *et al.* (1969), who also had suffered a previous episode of depression in association with hyperthyroidism, was depressed and suicidal. Miller (1952) described two patients without any apparent earlier history of mental illness who became profoundly depressed, one after thyroidectomy for carcinoma of the thyroid, the other for six months before her hypothyroidism was diagnosed. Both recovered with treatment for thyroid deficiency. Tonks (1964) reported on 18 patients with clear evidence of thyroid deficiency, 14 of whom had been psychiatrically ill for up to two years. Six were depressed, five showed an organic syndrome and five were schizophrenic. All these patients had been admitted to a psychiatric hospital and 10 had previous histories of mental illness. How many of the depressed patients were included in this number is not stated. Whybrow *et al.* (1969) observed that, in eight studies, 19 out of 42 hypothyroid patients were depressed and that many had received ECT before the endocrine disorder was diagnosed. Five of their seven hypothyroid patients were depressed, one being psychotic and paranoid. Depression in myxoedema was thought to be due to changes in catecholamines and electrolytes known to occur in this condition and not a reaction to the illness. There is also evidence that monoamine oxidase activity is increased in hypothyroidism. Jain (1972), who reviewed the literature, reported on 30 patients of his own. Thirteen were depressed and, although only two had past histories of depression, eight of 109 relatives had suffered from affective disorders. Whether the two patients with past personal histories of depression also had positive family histories is not stated. An unusual patient (Nordgren and Von Schéele, 1976), an adolescent who was chronically depressed with repeated suicidal attempts, recovered dramatically when treated with imipramine and tri-iodothyronine. She did not show the usual features of hypothyroidism but was thought to have a selective defect of thyroid stimulating hormone (TSH) release.

Thyroidectomy is sometimes followed by psychosis in association with hypothyroidism, a good example being the 50-year-old woman described by Libow and Durrell (1965). She became psychotically depressed two months after removal of a benign goitre. She recovered fully with tri-iodothyronine but relapsed when treatment was discontinued. There was no previous history of affective disorder in this patient.

Today, in many psychiatric centres, routine thyroid function tests are carried out on all patients, particularly older depressives. But, as Cropper (1973) has pointed out, in some elderly patients laboratory tests do not always reveal thyroid deficiency and reliance on clinical tests may be more effective when it comes to detecting the underlying endocrine disorder. In this context, Logothetis (1963) has observed that psychiatric symptoms may occur well before physical signs make the diagnosis obvious. Generally the picture is a minimal one of organic and depressive symptoms which may be masked by an overall impression of dullness and apathy.

In contrast with depression and mania in thyrotoxicosis (apart from apathetic thyrotoxicosis), there is rather less evidence of previous affective illness in hypothyroid patients who become depressed. The clinical picture often includes quite marked paranoid delusions and suspiciousness (Asher, 1949), but most psychiatrists will have treated middle-aged or elderly female patients who present with the characteristic features of endogenous depression. They do not often have a past history of affective disorder and respond well to treatment with thyroxine and antidepressant drugs once the diagnosis of hypothyroidism is established.

PARATHYROID DISORDERS

Hyperparathyroidism

Granville-Grossman (1971) has commented that, in addition to the physical symptoms of hyperparathyroidism, mild mental disturbances such as anxiety, depression and impairment of concentration and of memory commonly occur. Sachar (1975a) has noted how depression in hyperparathyroidism is associated with raised serum calcium and that removal of calcium by dialysis improves mood. Calcium is said to deplete noradrenalin and promote dopamine-beta-hydroxylase activity. Lishman (1978) comments that psychiatric disturbances are common in this condition, particularly confusion but also depression.

Karpati and Frame (1964) found that one-third of their patients showed nervousness, tension and irritability but four were severely psychotic and two were depressed. Boonstra and Jackson (1963), who commented more on fatigue and irritability, also noted mental depression in some patients and seven of Anderson's (1968) 30 patients gave a history of depression and loss of energy, which improved after surgical treatment. Flanagan et al. (1970) found that eight out of 10 investigated cases were depressed, three seriously so with suicidal ideas, and Frame (1976) reported on the frequency of depression which seemed to vary with the serum calcium levels. Some of Christie-Brown's patients (1968) showed depression, but six became increasingly depressed *after* parathyroidectomy in association with falling calcium levels. Although mental disturbance is by no means unusual after parathyroidectomy — Gatewood et al. (1975) mention confusion and psychotic behaviour — major affective syndromes are not often reported. On the other hand, Mikkelson and Reider (1979) have given details of a 52-year-old woman with a complex medical history who became manic after removal of a parathyroid adenoma which caused a rapid fall in her serum calcium. She recovered fully one month after the operation. In their review of the literature they record the psychiatric findings in six other patients, two of whom were agitated, depressed and paranoid.

Noble (1974) recorded an incidence of mental disorder in hyperparathyroidism ranging from 4.2–65 per cent, his own patient being a hypertensive female who became depressed on reserpine, recovered with ECT and drugs and then relapsed. A parathyroid tumour was removed without benefit to her affective illness, but she finally recovered with antidepressants. In this patient, presumably a constitutional manic-depressive, psychiatric illness seems to have been precipitated by a drug on one occasion, and by an endocrine tumour on the other. Petersen (1968) observed that the commonest psychiatric condition in his 36 patients was depression, which was severe in 15, sometimes with suicidal tendencies. The main symptoms were loss of initiative, irritability, depression, thirst and anorexia. Two of the five patients reported by Gatewood *et al.* (1975) showed features of endogenous depression. Both recovered after their parathyroid tumours were removed. The first patient had experienced an episode of severe reactive depression 10 years earlier after thyroidectomy, but the other patient apparently had not previously been mentally ill.

Most authors agree that depressed mood varies directly with calcium levels, a point noted by Crammer (1977) in a recent review. Varga and Kline (1973) observed a fall in urinary calcium in depressed patients who responded to ECT but not in those who failed to benefit from the treatment. They also observed an association between osteoporosis, osteoarthritis and depression, a finding which was more common in male patients in the USA. Carman *et al.* (1977) state that falls in serum and CSF calcium occur in depressed patients after three to five treatments with ECT, but Gerner *et al.* (1977), who gave depressed patients parathormone, failed to find any increase in depression despite a rise in calcium three hours after the hormone had been administered. This, however, was an acute, brief experiment and clearly different from the sustained high levels of serum calcium seen in patients with hyperparathyroidism.

The importance of magnesium deficiency as a cause of psychiatric symptoms in patients with parathyroid disease has been emphasized by Potts and Roberts (1958) and by Gatewood *et al.* (1975). The latter authors state that in patients who develop psychoses after parathyroidectomy, serum magnesium levels are low. Confusion and depression will improve once the patient has been treated with an infusion of magnesium. However, as Mikkelson and Reider have commented, by no means do all patients respond well to magnesium treatment.

The following patient illustrates some of the psychiatric features observed in patients with hyperparathyroidism.

C.W., female aged 69. This patient was referred for investigation of hyperparathyroidism diagnosed before coming to hospital. On admission she was complaining of thirst and constipation. She also had a number of urinary tract symptoms. On examination she was quite markedly retarded, depressed and somewhat confused. These symptoms improved over the ensuing two months until parathyroidectomy was performed. A large tumour was removed and following operation she became quite markedly depressed, slept poorly and looked extremely miserable. She presented a picture of pseudo-dementia with poor memory and concentration. These symptoms cleared up satisfactorily with doxepin.

Hypoparathyroidism

Although affective disturbances can occur with parathyroid deficiency they are rare, with the majority of hypoparathyroid patients showing organic syndromes (Denko and Kaebling, 1962; Frame, 1976; Lishman, 1978). However, seven of the patients described by Denko and Kaebling with idiopathic hypoparathyroid disease showed functional psychoses, mainly manic or schizophrenic. Fourman *et al.* (1967) described 18 patients with parathyroid insufficiency demonstrated by falls in already low calcium levels when parathyroid function was stressed. Eight of these patients were mild or moderately depressed and improved considerably when given supplementary calcium in their diets.

CUSHING'S SYNDROME

For the purposes of discussion, this section will be concerned with affective symptoms occurring in Cushing's *disease* in which adrenal hyperplasia develops secondary to ACTH stimulation from an over-active pituitary gland or tumour, and in Cushing's *syndrome* when the primary lesion is usually a benign or malignant tumour of the adrenal cortex. In addition, the syndrome can be the result of ectopic ACTH-producing tumours and in some heavy drinkers showing an alcohol-induced pseudo-Cushing's syndrome. In all these conditions psychiatric symptoms have been found to develop with an incidence varying from 21.1–66 per cent (Granville-Grossman, 1971), although in a recent study Cohen (1980) found that 86 per cent of his patients were depressed, whereas only 32.5 percent of those studied by Jeffcoate *et al.* (1979) were considered to be psychiatrically ill. However, only 26 of their 40 patients were investigated by the psychiatrist involved in this study, so possibly the figure for psychiatric disturbance is on the conservative side. Although any type of psychiatric illness can develop in these patients, there is an overwhelming preponderance of affective disorder, mostly depression, which can be sufficiently severe to cause suicide or suicide attempts.

The majority of papers describe typical patients with the syndrome or disease, but Friedman *et al.* (1966) have given details of nine patients with ACTH-secreting malignant tumours. One of these presented with a depressive illness before his endocrine disorder was discovered. The pseudo-Cushing syndrome (Smals *et al.*, 1976; Rees *et al.*, 1977) can also cause depression. One of the heavy drinking patients described by Rees *et al.* was depressed, as was one of the two patients with this condition mentioned by Jeffcoate *et al.* (1979).

Sometimes the psychiatric symptoms precede the appearance of physical signs as was the case with most of the patients described by Gifford and Gunderson (1970) and four of those presented by Jeffcoate *et al.* (1979). More often, the physical and psychiatric symptoms coincide, remitting together with appropriate treatment, although this is not an invariable outcome as Schindler and Schanda (1975) described a patient with Cushing's syndrome who became psychiatrically depressed *after* operation.

A patient with intermittent Cushing's syndrome, in whom relapses and remissions of physical and psychiatric symptoms occurred with periods of normality in between attacks, was described by Bochner *et al.* (1979). This 21-year-old woman had five bouts of severe suicidal depression associated with characteristic symptoms and signs of Cushing's syndrome. In the final episode her psychiatric symptoms and suicidal risk were so severe that a bilateral adrenalectomy was performed. Within a month after operation her symptoms had remitted and she has remained well over the subsequent six years (Lloyd, pers. comm., 1981) despite signs of increased secretion of ACTH and MSH (Nelson's syndrome). Neither the patient nor members of her family had suffered from affective disorder in the past.

The frequency of affective illness varies in different series. Table 7.1 shows the number of patients said to have been depressed and/or suicidal.

By no means all those said to be depressed were psychotic, but only in a relatively small number of papers are details sufficient to enable one to judge the severity of these illnesses. Jeffcoate *et al.* (1979) found that five of their patients were severely depressed, with another four being moderately depressed. Two other patients were described as frankly manic. Five of Cohen's patients were severely and 13 moderately depressed. In practically all these reports mention is made of suicidal behaviour or ideation in some cases. Rubin and Mandell (1966) comment particularly on the high incidence of depression and suicide in Cushing's syndrome, and a study not included in this table (Hurxthal and O'Sullivan, 1959) mentions that three of 34 patients were suicidal and that 13 showed "significant psychiatric illness", but does not specify the nature of these disorders.

Table 7.1

Incidence of Affective Disorders and Suicidal Behaviour in Cushing's Syndrome.

Author and Date	No. of Patients	Depressed or Suicidal	Percentage
Spillane (1951)	50	16	32
Spillane (1951)	7	2	28
Trethowan and Cobb (1952)	15	7	46
Starr (1952)	53	13	25
Mattingly (1968)	36	14	39
Arseni *et al.* (1968)	6	4	66
Starkman and Schteingart (1969)	35	26	74
Taft *et al.* (1970)	42	8	19
Gifford and Gunderson (1970)	10	8[a]	80
Regenstein *et al.* (1972)	7	3	43
Jeffcoate *et al.* (1979)	40	22[b]	55
Cohen (1980)	29	25	86
Totals	330	148	45

[a]Plus one hypomanic.
[b]Plus two manic.

Aetiology

The frequent occurrence of depression in Cushing's disease and its association with major endocrine abnormalities suggests that a better understanding of the pathogenesis of the condition might provide clues to the aetiology of affective disorder. So far, unfortunately, what might appear to be the answer in terms of over-activity of ACTH secretion is not wholly compatible with the clinical facts. Parenteral ACTH is said to cause depression, whereas cortisol more often results in euphoria (Relkin, 1969). In Cushing's disease depressed mood can correlate positively with serum levels of ACTH (Starkman and Schteingart, 1969), and Fleminger (1955) reported on a patient with psoriatic arthritis who became depressed with treatment with ACTH but euphoric when changed to cortisone.

On the other hand, it appears that depression occurs both with pituitary-dependent Cushing's disease when ACTH levels are high and also in those with the syndrome from primary adrenal tumours when cortisol will be high and ACTH low. Nonetheless, Cohen (1980) found that significantly more of his patients with pituitary-dependent Cushing's disease were depressed than those with adrenal tumours. Seven of the 29 patients with Cushing's disease or ectopic ACTH secretion examined by Jeffcoate *et al.* (1979) were moderately or severely depressed compared with one of the five patients with adrenal tumours, a difference which is statistically significant (chi-squared <0.04). Carroll (1976b), who summarized the findings in four other studies, found that 19 of 33 patients with pituitary-dependent Cushing's disease were depressed compared with four of 20 patients with adrenal tumours, again a highly significant difference. Furthermore, patients with Cushing's disease have higher suicide rates than those with the syndrome. In the majority of patients adrenalectomy or suppression of cortisol secretion with metyrapone (Jeffcoate *et al.* 1979) will usually result in remission of both physical and psychiatric symptoms, although some patients may remain depressed and suicidal for as long as six months after surgery.

Sachar (1975a) considers that the high incidence of depression in Cushing's disease might be caused by alterations in intra-cellular sodium and the metabolism of indole and catecholamines occurring in response to raised ACTH levels, and Maas (1972) observed that increased corticosteroids resulted in sodium retention and decreased synthesis of noradrenalin. Of considerable interest are the three patients reported by Pullan *et al.* (1980) with ectopic ACTH syndromes from carcinoid tumours resulting in Cushing's syndromes. One patient was manic and the other two seriously depressed. The authors found increased levels of beta-endorphin and methionine enkephalin in association with raised ACTH. When the tumours were removed the psychiatric symptoms and features of Cushing's syndrome disappeared. So far, at least, the possibility that endorphins may play a part in the symptomatology or aetiology of Cushing's syndrome has not been considered. However, massive over-secretion of ACTH following adrenalectomy — Nelson's syndrome — does not, at least as far as published cases reveal, cause depression, the patient described by Bochner *et al.* (1979) being a good example. Furthermore, in Addison's disease, to be discussed later, psychotic depression is unusual, although minor depressive and neurasthenic symptoms are fairly typical. Here again there is an over-secretion of ACTH with an absence of cortisol. Consequently it does appear that elevated ACTH and cortisol output together is more likely to be followed by severe affective disorder than excess of one hormone without the other. This still leaves a small number of patients who respond with depression to parenteral cortisone or high levels of circulating corticoids from primary adrenal tumours, but in all probability individual susceptibility and genetic predisposition may have some bearing on this phenomenon.

Quarton *et al.* (1955) found insufficient evidence to support or refute theories of affective disorder in Cushing's syndrome based on the supposition that genetic or personality factors were likely to predispose patients to this disorder. On the other hand, Regenstein *et al.* (1972) considered that a prior history of psychiatric illness largely determined the type of reaction which might develop in a patient with Cushing's disease. However, the details are insufficient on all of their seven patients to permit the reader to judge the merits of their case. Unfortunately, very few writers have provided adequate information on their patients' past personal and family histories, but Hall *et al.* (1979) could find no evidence that a positive family history or previous personal history of psychiatric illness increased the likelihood of psychoses developing in patients treated with prednisone. They described a variety of psychotic reactions, including affective disorders, and noted how these most often developed during the first five days of treatment and were related to dosage. Cohen (1980) found positive family histories of depression or suicide in eight of his depressed patients and considered that early loss of or separation from parents in five more patients might have contributed to their affective illnesses. On the other hand, Cohen did not mention any earlier attacks of depression in his patients independent of their endocrine disorders. At present it appears that the balance of evidence favours the hypothesis that affective disorders in Cushing's disease are directly caused by the abnormal levels of circulating hormones. All observers seem to agree that depression is not simply a reaction to the discomforts and disfigurements of the illness. The rapid resolution of symptoms when hormonal levels are controlled by appropriate treatment points to the conclusion that psychiatric and physical symptoms share a common pathogenesis, although the precise nature of this has yet to be determined.

Arseni *et al.* (1968) have postulated that Cushing's disease is a response on the part of the diencephalic–hypothalamic–pituitary axis to severe emotional upsets. Hurxthal and O'Sullivan (1959) claimed that six of their 35 patients became ill after "significant stress" and Gifford and Gunderson (1970) gave extensive details of 10 patients whose endocrine disorders emerged in a setting of disturbed personality and recurrent emotional crises. However, as Jeffcoate *et al.* (1979) point out, "An alternative view (to Gifford and Gunderson's hypothesis) is that the length of psychiatric history reflects an otherwise subclinical endocrine disorder which becomes manifest only at a later date." They also found that some patients who had been psychiatrically ill many years before the onset of Cushing's syndrome showed little clinical response to lowering of plasma cortisol and considered that in these patients the psychiatric and physical symptoms were unrelated. Cohen (1980), on the other hand, gives some support for the contrary opinion. Six of 26 patients had experienced major emotional disturbances shortly before the onset of Cushing's syndrome. Nonetheless, Cohen does not consider that this condition generally is likely to be a response to major life events of a disturbing kind.

Finally one has to conclude that, regardless of the differential effects of ACTH and cortisone on mood, the primary disturbance which is fundamental for both physical and psychiatric symptoms probably lies in the hypothalamus. Woolf *et al.* (1964), who described a patient with recurrent attacks of depression and Cushingoid symptoms lasting 3–5 days and coming on every one-and-a-half to three months, suggested that the source of the abnormal endocrine activity lay in the hypothalamus. In some cases one might also conjecture that emotional stress will be the activating force, whereas in others genetic and predispositional factors will cause these patients to develop severe depression in response to endocrine abnormalities which act as precipitants of the affective psychoses.

Steroid Psychoses

The number of psychoses following treatment with ACTH or corticosteroids varied from 0–24 per cent in nine papers summarized by Granville-Grossman (1971). As already mentioned, Quarton *et al.* (1955) considered that genetic and personality factors could not be clearly indicted as crucial in the aetiology of these psychoses, a point supported by Hall *et al.* (1979). Bearing in mind the frequency of affective disorder in conditions such as systemic lupus erythematosus, rheumatoid arthritis and multiple sclerosis, all of which are likely to be treated with steroids, it is not always easy to distinguish the hormonal effects from those of the disease.

ADDISON'S DISEASE

If the development of depression in Cushing's disease was secondary solely to the high output of ACTH, one would expect that in Addison's disease, which shares the same endocrine abnormality, but with low instead of raised corticosteroid output, depression would be common. However, as already discussed, excess secretion of ACTH clearly is not the sole factor determining the onset of affective disorder in Cushing's disease, but some writers have listed depression as one of the common psychiatric symptoms in adrenal insufficiency. Lishman (1978), for example, mentions depression, emotional withdrawal, apathy and loss of drive and initiative as the most frequently observed psychological features. Drake (1957), however, was inclined to regard the psychiatric picture of patients with Addison's disease as "neurasthenic" rather than depressive. Detailed analysis of the symptomatology was not discussed by this writer but psychotic depressive symptoms in Addison's disease appear to be unusual. Carroll (1976b) writes that 50 per cent of patients with Addison's disease are depressed and irritable, while Sorkin (1949) observed mental symptoms in 70 per cent of patients. He drew a distinction between asthenia and fatigue on the one hand and true depression on the other. Cleghorn (1951) also considered that about 50 per cent of patients with Addison's disease were depressed but later (1965) commented that psychotic depression is rare. Craddock and Zeller (1952), however, reported severe depression and suicidal tendencies in a patient who ultimately required ECT for his affective illness. Another patient with a 10-year history of Addison's disease described by Cumming and Kort (1956) became severely depressed and failed to respond to ECT until cortisone was added to the treatment. Mattson (1974), who described a patient with a paranoid psychosis and Addison's disease, says little about affective disorder in this condition but tended to emphasize neurasthenic symptoms as being more typical. Fortunately, once appropriate treatment of the endocrine condition is started the symptoms of apathy, fatigue, weakness and depression clear up in most patients.

PRIMARY HYPERALDOSTERONISM (CONN'S SYNDROME)

Rather surprisingly, in view of the effects of abnormal electrolyte and water metabolism, Mattingly (1968) states that affective disorders in this condition do not occur. However, Malinow and Lion (1979) have described a 29-year-old woman with no past personal or family history of affective disorder who became weak, insomniac, anorexic and depressed with associated loss of weight. She was found to be suffering from hyperaldosteronism and when her low serum potassium levels were corrected her symptoms abated.

OTHER ENDOCRINE DISORDERS

Although generally hyperglycaemia and hypoglycaemia do not cause depression, diabetes is a fairly common finding in older patients with affective disorders. Possibly the association of hypertension and cerebral athero-sclerosis are more responsible than the metabolic disorder for this phenomenon. Beumont (1979) has commented that psychiatric symptoms are not prominent in diabetics but that there is some evidence that they are prone to develop affective disorders. One might conjecture that an association between diabetes, hypertension and manic-depressive illness in members of the Jewish race would partly account for this observation. However, Waitzkin (1966), in his survey of patients in a mental hospital, where unsuspected diabetes was detected in 11.7 per cent of patients aged less than 50 but in 15 per cent of those aged 50–88, did not mention affective disorder among the diagnostic categories of these patients. The frequency of chronic schiz-ophrenia in the younger and organic psychoses in the older group probably has more to do with the nature of the hospital population than with the true incidence of diabetes in patients with manic-depressive psychosis.

Similarly, although insulinomas can cause psychiatric illness, including, on rare occasions, acute depression (Lishman, 1978), hypoglycaemia as such is not a cause of this kind of reaction. Lishman (1978) also discusses essential reactive hypoglycaemia in which minor psychiatric symptoms, including depression, can occur. However, this condition does not cause characteristic symptoms of endogenous or psychotic depression, and Ford *et al.* (1976), who found that one-third of their 30 patients with spontaneous hypoglycaemia showed features of depressive neurosis, concluded that these were not caused by hypoglycaemia.

Patients with pancreatic disease such as carcinoma and chronic inflammation often develop depression (Rickles, 1945; Savage *et al.*, 1952; Lawton and Phillips, 1955; Fras *et al.*, 1967) but there is no evidence that endocrine abnormalities play any part in the aetiology of the clinical picture.

One other condition, Simmond's disease, not surprisingly, in view of the very extensive endocrine disturbances found in this condition, can be associated with severe depression. Todd (1951) described a 54-year-old woman whose mood change responded well to hormone therapy. In this case, however, one might consider that hypothyroidism was as much responsible for her depression as the primary pituitary damage was.

Prolactin

Although there is little evidence that raised prolactin levels in depressed patients are anything other than a non-specific response to stress (Sachar *et al.*, 1973), Horrobin's (1977) comments are of interest. He observed how drugs such as reserpine, methyldopa and oral contraceptives, all known to precipitate depression, also cause a rise in prolactin, presumably on account of a reduction in available dopamine. Prolactin also stimulates prostaglandin synthesis which causes a fall in the synthesis of noradrenalin. It is worth noting that tricyclic antidepressants are also prostaglandin antagonists. With respect to reserpine, methyldopa and oral contraceptives, as will be shown in the next chapter, these drugs often precipitate depression in patients predisposed to this reaction by genetic or constitutional susceptibility. Less commonly, depression occurs in individuals on these drugs who have no past personal or family histories of affective disorders. In predisposed subjects one might conjecture that any role for prolactin in the pathogenesis of depression is likely to be subsidiary to the other more direct actions of these drugs on neurotransmitters, receptors and rate-limiting enzymes. In any case, the sharp rise in prolactin observed following ECT (Öhman *et al.*, 1976; O'Dea *et al.*, 1978) is hardly compatible with the notion that prolactin makes an important contribution to the aetiology of depression. No doubt individual variations occur, as Mendelwicz *et al.* (1977) observed different responses to levodopa as measured by changes in prolactin levels in unipolar and bipolar patients.

8

Drugs and Depression

Although Sim (1974) claimed that infections were the commonest precipitants of depression, today drugs appear to have overtaken viruses and bacteria as aetiological agents. In fact Sartorius (1974, p.19) has suggested that an apparent increase in depressive illness is due to "the currently raging epidemic of excessive medicament consumption", a phenomenon particularly evident in older patients and one which has not declined during the ensuing years. As, according to Tyrer (1980), 40 billion doses of benzodiazapines are being consumed each day, it is clear that the potential for adverse reactions to these and other drugs is considerable. Craig and Van Natta (1978) have commented on the steady increase in drug ingestion with age, with 10 per cent of those aged 60 and over taking at least four drugs daily. These patients obtained higher scores on a depression rating scale. Minor tranquillizers and sedatives appeared to be the prime offenders, but it was not clear whether these drugs were being given for depression or had contributed to it. This problem of drug intake by older patients has been discussed on a number of occasions (Gibson and O'Hare, 1968; Learoyd, 1972; Whitlock, 1977b), but its contribution to psychological depression requires closer examination.

The table of drugs alleged to cause depression includes some 90 preparations, some of which are more likely to induce this reaction than others (Table 8.1). Many of these have been discussed elsewhere (Whitlock and Evans, 1978; Whitlock, 1981b) and, taking as a working guide the biogenic amine-depletion hypothesis and the adrenergic–cholinergic imbalance theory proposed by Janowsky et al. (1972), it is possible to relate the psychological depressive effects of many drugs to one or other of these mechanisms. Other effects such as the induction of folate deficiency or electrolyte abnormalities are also relevant to the affective disturbances observed in some patients.

Table 8.1
Drugs that may Cause Depression[a]

Analgesics and Anti-Inflammatory Drugs	Cardiac and Anti-Hypertensive Drugs	Sedatives and Hypnotics
		Barbiturates
Fenoprofen	Bethanidine	Chloral
Ibuprofen	Clonidine	Chlormethiazole
Indomethacin	Digitalis	Clorazepate
Ketoprofen	Guanethidine	Ethanol
Opiates (morphine, etc.)	Hydralazine	Other benzodiazepines
Phenacetin	Methyl-dopa	Other non-barbiturate
Phenylbutazone	Prazosin	hypnotics and sedatives
Pentazocine	Procainamide	
Benzydamine	Propranolol	Steroids and Hormones
	Reserpine	
Anti-Bacterial and Anti-Fungal Drugs	Veratrum	ACTH
	Lidocaine	Corticosteroids
	Oxprenolol	Danazol
Ampicillin	Methosperidine	Oral contraceptives
Bactrim		Norethisterone
Clotrimazole	Neurological Drugs	Prednisone
Cycloserine		Triamcinalone
Dapsone	Amantadine	
Ethionamide	Baclofen	Stimulants and Appetite Suppressants
Griseofulvin	Bromocriptine	
Metronidazole	Carbamezapine	
Nitrofurantoin	L-dopa	Amphetamine
Nalidixic acid	Methsuximide	Fenfluramine
Sulphonamides	Phenytoin	Diethylpropion
Streptomycin	Phenidione	Phenmetrazine
Tetracycline	Tetrabenazine	
Thiocarlide		Miscellaneous Drugs
	Psychotropic Drugs	
Anti-Neoplastic Drugs		Acetazolamide
	Butyrophenones	Anticholinesterases
Azathioprin	Phenothiazines	Choline
6-azauridine	Fluphenazine decanoate	Cimetidine
1-asparaginase	Flupenthixol decanoate	Cyproheptadine
Bleomycin	Prochlorperazine	Diphenoxylate
Mithramycin		Disulfiram
Trimethoprim		Lysergide
Vinicristine		Methysergide
		Mebeverine
		Meclozine
		Metoclopramide
		Pizotifen
		Salbutamol

[a]After Myler's *Side-Effects of Drugs* (1972, 1975) and Annuals 1977–1979.

When considering drug-induced depression it is essential to ask whether one is witnessing a symptom, a syndrome, a transitory down-turn in spirits or sedation and apathy caused by the central action of the drug. Depression as a change in mood in the course of an illness needs to be distinguished clearly from the syndrome of depression characterized by feelings of hopelessness and despair, suicidal thoughts and actions, sleep disturbances, anorexia and feelings of guilt and self-reproach. Chronic illnesses, especially when accompanied by pain, as is the case with arthritis and malignant disease, may understandably cause feelings of hopelessness and disappointment at lack of response to treatment. Notwithstanding these contributions, a number of patients each year, usually the elderly, are admitted to hospital suffering from depressive illnesses which appear to have developed since the patient started treatment with one or more of the drugs shown in the table.

Do the drugs cause or precipitate illnesses? This is an important question with respect to the prevention of these reactions, as a number of investigators have demonstrated that a fairly large percentage of patients developing severe depression in response to drug treatment have past histories of affective disorders. This is particularly the case with antihypertensive drugs (Waal, 1967; Simpson and Waal-Manning, 1971; Snaith and McCourbie, 1974) and levodopa (Goodwin, 1972). Other patients may also have family histories of affective disorder. Consequently, genetic or constitutional predisposition could be the essential determinants of a depressive syndrome in which the drug or drugs act as precipitants rather than as essential causes. If this is a correct interpretation of the phenomenon we should, as far as possible, when placing a patient on a potentially depressing drug or combination of drugs ensure that he has not suffered from depression independently of physical illness or treatment in the past. Such a precaution might prevent a further attack of depression in patients with this kind of background.

To consider each of the drugs or group of drugs would be superfluous, and the reader is referred to the two reviews on the topic already mentioned. Certain substances, however, require further discussion, particularly antihypertensive drugs, oral contraceptives, psychotropic preparations, antiparkinsonian drugs, stimulants and appetite suppressants, alcohol and sedatives, anti-inflammatory drugs and a miscellaneous group of substances whose use has increased in recent years.

ANTIHYPERTENSIVE DRUGS

This class of drugs illustrates very clearly some of the difficulties encountered when trying to relate depression of mood to a particular chemical substance. Many variables have to be considered, including the genetic and constitutional makeup of the patient, the type and degree of hypertension, the effects of hypertension, particularly on cerebral circulation, the psychological response of the patient to his disease and its treatment, the class of drug being administered, and the effects of different drugs in various combinations and permutations. So far, a study taking all these factors into account has yet to be carried out. Only by including a very large number of patients would it be possible to give proper weight to the various factors contributing to depression in patients with raised blood pressure being treated with antihypertensive drugs. However, irrespective of claims for the absence of serious side effects, it is not uncommon for patients who are being treated with antihypertensives to be admitted to psychiatric wards with severe endogenous-type depressions.

Bulpitt and Dollery (1973) declared that the incidence of depressive reactions in patients being treated with antihypertensive drugs was relatively low, but a number of studies have expressed opinions contrary to this statement (Waal, 1967; Pariente, 1973; Bant, 1974; Snaith and McCourbie, 1974). Snaith and McCourbie found the occurrence of depression in patients on methyldopa to be 4–6 per cent, and Sainsbury (1955) noted that 28 per cent of his suicides had been on antihypertensive drugs. Because many patients who develop depression when being treated for hypertension have a past history of depressive illness (Waal, 1967; Simpson and Waal-Manning, 1971; Snaith and McCourbie, 1974), it is not easy to determine whether this is a causal or coincidental relationship, particularly as hypertension and antihypertensive drugs can both produce symptoms resembling depression.

Reserpine

Treatment with reserpine, according to Granville-Grossman (1971), who reviewed a number of studies, is followed by depression in 10–15 per cent of patients. Rawolfia alkaloids reduce the availability of 5-HT and noradrenalin but also potentiate acetylcholine (Sulser *et al.*, 1964). In common with methyl-dopa they also cause a rise in prolactin, presumably by reducing the dopaminergic control of prolactin-inhibiting factor, although this is unlikely to have much bearing on mood disturbances. Another possible relevant action of reserpine, particularly when combined with diuretic therapy, is alteration in electrolyte levels (Lewis, 1971). Clinical studies of rawolfia alkaloids confirm their depressive effects. Quetsch *et al.* (1959) compared 185 hypertensive patients on non-specific treatment with 202 on rawolfia alone or combined with other drugs. Four per cent of those on non-specific therapy developed moderate to severe depression compared with 10 per cent on rawolfia alone and 12 per cent on combined treatments. Nineteen of the patients on rawolfia had a past history of depression and 11 of these became depressed on the drug. Age, sex, duration and severity of the hypertension, complications of the disease and the results of treatment were not regarded as relevant factors.

Layland *et al.* (1962) found that 22 of 119 patients on methosperidine became depressed, but most recovered when the drug was withdrawn.

Ayd (1958) has drawn attention to the important issue of whether patients on a variety of drugs are depressed or are showing a pseudo-depressive picture of sedation, fatigue and retardation. Twenty-three of 70 patients allegedly depressed from reserpine or thioridazine were, in fact, pseudo-depressives. There was a higher incidence of past psychiatric treatment in those with true depression compared with the pseudo-depressives. Some patients were probably depressed before starting the drugs and the majority, not surprisingly, were in the 40–70 age range. Bunney and Davis (1965) reviewed 50 studies of hypertension treated with reserpine and found an overall incidence of depression of 15 per cent. In one study 85 per cent of the depressed patients had a past history of psychiatric care. Jensen (1959), in a similar review, recorded depression in 8–10 per cent of patients on reserpine. Two of his 11 depressed patients had past histories of recurrent depression and one had made a suicidal attempt. Goodwin *et al.* (1972) who reviewed 60 investigations and found an overall incidence of depression of 20 per cent, including seven per cent with severe depression, remarked (p.85), "The single variable that most reliably predicts who will develop depressive symptoms when on reserpine is a past history of depressive illness." Similarly, Goodwin and Bunney (1971) felt that the more reserpine-induced illness resembled endogenous depression the greater the likelihood that the patient would have a past history of a similar illness. Schwartz *et al.* (1973) compared patients on reserpine with others on clonidine or placebo. Using a rating scale, depression was more frequently recorded in the reserpine-treated patients. On the evidence, it would be difficult to refute the capacity of rawolfia alkaloids for causing depression and that individuals with a past history of depression are more liable to this drug-induced state than those lacking any such predisposition.

Methyl-Dopa

Methyl-dopa is regarded as second only to reserpine in its capacity for causing depression, and it has been recommended that patients with a past history of depression should not be treated with it (*British Medical Journal*, Editorial, 1966). However, in the six cases described by Johnson *et al.* (1966), none had a past history of depression. In a review of 12 studies Granville-Grossman (1971) found an incidence of depression of 5.7 per cent. However, only nine of the 308 adverse reactions to methyl-dopa reported from Sweden were depressive (Furhoff, 1978) but the true extent of this response could not be accurately assessed by this type of investigation. Of the 15 cases reported by Bunney and Davis (1965), nine of the 10 for whom sufficient information was available had a past history of depression. The symptoms were classically endogenous in type with suicidal thoughts often present, but stopping the drug usually resulted in prompt remission. Like reserpine, methyl-dopa, which passes the blood–brain barrier (Nies, 1975), depletes the brain of catecholamines by inhibiting dopa-decarboxylase (Oates *et al.*, 1965; Sourkes, 1965; Goodman and Gilman, 1975).

Alpha-Adrenergic and Beta-Adrenergic Receptor-Blocking Agents

Both guanethidine and bethanadine apparently cause depression in hypertensive patients (North, 1969, p. 117). Prichard *et al.* (1968) observed mild depression in seven per cent of patients on bethanadine and 21 per cent on guanethidine, despite the very limited capacity these drugs have for passing the blood–brain barrier. In another two patients on methyl-dopa the depression was severe but cleared when the drug was stopped. Dollery *et al.* (1960) recorded complaints of weakness, tiredness and depression, but two of their 80 patients on guanethidine became severely depressed and suicidal. Four of the 28 patients reported by Bauer *et al.* (1961) became depressed and one, a cyclothymic personality, committed suicide. Three of these patients had past histories of depression, with two becoming ill following the use of reserpine. Rather surprisingly, Bant (1974) found a higher incidence of depression in patients on alpha-adrenergic blocking agents than in patients on methyl-dopa and reserpine.

Guanethidine interferes with catecholamine metabolism at the synaptic nerve endings and, like reserpine, causes retention of salt and water (Bauer *et al.*, 1961). According to Dollery *et al.* (1960) guanethidine is distributed in rat brain in much the same concentration as in plasma, and Goodman and Gilman (1975) mention that the drug releases serotonin from central and peripheral sites although its major action appears to be adrenergic blockade.

Apart from Waal's report on propranolol (1967) in which 26 of 89 patients became depressed, there have been few reports on affective disturbances in patients on this drug. Of Waal's 26 patients (including two suicides) 11 of 13 who had been previously depressed when treated with reserpine became depressed when taking propranolol, whereas none of the patients who had not reacted to reserpine in this manner did so when changed to the beta-blocker. The severity of depression increased with dosage of the drug. In a review of 303 patients (Zacharias *et al.*, 1972) only two patients became depressed, but only one sufficiently so to require withdrawal of the drug. Prazosin causes depression in 1.8 per cent of patients (Simpson *et al.*, 1977), and in a recent short review Harris and Richards (1978) recorded depressive symptoms in 5.5 per cent of patients on oxprenolol, 2.7 per cent on acebutalol and 0.07 per cent on labetol, although the last figure increased to

2.7 per cent when the drug was taken in higher dosage for longer periods of time. In a report by Hua *et al.* (1980) on acebutalol, one patient with a past history of depression became severely and another patient mildly depressed.

I have recently seen two patients who became depressed after being placed on metoprolol for labile hypertension. Both recovered promptly when the drug was stopped. In one case there was a possible episode of depression some 15 years earlier, and the other patient had qualities suggestive of cyclothymia. Both patients had first degree relatives who had been treated for depression or manic-depressive psychosis.

Clonidine

A number of reports mention depression as a side effect of clonidine, a drug which causes alpha-adrenergic blockade and also inhibits the release of noradrenalin (Ng *et al.*, 1967; Kellett and Hamilton, 1970; Simpson, 1973). Clayden *et al.* (1974), however, comparing clonidine with placebo for the treatment of menopausal flushing, found the same incidence of side effects — including depression — in both groups of patients. Schwartz *et al.* (1973) also reported that clonidine caused depression no more frequently than placebo. Nonetheless, in a general review of the drug, Brogden *et al.* (1975) recorded depression, drowsiness, dryness of mouth and anxiety among the common side effects.

The use of clonidine for conditions other than hypertension is not free from side effects, and Roberts (1977) reported on a patient given dixarit as a prophylactic against migraine. She developed an agitated depression which cleared within ten days when the drug was stopped. I recently saw an identical case, a young woman who became depressed when given dixarit for her migraine. In her case there was a past history of depression independent of the drug.

On the evidence it seems clear that antihypertensive drugs are more likely to cause depression in patients who have had previous episodes of affective disorder. These illnesses indubitably occur but may seem infrequent if surveys are made only on patients attending hypertension clinics. Bulpitt and Dollery (1973), for example, found little evidence of depression in 477 patients being treated with a variety of drugs including alpha and beta-blockers and methyl-dopa. Nevertheless, despite many observations which relate depression in patients receiving antihypertensive drugs to their past histories of affective disorder, Snaith and McCourbie (1974), Snaith (1976) and Bant (1974) considered that the severity of the disease was more causative of depression than the drugs. In a more recent paper, however, Bant (1978) compared hypertensive patients with a control group suffering from a variety of chronic illnesses. Both groups were similar with respect to past psychiatric disorders but, during the follow-up period, rather more of the hypertensive patients suffered depression although those on methyl-dopa more often had suffered from earlier attacks of affective illness.

Summary and Conclusions

If the disease rather than the drug is responsible for depression, one has to ask why some antihypertensive drugs apparently are associated with a much higher incidence of the illness than others. It is reasonable to assume that all the drugs listed have now been used on large numbers of hypertensive patients, regardless of the severity of their illnesses. Hence, the greater frequency of depression in patients on reserpine, methyl-dopa and the alpha-blockers compared with patients treated with beta-blockers and clonidine surely implies that the drugs are contributing to the depression regardless of the effects of hypertensive illness. Nonetheless, the most important contribution comes from predisposition to affective disorder in the shape of previous attacks of similar breakdowns. Hence the conclusion that the drugs have precipitated rather than directly caused depression in the majority of these patients. Presumably this is the result of their effects on subjects with cerebral mechanisms which are more susceptible to depletion of neuro-transmitters by these agents.

STEROID HORMONES AND ORAL CONTRACEPTIVES

Steroid Hormones

Some of the effects of ACTH and corticosteroids on mood have been discussed in the previous chapter. Although any type of psychiatric reaction can develop following the use of these drugs, affective disturbances predominate. It has been thought that patients with past histories of mental illness or disturbed personalities are particularly at risk, but this point was disputed by Lewis and Fleminger (1954) and by Clark *et al.* (1953). The Boston Collaborative Drug Surveillance Program (1971) reported 21 acute reactions in 676 patients. Eight patients were euphoric and 13 psychotic. Of the psychotic patients, two were depressed and six manic. A rather atypical pattern of psychosis was the rule rather than the exception. On occasions psychoses can develop when steroids are stopped too abruptly and Gifford *et al.* (1977) described a patient who became depressed and amnesic in a setting of "fugue-like" behaviour when prednisone was withdrawn.

Oral Contraceptives

Since oral contraceptives became widely used, there have been numerous reports on their effects on mood. These steroids share with antihypertensive drugs some of the methodological problems which have to be considered before concluding that they can directly cause depression. Once again, the genetic and constitutional make-up of the subject might be of critical importance. Other factors will include the woman's attitude to contraception generally and oral contraceptives in particular, any anxiety she might have about their alleged hazards, her wish for or fears of pregnancy, the marital relationship and sexual adjustment, her experience of pre-menstrual tension and depression and the type of oral contraceptive being used. Finally, one has to ask whether depression as a psychiatric syndrome is being experienced or whether the subject manifests a transitory down-turn of spirits unaccompanied by the more severe symptoms of melancholia.

In the face of these uncontrollable variables the precise role of oral contraceptives in the aetiology of depression is still far from clear (Herzberg *et al.*, 1971; Kutner and Brown, 1972; The Royal College of General Practitioners, 1974). Many authors (Nilsson *et al.*, 1967; Kane *et al.*, 1969; Lewis and Hoghughi, 1969; Hertzberg *et al.*, 1971; Parry and Rush, 1979) consider that women with past histories of affective illnesses or abnormal personalities have a greater liability for developing severe depression with oral contraceptives. However, the frequency of these adverse reactions, varying from 5–7 per cent of patients (Malek-Ahmadi and Behrman, 1976; Hertzberg *et al.*, 1970) to 5–30 per cent (*British Medical Journal*, Editorial, 1969c), indicates a far higher frequency of affective disorders than would be found in the general population. On the other hand, only a minority of these patients would be showing the typical features of endogenous depression, although in some series suicide or attempted suicide have been recorded in association with oral contraceptive use. Kutner and Brown (1972), in contrast with other opinions, did not feel that earlier episodes of affective disorder were relevant to the onset of depression in patients on oral contraceptives.

Equally contradictory opinions have been expressed about the effects of different types of steroid combinations, with some claiming that oral contraceptives with a high progestagen content are more liable to cause depression (Lewis and Hoghughi, 1969). Others have declared that the progestagen content is irrelevant (Nilsson and Sölvell, 1967; Kutner and Brown, 1972), but Grant and Pryse-Davies (1968), after observing that a fall in oestrogen with a concurrent increase of progestagen leads to a rise in monoamine oxidase activity, considered that oral contraceptives with a high progestagen content were more likely to cause depression and loss of libido as a consequence of their probable effects on this enzyme. In support of the belief that patients taking high progestagen-type oral contraceptives were more likely to become depressed, Lewis and Hoghughi (1969) compared 50 female patients on oral contraceptives with 50 controls. Both groups had equal numbers with past histories of depressive illness, but 19 of the oral contraceptive users compared with three controls experienced severe or mild depression, with those on high progestagen content contraceptives being the more depressed.

A good many of the disputes in this area may hinge on what is meant by depression in the context of oral contraceptive use. Feelings of oppression, irritability and fatigue should not be regarded as synonymous with melancholia and, consequently, few users are likely to develop symptoms sufficiently serious to justify a diagnosis of severe depression. Fleminger and Seager (1978) compared three groups of patients, those taking oral contraceptives, those who had taken them in the past and those who had never used them. The incidence of depression, using a rating scale, was about the same in all three groups but it tended to increase with age. Past takers had higher neuroticism scores on the Eysenck Personality Inventory (EPI), and the authors concluded that depression observed in patients on oral contraceptives had more to do with personality and the house-bound housewife syndrome than with the steroids. Full-time housewives had higher depressive scores on the rating scales, but again one has to ask whether it is true depression that is being measured, or simply a combination of being fed-up, miserable or unhappy for a number of reasons unrelated to either housewifely status or the ingestion of steroids. Even so, there can be no doubt that some women on oral contraceptives do suffer severe depression even to the point of feeling suicidal; and, on the evidence, mixed as it is, one might conclude that patients with past histories of moderate to severe depression are the ones most at risk for this response. A Committee of the Royal College of General Practitioners (1974), after reviewing a large number of papers, concluded that severe depression in women taking oral contraceptives occurred no more frequently than in non-users and that an increase of 30 per cent in depression in users of oral contraceptives was an excessive estimate. This study, however, did appear to show that users and ex-users had fairly high admission rates to hospital on account of depression.

Theories concerning the possible modes of action of these hormones have been reviewed by Parry and Rush (1979). As already mentioned, Grant and Pryse-Davies (1968) observed that in the normal menstrual cycle there is a rise in endometrial MAO activity in the late secretory phase associated with a fall of oestrogen and increased pre-menstrual tension. Pills containing pro-gestagens cause an earlier rise in MAO, but whether this implies similar activity in the brain is not clear. Madsen (1974), after taking note of the effects of pregnancy, the stage of the menstrual cycle and combined oestrogen and progestagen oral contraceptives on the kynurenine pathway, studied the excretion of 5-HIAA in 11 subjects on combined preparations. In eight there was a rise in 5-HIAA excretion and three subjects stopped taking the contraceptives on account of depression. The highest rate of 5-HIAA excretion was associated with the most severe depression. Leeton (1974), who also felt that women with past histories of affective symptoms were more liable to suffer from depression when taking oral contraceptives, considered that progestagen deflected the metabolism of tryptophan into the kynurenine pathway leading to a fall in serotonin. This process can be prevented by giving pyridoxine but, considering the heterogeneity of affective disorders, it is unlikely that any single explanation of the depressive effects of oral contraceptives will suffice. What does seem clear is that a not insignificant number of women taking these preparations become depressed, sometimes to the point of feeling suicidal, and that on the evidence it is those with past histories of depression who are most likely to react in this way. Consequently, it seems sensible to advise these women to avoid oral contraceptives, particularly those with a high progestagen content, and to adopt some other mode of contraception (*British Medical Journal*, Editorial, 1970b).

ANTIPSYCHOTIC DRUGS

Most of the unwanted effects of antipsychotic drugs are well known, but controversy persists over the question of whether the long-acting preparations such as fluphenazine decanoate and flupenthixol cause severe depression in some schizophrenic patients. Ayd (1975) has written, "All neuroleptics may produce a syndrome which closely resembles an endogenous depression. There is now general agreement that mild to severe depression that may lead to suicide may happen during treatment with any depot neuroleptic, just as they might occur during treatment with any oral neuroleptic." The question of symptomatic depression in the course of schizophrenia will be deferred to a later chapter, but De Alarcón and Carney (1969) described 16 patients receiving intramuscular fluphenazine who became severely depressed. Five committed suicide. Johnson (1973) found that 15 per cent of patients on fluphenazine decanoate required treatment for depression, although he expressed doubts about whether the drug was responsible. In a later investigation Johnson and Malik (1975) observed that patients with acute relapses of schizophrenia showed a definite euphoria when treated with flupenthixol, whereas those on fluphenazine decanoate experienced a downturn in mood, although this did not amount to serious depression. Corbett (1975) also observed depressive episodes in many acute schizophrenic patients being treated with fluphenazine.

Carney and Sheffield (1975) found that 15 per cent of patients treated with depot flupenthixol became depressed, and in 10 per cent this was severe enough to require specific treatment. Six of 199 patients withdrew from treatment because of depression and one committed suicide. Seven per cent had transient episodes of hypomania. In a later paper the same authors (Carney and Sheffield, 1976) claimed that, compared with fluphenazine enanthate and decanoate, flupenthixol decanoate has a lower incidence of severe depressive side-effects. It is likely that these severe mood changes are caused by the drug's capacity for blockading dopamine and noradrenalin receptors.

In contrast with other investigators, Hirsch *et al.* (1973) found only a low incidence of depression in patients successfully maintained on fluphenazine but, in a later study, Knight *et al.* (1979), who compared patients treated with either fluphenazine or flupenthixol, recorded that 53 per cent became depressed, with no differences between the two drugs. Twenty-seven per cent had to receive treatment with antidepressants. Falloon *et al.* (1978), who compared fluphenazine with pimozide for the long-term treatment of schizophrenia, reported that nearly half their patients became depressed. This occurred rather more often with fluphenazine than with pimozide. On the other hand, McCreadie *et al.* (1980) found little evidence of depression in two groups of schizophrenic patients treated with pimozide or fluphenazine.

Two brief reviews of drugs by the American Medical Association Council on Drugs (1968) mention depression in association with the use of butaperazine and haloperidol. Achté (1974) also states that butyrophenones are particularly liable to cause depression, a complication which is due to the drug's capacity, along with other antipsychotic substances, to block catecholamine receptors (Fuxe *et al.,* 1970).

The cause of neuroleptic-induced depression is not entirely clear, for, as Weinstein (1980) has pointed out, there seems little reason why all patients on these drugs should not become depressed as a result of their action on catechol and indoleamine receptors. Possibly diagnostic inaccuracy plays a part, and there seems little doubt that some patients treated as schizophrenics have been examples of manic-depressive psychosis. Blum (1980) has commented on this and found that patients most likely to develop depression when treated with depot neuroleptics more often have psychoses of sudden onset with associated confusion, absence of emotional blunting but with feelings of guilt and thoughts of suicide and death. Such a clinical picture sounds more typical of manic-depressive psychosis than of schizophrenia. Nevertheless, most patients who became depressed when receiving depot neuroleptics were unequivocally schizophrenic and, although a change in psychosis from schizophrenia to manic-depressive psychosis can occur (Sheldrick *et al.,* 1977), this is unlikely to occur sufficiently often to account for the majority of patients with neuroleptic-induced depression.

STIMULANTS AND APPETITE SUPPRESSANTS

Amphetamines

Although drugs in this group do not usually cause depression when being consumed, severe depression can occur when they are stopped. In a review of amphetamine psychosis, Siomopoulos (1975) stated that the main effect of amphetamine was to block the re-uptake of noradrenalin and dopamine, thereby releasing these transmitters and, at the same time, inhibiting their destruction by monoamine oxidases. Hence, when amphetamines are withdrawn, a relative decrease of available transmitter amines may be responsible for the depressed mood.

Connell (1958) observed withdrawal depression in seven of his 30 amphetamine addicts, and four were depressed during their psychotic states. Although six of the 30 patients had past histories of depression, it is not stated how many of these became depressed when taking or after withdrawal of amphetamines. None of the addicts had positive family histories of affective disorder. Edison (1971) described one patient who had suffered mild anxiety and depression in the past but became severely depressed and suicidal when she stopped using an amphetamine–barbiturate preparation.

Fenfluramine

Fenfluramine causes depression when the drug is stopped, a reaction which has now been recorded by a number of authors (Gaind, 1969; Imlah, 1970; Golding, 1970; Harding, 1971, 1972; Steel and Briggs, 1972; Oswald, 1974; Levin, 1975; Innes *et al.*, 1977). Like amphetamines, fenfluramine alters brain catecholamines but also stimulates the release of 5-HT and blocks its re-uptake (Innes *et al.*, 1977) with consequent depletion of brain serotonin (Sanders-Bush *et al.*, 1974; Duhault *et al.*, 1975; Clineschmidt *et al.*, 1976). Oswald *et al.* (1971) found that a down-turn in mood was most pronounced four days after stopping the drug, an observation that was confirmed by Steel and Briggs (1972). Some patients who become severely depressed when fenfluramine is discontinued have previous histories of affective disorder (Golding, 1970; Harding, 1971), but Harding (1972) described three patients with withdrawal depression, only one of whom had suffered from a neurotic depressive reaction some two years earlier.

Other Appetite Suppressants

Van Praag (1968) has reported depression following the use of phenmetrazine, and Louria (1972) mentioned severe depression, sometimes resulting in suicide, when this drug was withdrawn. In a general review, Connell (1975) has reported on the CNS side effects of many appetite suppressant drugs. It is probably correct to say that although most patients experience some euphoria when taking these drugs, a significant minority can become depressed but a far larger number experience depression when the drugs are withdrawn. Silverstone (1974) recorded an incidence of depression in 4.2 per cent of patients on diethylpropion, and Steel *et al.* (1973) observed depression in patients on phentermine, although this was less frequent than in patients on fenfluramine. Carney and Harris (1979) have given details of six patients with psychoses following excessive use of diethylpropion. Three of these experienced withdrawal depression, but two of them had long histories of personality disorder and multiple drug use, including alcohol. The second patient had no past history of affective disorder.

Although complete data are not available, it is clear that some patients experiencing severe depression when stimulants and appetite suppressant drugs are stopped have past histories of affective disorders. Many of those who become addicted to these drugs will have abnormal personalities and, not infrequently, records of multiple drug abuse. In some of these it is probable that affective symptoms will have been experienced in the past. On the other hand, there are undoubtedly some patients without evidence of former psychopathology who become severely depressed, largely, one presumes, on account of the depletion of catecholamines brought about by the drugs.

ALCOHOL AND SEDATIVES

Alcohol

Of all the drugs with a capacity for inducing depression ethanol is probably the best documented. "Boozer's gloom" is a well recognized syndrome occurring, as a rule, after heavy bouts of drinking when blood-alcohol levels are falling. Suicide and attempted suicide rates of heavy drinkers are very much higher than those found in the general population, possibly because of the higher incidence of depressive illness, which may be secondary to the alcohol consumption though likely to be aggravated by other drugs (Baker *et al.*, 1977).

Pottenger *et al.* (1978) found that 14.7 per cent of 61 heavy drinkers/alcoholics were moderately or severely depressed. Of the whole series, 41 had received psychiatric treatment in the past and 69 per cent had positive family histories for psychiatric illness — mainly alcoholism — although 12 per cent of the patients' mothers were said to have been depressed. How many of the depressed alcoholics had positive family histories of affective disorder or had suffered from depression themselves independently from their alcoholism was not stated. Keeler *et al.* (1978) found that, when assessed clinically, 8.6 per cent of 35 male alcoholics were depressed. They were critical of the use of rating scales for estimating the quality and degree of depression in alcoholic patients.

A number of authors (Davis and Walsh, 1971; Feldstein, 1971; Israel and Mardones, 1971; Geller *et al.*, 1973; Takaishi *et al.*, 1974) have shown that heavy intake of alcohol results in falls in the quantities of serotonin and noradrenalin in the brain and that the release of acetylcholine is inhibited while blood-alcohol levels remain high. In animal experiments the evidence is somewhat contradictory (Feldstein, 1973), but Shaw *et al.* (1967) noted the low quantities of serotonin in the hind brains of alcoholic suicides and Takaishi *et al.* (1974) found reduced amounts of 5-HIAA and homovanillic acid (HVA) in the cerebrospinal fluid of alcoholics during withdrawal. The increased availability of acetylcholine as blood alcohol falls may be responsible not only for depression, but also for the tendency of some alcoholics to experience epileptic fits during this phase. Such a picture may be too simple as it takes no account of other metabolic effects of ethanol but, in broad terms, the evidence for depression in alcoholics as a result of interference of the drug with biogenic amines is sufficiently strong to justify this working hypothesis.

Nonetheless, a drug like alcohol will affect many bodily systems with, possibly, changes in transmitter amines in the brain as one of the end products. In a review of some of the biochemical changes in alcoholics, Mendelson (1970) mentioned that alcohol causes a rise in catecholamine receptor thresholds with increased loss of these neurotransmitters. Alcohol also activates adrenal cortical function through increased release of ACTH. During drinking and the early withdrawal phase, alcoholics have a raised output of cortisol with the figures for serum cortisol being correlated with the levels of blood alcohol (Mendelson *et al.*, 1971). These findings could be relevant to the alcohol-induced pseudo-Cushing syndrome and its associated mood of depression.

Barbiturate and Non-barbiturate Sedatives

The barbiturate and non-barbiturate sedatives and hypnotics not only potentiate the effects of ethanol, but also have rather similar pharmacological effects and withdrawal symptoms (Williams and Salamy, 1972). As with alcohol the risk of depression and suicide among patients dependent on these compounds is well known (Whitlock, 1970).

Chadwick *et al.* (1975) noted an increase of 5-HIAA and HVA in epileptics treated with phenobarbitone and dilantin and that animals in whom 5-HT is reduced have lower seizure thresholds. Caldwell and Sever (1974) observe that barbiturates impair the release of acetylcholine in the CNS and that withdrawal seizures are associated in rats with falls in 5-HT. The frequency of these seizures could be reduced by intracisternal injections of 5-HT, suggesting that a deficiency of this compound had occurred. Goodman and Gilman (1975) comment on an antiadrenergic action of barbiturates, although they warn that this should not be construed as evidence of a special affinity of the drugs for adrenergic receptors. Christian (1972) found that barbiturates increased both the bound and free acetylcholine in the brain.

Achté (1974), in a review of somatic symptoms in depression, mentions alcohol and tranquillizing drugs as common causes of the illness. Glatt (1974, p.149) states that "barbiturates taken in fairly high doses for some time may lead to a state of depression". However, it should be remembered that, as with other addictive drugs, in some patients the depression will be the consequence of withdrawal at least as frequently as from the direct pharmacological action of the drug on brain mechanisms. It will be recalled that phenobarbitone, as well as alcohol and diphenylhydantoin, is capable of causing folate deficiency which itself may be manifested by depression as one of its symptoms (Hunter *et al.,* 1969; Reynolds *et al.,* 1970). Finally, the severity of depression observed in barbiturate-dependent patients will probably depend to some degree upon their genetic and constitutional qualities. Many of these patients will be multiple drug users who will also show much psychosocial disturbance in their personal lives and family backgrounds. Possibly the combination of these qualities with the biochemical effects of the drugs is responsible for the severe depression and suicidal behaviour shown by many barbiturate addicts. In addition, some multiple drug abusers show signs of organic brain damage (Judd and Grant, 1975; Grant *et al.,* 1978) which could also contribute to their affective disturbances. Fortunately, the decline in barbiturate prescribing has led to a reduction in the frequency of the dependence syndrome which formerly was most often seen in middle-aged women (Whitlock, 1970).

ANTI-INFLAMMATORY DRUGS

The more recently developed analgesic and anti-inflammatory substances such as phenylbutozone, indomethacin and ibuprofen are all said to cause depression in some subjects (Prescott, 1972; Cochrane, 1973; Blechman *et al.,* 1975). Thompson and Percy (1966) observed severe depression in four of 70 patients taking indomethacin, one of whom became suicidal. All had been treated for long periods of time and all recovered when the drug was stopped, without relapse when it was reinstituted at a lower dosage. Presumably none of these patients had suffered from a depression before taking indomethacin.

Robinson (1965) reported that seven patients on this drug became depressed and that one took her life. In a later paper, (1966) the same author commented that depression is a very real problem in susceptible or unstable persons. This seems to imply that premorbid traits or earlier affective illnesses are significant contributors to this reaction, but no details of personality or family history were given. O'Brien (1968) also mentions depression and suicide amongst patients on indomethacin.

The mode of action of indomethacin as a cause of affective disorders is obscure. According to Bianco *et al.* (1965) it has no direct effect on the vasoconstrictive actions of indoleamines and catecholamines. Neither is the metabolic pathway of tryptophan altered by indomethacin (Speira, 1966). In the absence of crucial studies of the effects of the drug on neurotransmitters in the brain, one can only speculate about any possible interactions.

Compared with indomethacin the newer anti-inflammatory drugs such as ibuprofen, fenuprofen, ketaprofen and naproxen appear to be relatively free from side effects of all kinds (Huskisson *et al.*, 1976) although in one study of naproxen (Castles *et al.*, 1978) ten of 132 patients complained of depression. No details of these patients or the quality of depression are mentioned. It should be remembered that arthritic disorders are apt to cause depression in their own right and, in many instances, it would be difficult to apportion out the contributions of drug and disease. Nonetheless, accurate clinical investigation including specific assessment of mood change would probably reveal more drug-induced depression in these patients than is apparent from current reports.

DRUGS USED IN THE TREATMENT OF EXTRAPYRAMIDAL DISORDERS

The psychiatric side effects of L-dopa have been examined in Chapter 5 (pp. 61–62), but two newer drugs, tetrabenazene and bromocriptine, require some discussion. The traditional anticholinergic preparations used in the treatment of Parkinson's disease commonly cause confusion and visual hallucinations, particularly in elderly patients, but depression is unusual. Tetrabenazene, on the other hand, has been used for the treatment of a number of basal ganglia syndromes, particularly Huntington's chorea (McClellan, 1972; McClellan *et al.*, 1974; Swash *et al.*, 1972; Toglia *et al.*, 1978; Kingston, 1979). The commonest psychiatric side effects have been drowsiness and depression, both of which are probably caused by the depletion of catecholamines and indoleamines by this drug (Pletscher, 1953; Zbinden, 1962). In this respect it closely resembles reserpine, also a potent cause of depression in hypertensive patients. The incidence of depression in a number of studies is in the region of 10–16 per cent, but unfortunately none of these reports discusses the likely contribution of premorbid personality to this reaction. However, many patients with Huntington's chorea are prone to depression independently of any treatment received, and Soutar (1970) reported one of two patients (who also had diabetes) became depressed, but improved when treated with isocarboxid.

Bromocriptine has caused a number of psychiatric reactions including depression (Boyd *et al.*, 1977). This drug which structurally resembles lysergide, is a dopamine agonist and might, in theory, be expected to cause symptoms similar to those seen following treatment with L-dopa.

SULPHONAMIDES AND ANTI-TUBERCULOUS DRUGS

Sulphonamides

The older sulphonamides, particularly sulphapyridine, were well-known causes of depression (McClelland, 1973). Newer compounds such as sulphamethoxazole, which is contained in Septrin (Wellcome Australia) and Bactrim (Roche), appear less likely to cause depression, but this does occur (Goodman and Gilman, 1975). Sulphonamides act by competitive antagonism of para-aminobenzoic acid which conceivably could result in a reduction of available folic acid. In elderly patients, at least, depression could be one of its consequences. This action might be particularly important in the case of Bactrim (trimethroprim and sulphamethoxazole) which inhibits more strongly the incorporation of para-aminobenzoic acid into folic acid (Goodman and Gilman, 1975). Reynolds *et al.* (1970) found that 24 per cent of depressed patients had low levels of folate, although this did not appear to be related to drug intake or inadequate diet. They pointed out that folate was needed as a co-factor for tyrosine hydroxylase and the synthesis of catecholamines and 5-HT. I have known elderly patients being treated with Bactrim for urinary tract infections who have become depressed without any previous experience of affective disorder.

Anti-Tuberculous Drugs

Wallach and Gershon (1972), in a review of the psychiatric effects of drugs used in tuberculous therapy, mention isoniazid-induced depression responding to vitamin B complex and nicotinic acid. In fact, the clinical picture has much in common with pellagra. Iproniazid, which inhibits monoamine oxidases, may cause euphoria, which can change to depression when the drug is withdrawn. Goldman and Braman (1972) found that isoniazid more commonly caused acute psychoses with manic-type symptoms but also observed that some patients complained of lethargy, depression, drowsiness and impaired memory.

Newton (1975), in a brief review of the side effects of drugs used in the treatment of tuberculosis, mentions mental disturbances with isoniazid and cycloserine, and Goodman and Gilman (1975) warn that cycloserine might be dangerous if given to patients with a past history of depression. This drug causes a variety of psychiatric symptoms including depression. Pasargiklian and Biondi (1970) and Helmy (1970) observed that among 13 of 133 patients treated with cycloserine who developed psychiatric symptoms, three were depressed. Verbeist *et al.* (1966) described 11 cases of depression in patients treated with cycloserine in combination with isoniazid and para-aminosalicylic acid, and Leston *et al.* (1970) reported that 13 per cent of patients in one series and seven per cent in another became depressed on cycloserine. Granville-Grossman (1971) has reviewed the adverse psychiatric reactions to cycloserine. These include confusion, paranoid psychoses and depression, sometimes sufficient to result in suicide. The frequency of these reactions varies, but increases sharply to about 50 per cent with doses in the range of 1.0–1.5g daily. If the dose is restricted to 0.5g daily, psychiatric reactions occur in less than eight per cent of patients.

Although all the drugs mentioned are effective in the treatment of tuberculosis, surprisingly little seems to be known about their biochemical and pharmacological properties. Numerous untoward effects on the central nervous system have been recorded, and one presumes that depression is not a specific consequence of any of these preparations. Clark (1976), however, has pointed out that both cycloserine and isoniazid lower serum folate levels and this could be one possible cause of depression in patients taking these drugs.

MISCELLANEOUS DRUGS CAUSING DEPRESSION

Antihistimines

Most antihistimines, particularly if taken in excess, cause sedation and visual hallucinations, the consequences of their anticholinergic properties. The commonest reported side effect of the H2-receptor blockading drug cimitidine is confusion but acute depression can also occur (Jefferson, 1979; Johnson and Bailey, 1979; Petite and Bloch, 1979; Crowder and Pate, 1980). These patients had not previously suffered from episodes of depression, but the findings are difficult to reconcile with the hypothesis that anti-depressant drugs can alleviate symptoms by virtue of their ability to block H2-receptors in the brain.

Baclofen

Baclofen, used to control muscle spasm in a number of neurological disorders, particularly multiple sclerosis, can cause depression in some patients (Brogden *et al.,* 1974). Pinto *et al.* (1972) mentioned that depression occurred in 3.9 per cent of patients but that a previous history of depression might be an important contributory factor. A depressive illness precipitated by baclofen in a manic-depressive patient was also described by Korsgaard (1976).

Disulfiram

In a review of the literature Liddon and Satran (1967) found reports on 52 patients with psychosis following the use of Antabuse (Ethnor). Thirty-five developed delirious reactions and nine of the 52 were significantly depressed. There were nine attempted suicides and five successful suicides. Four patients were manic or hypomanic.

Goodman and Gilman (1975) mention hypotension affecting patients suffering from a disulfiram-ethanol reaction. Apparently the drug inhibits dopamine-beta-hydroxylase with a consequent fall in noradrenalin synthesis. Kane (1970) also commented on the capacity of disulfiram for inhibiting noradrenalin synthesis, resulting in falls of this neurotransmitter in the brain. The patient he described, who became depressed when taking antabuse, had a past history of a similar illness.

FREQUENCY OF DRUG-INDUCED SYMPTOMS AND CONCLUSIONS

Figures for the frequency of drug-induced depression vary according to the type of drug involved from about 1–10 per cent of patients. The likelihood of an adverse reaction developing increases when two or more potentially depressing drugs are being taken together, for, as Prange (1973) has commented, "drug combinations should always be approached with caution, especially in the elderly, since benefits may add while side effects will multiply." N. Hurwitz (1969) demonstrated this phenomenon, which was far commoner in older patients who, in any case, may be taking more drugs than younger subjects.

Although some drugs appear to cause depression in a percentage of patients who have no genetic or constitutional predisposition to affective disorder, the evidence reviewed in this chapter shows that in most cases a family history or past personal history of depression are the decisive factors causing a relapse when a drug which can affect levels of available neurotransmitters is prescribed. Cessation of the drug often leads to a prompt remission, but some patients require appropriate anti-depressant treatment.

Additional to the direct action of these drugs are their effects on vitamin levels. Ovesen (1979) has reviewed drug-induced avitaminoses which often are caused by interference with absorption from the gastro-intestinal tract. Vitamins of the B-group are the ones most typically reduced by drugs, among which should be mentioned anticonvulsants, antituberculous drugs, L-dopa, antineoplastic drugs and oral contraceptives. No doubt these substances will have many other actions contributing to the onset of adverse side effects, but the combination of a susceptible patient, reduced vitamin levels and the drug's specific action on neurotransmitters will sometimes be sufficient to precipitate severe depression which may lead to suicide.

9

Affective Disturbances Following Childbirth and Surgical Operations

CHILDBIRTH AND AFFECTIVE DISORDER

Leaving aside the alleged depressive effects of oral contraceptives, interest in affective disorders in obstetrics and gynaecology is focused mainly on the premenstrual tension syndrome, post-partum affective disorder and the downturn in mood commonly experienced after delivery, sometimes known as third-day or maternity "blues". The premenstrual tension syndrome can certainly be characterized by quite severe depression of mood, but this is rarely a depressive syndrome in the strict sense of that term.

Post-Partum Affective Psychosis

Granville-Grossman (1971), summarizing the findings of four studies on post-partum psychosis, noted an incidence of 1.4–1.9 per thousand live births. In six studies the frequency of affective disorder ranged from 15 to 54 per cent of all cases of psychosis. The rates vary considerably, depending to some extent on diagnostic fashions and the number of toxic psychoses associated, in the past, mainly with puerperal infections. Brockington *et al.* (1978) provide a table showing the high levels of toxic psychoses in the first quarter of this century compared with the very low levels in developed countries over the past 30 years. Consequently, the proportion of affective psychosis has varied from three to 70 per cent. Often enough the picture is atypical, with a mixture of

121

schizophrenic-like symptoms and confusion distinguishing these illnesses from manic-depressive psychosis occurring independently of the puerperium. Grundy and Roberts (1975) recorded an incidence of post-partum depression of 30–100 per thousand live births in three studies but, in view of their finding of only 1.9 per thousand for all post-partum psychoses, it is clear that the term "depression" is being used differently by different authors. Meares *et al.* (1976) distinguish clearly between depressive illness, depressive symptoms and maternity blues characterized by emotional lability and crying spells.

Genetic factors in the aetiology of post-partum affective psychosis have been discussed by Steiner (1979), who mentions reports claiming a high incidence of similar illnesses in the relatives of patients. None of these studies are particularly convincing, and Protheroe (1969), who gave details of 91 patients with post-partum affective disorder, found no increase in the incidence of similar puerperal illnesses in relatives, and considered the genetic loading to be the same as that for patients with non-puerperal manic-depressive psychosis. In fact, there is better evidence for a relationship between bipolar affective disorder and post-partum depression or mania (Bratfos and Haug, 1966; Reich and Winokur, 1970; Baker *et al.*, 1971; Steiner, 1979). Baker *et al.* (1971) considered that there was little difference between post-partum depression and depression occurring independently of pregnancy, but in their patients there were no family histories of affective disorder. Patients with bipolar affective disorder were more liable to post-partum depression than unipolar patients. Bratfos and Haug (1966) found that women with a history of manic-depressive psychosis had ten times the risk of developing post-partum depression. In patients who developed this condition the symptoms and signs were similar to these experienced when it occurred unrelated to pregnancy, a point made by Herzog and Detre (1976), who also mentioned the added element of confusion in puerperal depression. Reich and Winokur (1970) concluded that patients who suffered from recurrent attacks of manic-depressive psychosis are more likely to develop post-partum affective disorder. On the other hand, Kadramas *et al.* (1979) have given details of 21 patients with bipolar affective illnesses, 20 of whom developed post-partum mania. Compared with nonparturient bipolar females, puerperal cases had fewer relatives with affective disorder and fewer relapses during the ensuing three years. The authors consider the possibility of puerperal mania being different in type and origin from the usual variety of bipolar affective disorder.

It is difficult to predict who will suffer post-partum depression (*British Medical Journal*, Editorial, 1969a), although some association with an abnormal obstetric history has been observed. Hegarty's patients (1955) had suffered a variety of stresses in the shape of infections and psychosocial misfortunes during pregnancy, but some also had past histories of depression. Tod (1964), in a survey of 312 first pregnancies, observed depression in 2.9 per cent of the patients. He found that these patients more often had histories of psychiatric illness, abnormal obstetric records and less satisfactory marriages. Pitt (1968) reported an incidence of psychotic depression of one in five-hundred births. In his study of 37 patients with third-day blues only one showed a classic endogenous depressive picture, but 12 of his patients were still depressed after one year. Dalton (1971a) found an incidence of post-partum depression in 7 per cent of patients who also, subsequently, were prone to premenstrual tension with depression. In a further study, contrary to most other writers, Dalton (1971b), comparing the depressed post-partum patients with non-depressed controls, found no greater frequency of previous psychiatric illness. She felt that a disturbance of hormonal function was an important cause, a point of view shared by Kendell *et al.* (1976). They recorded a sharp increase in psychiatric consultations during the first three months after delivery. Among the 2257 mothers there were nine cases of psychiatric illness, seven of whom were depressed.

There seems to be a fair measure of agreement — there are exceptions — that patients with past histories of affective illness are more likely to suffer post-partum depression, and that the clinical picture is not greatly different from depression observed independently of pregnancy. Kaij and Nilsson (1972) state firmly that, with respect to schizophrenia and manic-depressive psychoses developing during the puerperium, pregnancy and childbirth are at most precipitating factors, but the question of pathogenesis has yet to be settled, and it is unlikely that any single cause can be delineated. Treadway *et al.* (1969), for example, found that depression in pregnancy in the early puerperium was associated with low urinary excretion of noradrenalin, while Thornton (1977) described a patient who was depressed, suicidal and withdrawn after delivery, but who was found to have a low serum folate. Treatment with folic acid brought about a remission within 10 days. G. Stein *et al.* (1976) claimed that 50–70 per cent of women had mild post-partum depression, but undoubtedly this included the patients with third-day blues. These authors found a low plasma tryptophan similar to that observed in non-pregnant depressed patients. Possibly this might cause low levels of serotonin in the brain, but the reason for the fall in tryptophan is not known. Handley *et al.* (1977) also found a positive correlation between plasma tryptophan levels and mood. In 18 patients studied 2–5 days after delivery, tryptophan tended to rise and cortisol to fall. None of these patients were severely depressed and most showed a mild euphoria.

The pathogenesis of post-partum depression must also take into account the massive hormonal changes occurring after delivery. These will include a sharp fall in progesterone and oestrogen, which might increase monoamine oxidase activity with consequent depletion of catecholamine transmitters. It is interesting in this context that many subjects feel particularly well during pregnancy, a state of mind which conceivably could involve inhibition of

MAO as one contributory factor. After delivery, the sharp rise in prolactin might be a further factor which, in patients made susceptible by heredity and constitution, would precipitate an attack of depression, leaving those not so predisposed more or less immune. Gelder (1978) commented on the delay of two days before the onset of psychosis. He pointed to similarities between this phenomenon and observations made on the delay between surgery and post-operative psychosis (Stengel *et al.,* 1958). This latent period and its relationship to the hormonal changes suggest that they are the important precipitating factors, although psycho-social stresses might well contribute to the onset of severe depression. Nonetheless, at present the precise mechanism whereby hormonal changes cause affective disturbances is not fully understood. As Steiner (1979) has written, "We do know of some specific hormonal changes occurring at the time of the partal events . . . The temporal interaction of these hormones, the possibility of a synergistic effect between prolactin and steroids and their correlation with other mental disorders specific to women should be an important aim of further research."

Third-Day Blues

The main reason for discussing this mild but common phenomenon is to see what light, if any, it might throw on the aetiology of more serious post-partum affective disorders. Pitt (1968, 1973) has stated that 80 per cent of parturient women suffer maternity blues, which he attributes to the sudden fall in oestrogen and progesterone. Of these patients, 10.8 per cent continue to be depressed for two weeks or more and the condition can, to some degree, be disabling. Pitt has listed the main clinical features, which include "confusion", in the form of impaired concentration, memory and learning. He suggested that this element, in the absence of personality predisposition or major psychological stresses, might indicate an organic factor stemming from endocrine changes after delivery. Dalton (1971b) did not find that the pregnancies of women who developed maternity blues differed from those of normal women, but she did find a high incidence of difficulties with the babies. However, bearing in mind that most women show this disorder on the third to fifth day after delivery, it is difficult to see how anxiety over the babies' behaviour could be playing a major role at this stage.

Enough has been said about the effects of oestrogen on monoamine oxidase and the additional factor of prolactin during the post-partum period to give some support to the endocrine origin of the condition. Dalton comments on the higher incidence of the premenstrual syndrome in women who develop puerperal depression, suggesting again a variability of hormone activity that seems to conduce to depression in these patients. Meares *et al.* (1976) agreed with Pitt (1973) that the condition is more likely to have a hormonal basis and that this, taken in conjunction with other psycho-social stresses, might be responsible for the more severe depressions seen in some patients. Paykel *et al.* (1980) considered that maternity blues occurring independently of undesirable life events are probably related to the massive hormonal changes occurring at this time, but Gelder (1978), comparing 30 patients with "blues" with 16 other women unaffected by the condition, found no changes in oestrogen, progesterone, LH, FSH or prolactin to distinguish the depressed mothers from the control group. Nonetheless, if 80 per cent of women experience this downturn in mood three days after delivery, it seems reasonable to conclude that hormonal changes are important aetiological agents.

In the light of the changes in prolactin after delivery and the possible relationship of this hormone to depression, it is interesting to note two patients precipitated into *mania* by bromocriptine used to suppress lactation (Brook and Cookson, 1978; Vlissides *et al.,* 1978). Velissides *et al.'s* patient had not suffered from affective disorder in the past. Bromocriptine is a dopamine agonist and, as such, promotes the activity of prolactin-release inhibiting factor. The role of dopamine in affective disorder has yet to be clearly defined, but observations of this kind support the possibility that falls in dopamine may directly or indirectly cause depression, whereas increases could be related to manic excitement.

POST-OPERATIVE AFFECTIVE DISTURBANCES

Although the most common reaction to anaesthesia and surgery is delirium, one often sees deeply depressed patients who date their illnesses from recent operations; and suicide post-operatively is not infrequent, particularly in older patients (Dorpat *et al.*, 1968; Whitlock, 1977b).

Stengel *et al.* (1958) reported on 80 post-operative patients admitted to a psychiatric ward. Thirty-six were depressed and nine manic. The effects of aneasthesia, it was felt, were not responsible for these reactions, which occurred more often after hysterectomy. The authors considered that the frequency of post-operative psychosis did not exceed chance expectation. Hackett and Weissman (1960) remarked on the tendency for post-operative depression to develop some weeks after surgery rather than as an acute response. Only one of their 10 patients with a post-operative psychosis was depressed, a reaction which they interpreted along psychodynamic lines. Lindemann (1941) studied 40 women undergoing abdominal surgery and found that, although 25 were unaffected at follow-up some 10–18 months later, 15 showed signs of psychiatric disturbance. Thirteen of the patients exhibited a picture of agitated depression which had been experienced by four of them some time before their surgery. Patients who had undergone pelvic operations were more likely to be depressed than those who had had cholecystectomies, a point amply confirmed by Barker (1968).

Although any type of surgical operation can be followed by an adverse psychiatric reaction, including depression, these adverse consequences have been examined more frequently in association with three types of operation: hysterectomy, mastectomy and open-heart surgery.

Hysterectomy

The frequency of depression after hysterectomy varies from 4.6 per cent (Melody, 1962) to 36.5 per cent (Richards, 1973), although the majority of the patients in Richards' study would not have shown the major features of an endogenous type of illness. In fact, over the three years following operation, only nine required hospitalization for psychiatric treatment. Aspects of post-hysterectomy depression have been reviewed by Ananth (1978) and by Turpin and Heath (1979).

From these reviews it is apparent that women who become depressed after hysterectomy more often have had past episodes of affective illness or shown abnormal personality qualities which, not surprisingly, are often called hysterical. An important investigation by Barker (1968) compared 729 women who had undergone hysterectomy with 280 patients who had had cholecystectomies. Significantly more of the hysterectomy patients (53, 7 per cent) than the cholecystectomy group (9, 3 per cent) required psychiatric treatment within four-and-a-half years following operation. Eighty-five per cent of the post-hysterectomy psychiatric referrals were described as depressed (manic-depressive, depressed and neurotic depressive reactions) and 15 depressed patients had taken drug overdoses requiring admission to hospital. The risk of post-operative psychiatric illness was ten times greater for patients with past episodes of psychiatric illness. An interesting finding was the significantly greater number of patients becoming depressed who, at the time of operation, were devoid of significant pelvic pathology. Those with malignant or benign tumours of the uterus or ovary were less likely to develop post-operative psychiatric complications.

The findings of Barker (1968) and others suggest that hysterectomy acts as a precipitant of depression in women who have suffered from affective illnesses in the past, although Ananth (1978) mentions that removal of the uterus can cause a fall in oestrogen with a parallel drop in plasma tryptophan. Nevertheless, he considers a past history of depression to be an important factor. Furthermore, hormonal changes seem to be relatively unimportant as oophorectomy in conjunction with hysterectomy is not followed by more psychiatric disturbances than when hysterectomy alone is performed (Barker, 1968; Chynoweth and Abrahams, 1977). Turpin and Heath, who comment specifically on the time-lag of two to three years between operation and subsequent depression, clearly favour psychological explanations of the phenomenon. "Depression occurring after hysterectomy is more likely to be associated with social and psychological consequences of organ removal than with the operative procedure itself and, therefore, one may not expect the condition to become clinically obvious for anywhere from six months to two years postoperatively."

Mastectomy

In recent years many papers have discussed adverse psychiatric sequelae to mastectomy and other operations of a mutilating kind. P. Maguire (1976, 1978) has discussed a number of psychological reactions following mastectomy. He found (1976) that 26 per cent of these patients experienced moderate and six per cent marked symptoms of depression in the first three to four months after operation. Some who had been depressed for the whole time were also troubled by suicidal ideas. Maguire *et al.* (1978) also found that one year after mastectomy for breast cancer, 19 of 75 women required treatment for anxiety, depression or both. The authors mention the likely contribution of radiotherapy to depressed mood but, unfortunately, they say nothing about whether the patients had experienced earlier episodes of affective disorder.

In their most recent study, Maguire *et al.* (1980) found that four of 152 patients who underwent mastectomy were moderately depressed before operation but that 16 were moderately and two severely depressed 12–18 months later. Seventy-five of the patients received expert counselling before and after surgery, with the other 77 receiving normal surgical follow-up care. Although there were fewer depressed patients in the counselled group who were psychiatrically ill for a shorter time, the main value of continued specialist-nurse supervision was the earlier recognition and treatment of patients showing signs of psychiatric disturbance. It is not clear how many depressed patients in each sample had suffered previously from affective disorders, although the two groups were said to be well matched with respect to the frequency of psychiatric illness before their surgical treatment.

In contrast to most authors who emphasize the effects of mastectomy on the woman's self-image, her sexuality and loss of femininity, Worden and Weissman (1977) found that depression was no more common in women after mastectomy than after other major operations. However, they noted some increased emotional distress in the mastectomy patients some two to three months after operation.

The emphasis on the purely psychological aspects of mastectomy to the exclusion of other possible causes of depression does small justice to the

128 *Symptomatic Affective Disorders*

complexity of this problem. None of the authors, including Asben (1975), who reviewed the earlier literature on the topic, mention any likely contribution to post-mastectomy depression from genetic or constitutional predisposition. In addition one would need to consider the likely effects of a malignant tumour (to be discussed later) and the consequences of other treatments, particularly radiotherapy and antineoplastic drugs. Unless all these factors are taken into consideration it seems premature to regard affective disturbances following mastectomy as wholly psychological in origin.

Open-Heart Surgery

The commonest psychiatric disturbance following open-heart surgery is delirium, and most authors have concentrated their attention on this reaction. However, some patients do become significantly depressed after operation. Egerton and Kay (1964), reporting on 60 patients followed up for three months, found that five patients were troubled by depressive ideas. One of these had a depressive psychosis. On the other hand, two patients were sufficiently depressed before operation to require psychiatric treatment, and another was hypomanic. It is not clear whether these three patients were among the five post-operatively depressed cases.

Freyhan *et al.* (1971) found that 58 of 150 patients experienced mood disturbances following open-heart surgery. Thirty-one of the whole group showed signs of pre-operative psychiatric illnesses, including 25 with organic brain dysfunction. The authors commented that depression in this context differed from typical endogenous depression in that their patients were less likely to have feelings of guilt or suicidal ideation. Of two patients who became depressed following coronary bypass surgery (Rabiner *et al.,* 1975), one was reacting more to a major family misfortune than to his operation. The other, as far as one can tell, did not have any previous history of affective disorder. In a later investigation Rabiner and Willner (1976) followed up 46 patients 18 months after coronary bypass surgery. One who became depressed ultimately committed suicide. Three other patients were depressed, and two also showed evidence of organic brain impairment. Two were suicidal and another patient, who took her life, had suffered severe depression in the past. From the findings it did appear that these depressive illnesses following surgery had more to do with factors other than the operation itself. These included earlier episodes of depression, organic brain impairment and, in one patient, an attack of hepatitis which precipitated depression and suicidal feelings.

Blacher (1972) has commented on what he refers to as concealed psychosis following heart surgery. Symptoms of psychiatric illness were often overlooked by members of the cardiac surgery team. In a later paper Blacher (1978) described 20 patients who were depressed after heart surgery. Two had previous histories of affective disorder. The author interpreted these reactions in psychodynamic terms which involved guilt feelings on account of survival when others had been less fortunate.

As is the case with other major surgical operations, depression following open-heart surgery is more likely to occur in patients with previous histories of affective disorder. The type of operation and certain technical aspects of after-care do not appear particularly relevant, although they may be more significant as causes of delirium. Summers (1979) reported on 26 patients undergoing open-heart surgery, eight of whom developed post-operative psychoses. Six were delirious and two had affective illnesses coming on about three days post-operatively and lasting four days. Comparing patients who had post-operative psychoses with those who did not, Summers was unable to find any differences in terms of previous episodes of psychiatric disorder or positive family histories of psychiatric illnesses. The only significant difference was the greater quantity of psychotropic drugs being taken before and after surgery by those who became psychiatrically ill. In an earlier series of investigations Kimball (1969, 1972) found that patients showing pre-operative anxiety and depression were more likely to develop a syndrome of apprehension, agitation, irritability and disruption of sleep following surgery. Patients who had been depressed before operation had higher mortality rates immediately after operation and during the follow-up period. To what extent the depression and deaths were related to possible cerebral damage cannot be determined from these studies.

10

Cancer and Depression

Galen considered that melancholy women were more prone to cancer than those of sanguine temperament, an observation to be repeated by others over the past 220 years. Herbert Snow, for example, (1893, p.33), wrote, "We find that the number of instances in which malignant disease of the breast and uterus follows immediately antecedent emotions of a depressing character is too large to be set down to chance." Earlier, Guy (1759) stated that women who suffered from melancholy were more liable to develop breast cancer, citing two cases of the disease following attacks of depression in support of his thesis. Somewhat similar observations were made by Sir James Paget (1863) and by Parker (1885). Needless to say, clinical insights of this kind were not backed up by epidemiological investigations, but they point to a link between depression and cancer which only recently has been investigated. A number of questions about this relationship need to be examined and, if possible, answered. Can severe depression predispose to the development of cancer? Can depression be the presenting symptom of cancer? Does cancer itself cause affective disturbances which are distinguishable from the understandable reactions of some patients to being told that they are suffering from a potentially fatal and possibly painful disease? Finally, is there a "cancer-prone" personality whose characteristics can be detected well before cancer is diagnosed?

Many investigations have addressed themselves to the last of these questions, and consequently, their findings suffer from the disadvantage of being retrospective in nature (Le Shan and Worthington, 1956; Kissen, 1963; Brown, 1966). Those claiming to have demonstrated a connexion between personality and preceding stress on the one hand and the development of a malignant neoplasm on the other, have been criticized on a number of grounds, such as inadequate controls, the use of patients whose cancers had already been diagnosed and reliance on personality or interpretive psychological tests (Hurst *et al.*, 1976; Surawicz *et al.*, 1976; Watson and Schuld, 1977). To circumvent some of the difficulties inherent in retrospective investigations, Schmale and Iker (1966) examined a number of women before they underwent cone biopsies of the cervix. On the basis of clinical examination and the results of the MMPI test, they were able to predict correctly in a substantial number of instances which women would be free from cancer and which would be cancer-positive. Those who had positive biopsies more often showed features of depression and hopelessness which the authors tended to relate to certain personality characteristics of the patients. On the other hand, it could be argued that their depressed mood was being caused by developing neoplasms which had not yet presented with diagnosable signs and symptoms.

In contrast to the retrospective investigations there have been reports on associations between cancer in particular sites and symptoms of depression. For example, Fras *et al.* (1967), found that 76 per cent of a group of patients with carcinoma of the pancreas were suffering from depression. In half of them, the psychiatric illnesses preceded the physical symptoms of malignancy. Other writers (Yaskin, 1931; Rickles, 1945) also described cases of severe depression developing some months before pancreatic carcinomas were diagnosed. None of their patients had previous histories of affective disorder. A patient described by Wallen *et al.* (1972), a 63-year-old man who became depressed, ultimately died from a cancer of the pancreas. No macroscopic lesions were found in his brain at autopsy. In older patients, Benos (1974) regarded depression, insomnia, anorexia, weight loss, restlessness and abdominal pain as symptoms which together might indicate a pancreatic carcinoma. Jacobson and Ottosson (1971), who reviewed the literature on this topic, found that in 10 per cent of the patients psychological symptoms preceded physical symptoms of malignancy by some months. They also found increased excretion of 5-HIAA in patients with pancreatic tumours, some of which contained excessive quantities of 5-HT. However, there is no reason for thinking that the biochemical changes are necessarily relevant to the affective symptoms in these patients. The importance of pancreatic disease as a cause of depression was emphasized by the association between depression and other psychoses and chronic relapsing pancreatitis (Savage *et al.*, 1952; Lawton and Phillips, 1955; Schuster and Iber, 1965). In this condition, one might conclude that alcoholism played a part in the development of depression in some of these patients.

The relationship between cerebral neoplasm and depression or mania has been discussed in Chapter 5 (pp. 48–57) and, as already mentioned, depression following mastectomy might not always be a psychological response to a mutilating operation. Goldfarb *et al.* (1967) described three depressed patients with carcinoma of the breast, one of whom made a suicidal attempt. She made a good recovery with ECT and antidepressants, with apparent regression of her tumour.

There have been other reports of patients with cancer whose diagnoses had been preceded by depression. Andersen and McHugh (1971) described such a patient who became depressed and suicidal in association with Cushing's syndrome, secondary to a carcinoma of the lung. Solomon and Solomon (1978) described a female patient who had suffered three previous attacks of depression, which always cleared with anti-depressant drugs. After her fourth episode she was found to have a carcinoma of the lung, a warning that physical illness can occur either as a cause or as a consequence of depression, even when previous attacks have shown no evidence of physical illness.

Two investigations, one in Newcastle, England (Kerr *et al.*, 1969) and the other in Brisbane, Australia (Whitlock and Siskind, 1979) have found a higher than expected number of deaths from cancer in male patients followed up for four years after an episode of fairly typical depressive illness. At the time of their admissions, no evidence of malignancy was discovered. In the Newcastle study, none of the patients had previous histories of affective disorder, but in the Brisbane investigation, one male and one female patient who died from cancer had suffered from depression on one occasion in the past. The Newcastle patients did not show the classic symptoms of guilt, feelings of worthlessness and suicidal ideation, but the Brisbane cases were more typical examples of unipolar depression. All these patients were aged over 40, but although there was a significant excess of deaths in male patients, this was not found during the follow-up period in the female patients.

Two other investigations give some support to these observations. Varsamis *et al.* (1972) carried out a six-year follow-up study of older psychiatric patients and found a relatively high incidence of malignant disease in 24 patients who had suffered from affective psychoses. Unfortunately, they did not carry out a statistical analysis of these findings, but three of seven patients with affective disorder who died did so from malignant disease, and another three survivors had developed cancers. Niemi and Jääskeläinen (1978) investigated cancer morbidity rather than mortality and, although rather more men than expected developed malignant disease, the finding was not statistically significant. There was no increased cancer morbidity among the female patients.

On the other hand, Evans *et al.* (1974), using the facilities of the Oxford Record Linkage System, failed to confirm the findings of Kerr and his colleagues. However, the two investigations are not strictly comparable. Although the Oxford investigation included a far larger number of patients suffering from affective disorder, follow-up interviews were not carried out.

No names of patients in the Oxford study appeared on death certificates that indicated cancer as the cause of death, and this was taken as evidence that none of them had died from cancer during the four-year follow-up period.

CANCER AND SUICIDE

An association between suicide and cancer has been demonstrated by a number of epidemiological studies. Sainsbury (1955) found that physical illness was a factor in 29 per cent of his suicide cases. He estimated that the incidence of cancer was 20 times greater than in the general population. Dorpat *et al.* (1968) found cancer in eight per cent of 80 cases of suicide, compared with 0.43 per cent in the general population. These authors also noted that physical illness was a common precipitant of suicide, particularly in male victims. Surgery, or the prospect of surgery for cancer apparently added to the suicide risk. In this context, urological surgery in males may be particularly important (Fawcett, 1972). However, it is not clear from these studies how many of the victims knew they had cancer or whether it was discovered in the course of autopsy. Barraclough (1971) found a high incidence of terminal malignancy and other conditions likely to be fatal within two years in a group of 30 suicides aged 65 and over, when matched with a control group who had sustained accidental deaths. Not all the cancer cases had been diagnosed before death.

Whitlock (1978) compared suicide victims with individuals who had died as a result of violence (mainly through motor-vehicle accidents). Seventeen suicide victims, compared with two control cases, were found to have malignant disease at autopsy. Cancer had not been diagnosed before death in seven of the suicide victims and one of the control cases, but not all those in whom cancer had been detected were aware of their condition. Hence, one cannot conclude that suicide was a reaction on the part of the patient to the knowledge of a terminal disease. The frequency of depression as the precursor to suicide is a well-established fact, particularly in older patients where depression may account for 70–80 per cent of the diagnoses (Sainsbury, 1962; Barraclough, 1971). Although details of the patients' mental states before their deaths were available for only a percentage of the suicide victims, there was some evidence in the Brisbane suicide cases of depression which had been treated either shortly before their deaths or at some time in the past (Whitlock, 1978).

AETIOLOGICAL RELATIONSHIP OF CANCER TO DEPRESSION

Precisely how depression can be caused by an unsuspected cancer is far from clear, but Kerr *et al.* (1969) and others (*British Medical Journal*, Editorial,

1970a; Joynt, 1974) have considered some possible mechanisms. Firstly, depression — or mania (Jamieson and Wells, 1979) — might be the first symptom of a small cerebral metastasis or, as has been discussed earlier (Chapter 5, pp. 48–57), of a primary brain tumour. The following patient is a good example of this association.

D.B., female, date of birth 1936. This patient first became ill with depression following, possibly, a viral infection at the end of 1974. Her symptoms were characterized by nausea, abdominal pain, depression, misery and dysphagia. She received treatment in the shape of anti-depressant drugs and ECT over the ensuing three years, during which time her depression remained fairly constant and was complicated by a number of suicidal attempts by drug overdose. A cerebral tumour was finally diagnosed early in 1978, at the age of 41. This followed an overdose of phenothiazines and the appearance of neurological signs for the first time. There was no prior history of mental illness and the family history was also negative. In February 1978, a large astrocytoma involving the right temporal middle gyrus and hippocampus was partially removed. Unfortunately, the tumour continued to progress and the patient remained depressed and suicidal. She died in October 1978.

Secondly, depression might be the presenting symptom of a hidden carcinoma, analogous to the carcinomatous neuropathies and myopathies (Brain and Henson, 1958). With this possibility in mind, Solomon (1969) mentions a patient with "a severe mental disturbance bordering on psychosis" with myasthenia and peripheral neuritis. A bronchogenic carcinoma was discovered, successfully removed, and the patient's mental symptoms disappeared. The nature of these symptoms, however, whether depressive or otherwise, was not stated. The mechanism whereby small cancers can cause major effects on the central nervous system is not known, but Corsellis *et al.* (1968) have demonstrated a similarity between the neuropathology of carcinomatous neuropathy and viral encephalitis. All three of their cases had lung cancers and all showed anxiety and depression as early symptoms. Although the brain histology resembled the picture seen in herpes simplex encephalitis, these writers did not favour a latent virus infection released by the presence of cancer as a likely explanation. Nonetheless, there is a striking resemblance between these patients and three cases of sub-acute encephalitis described by Brierley *et al.* (1960), two of whom were severely depressed in the initial stages of their illnesses.

Thirdly, the endocrine effects of some tumours can cause symptoms of hyperparathyroidism (Gordan, 1974) and Cushing-like syndromes, which are seen in some patients with bronchogenic carcinomas (Armatruda and Upton, 1974). Depression in the course of Cushing's syndrome secondary to ectopic production of ACTH from a malignant neoplasm might explain the cancer–affective disorder association, although none of the patients described by Kerr *et al.* (1969) or by Whitlock and Siskind (1979) showed any Cushingoid features.

A fourth possibility is that an attack of depression in an elderly patient would reduce that individual's immunocompetence, thus allowing neoplastic cells to gain lodgement and proliferate. Studies of patients with cancer of all kinds (Le Shan and Worthington, 1956) and with uterine cancer (Schmale and Iker, 1966) have demonstrated a relationship between the disease and preceding stress. Furthermore, the possibility of an immunological basis for the relationship is suggested by Bartrop *et al.* (1977), who found a depression of immunological mechanisms following bereavement. The reduction in immunological surveillance in association with increasing age and its particular importance for carcinogenesis have been discussed by Burnet (1976), while changes in immunoglobulins in association with breast cancer have been examined by Pettingale *et al.* (1977). M. Stein *et al.* (1976), who reviewed the evidence for disturbances of the central nervous system influencing the immune system, feel that an hypothesis relating depression to cancer by virtue of the effects of stress and psychiatric illness on the patient's immunological defences is not beyond the bounds of possibility.

Finally, one might have to consider some genetic linkage between cancer, depression and ageing. Munro's (1966) observation of an unexpectedly higher incidence of cancer in the mothers of patients with depression could be relevant to such a relationship.

Most psychiatrists will have treated depressed, elderly patients who are convinced that they are suffering from cancer. Although the belief may be delusional, in some instances the patient is correct. Director (1980), for example, has described a psychotically depressed and suicidal man who believed he had cancer of the throat. He was ultimately found to have carcinoma of the lung. Appropriate treatment of his depression and neoplasm resulted in a successful recovery.

Although an association between cancer and affective disorder has been demonstrated in older men, this does not appear to be as common in female patients. The characteristic symptoms of severe depression are not always present, and the majority of patients have not suffered from depression in the past. Consequently, a middle-aged or elderly male who becomes depressed for the first time in his life without, as far as can be ascertained, sufficient cause, should be thoroughly examined to make sure that he is not harbouring a developing cancer. In the absence of positive findings it is prudent to follow up such a patient over the next four years to ensure that early treatment of the cancer can be given should the need become apparent.

11

Affective Illnesses Associated with Immunological Diseases

At the present time it is almost impossible to decide whether depressed mood causes deficiencies in the body's immune defences or whether alteration in these defences can cause depression. Stein *et al.* (1976) have reviewed evidence showing that lesions in the hypothalamus in experimental animals can modify the immune response, and one can only speculate whether profound emotional disturbances can produce similar changes in humans. Some support for this possibility has been given by Bartrop *et al.* (1977) who described impaired lymphocyte function following bereavement.

Depression in the course of auto-immune disease has been studied, particularly in systemic lupus erythematosus (SLE) and rheumatoid arthritis. Additionally, in recent years, the finding that depressed patients have raised titres of antinuclear factor (ANF) more frequently than controls has aroused interest and controversy. Von Brauchitsch (1972) found 18 of 26 patients with positive ANF titres and similar observations were recorded by Debert *et al.* (1974, 1976). Other writers have argued that positive ANF titres are due to drugs given to psychiatric patients and Alarcon-Segovia and Fishbein (1975) claim that 40 per cent of patients on chlorpromazine have positive titres. Johnston and Whalley (1975) considered that lithium was a cause, but one would need a larger series of patients to be certain that this was the case. Gottfries and Gottfries (1974) were unable to confirm the earlier findings of positive ANF titres in depressed patients but again blamed chlorpromazine. Nonetheless, it is interesting to discover how many drugs capable of causing depression also have the capacity to induce the antinuclear factor.

Plantey (1978) is strongly critical of the alleged association of depression and ANF as none of his 25 patients had positive titres. An unpublished study by Young and Whitlock, who compared groups of depressed, schizophrenic and alcoholic patients, found a number of depressed patients with positive ANF titres which turned out to be no higher than in the other groups. On the other hand, the drugs being consumed by all three groups of patients did not appear to be making any obvious contribution. However, changes in immunity are hardly likely to be direct causes of psychiatric disturbances, which in all probability follow brain damage brought about by vasculitis and other sequelae of immunological reactions.

SYSTEMIC LUPUS ERYTHEMATOSUS (SLE)

Systemic lupus erythematosus is an auto-immune disease with a high incidence of psychiatric disturbance as one of its major manifestations. These follow cerebral damage, but steroid therapy is not a major cause. In fact, increasing the dosage of steroids will often relieve neuro-psychiatric symptoms (O'Connor, 1959).

Estimates of the frequency of psychiatric illness in patients with SLE vary considerably, depending to some extent on the source of the reports and what is regarded as being sufficiently disturbing to justify inclusion. Papers by physicians concentrate more on the complex immunological changes, the neuro-psychiatric symptoms and pathological findings in their patients. Despite modern treatment methods there is a high mortality, those with neuro-psychiatric symptoms tending, in general, to have worse prognoses.

In a review of seven studies Granville-Grossman (1971) found that psychiatric illness was mentioned in 8–51 per cent of the patients. O'Connor and Musher (1966) gave figures of 5–63 per cent, based on 13 reports. In their own investigation 51 per cent of cases had mental symptoms at some time in the course of their illnesses. Although the majority of patients suffer delirious and other organic syndromes, the frequency of affective disturbances is high. Sometimes these emerge in the course of an organic psychosis, but they can be characteristically manic-depressive in nature. Other patients develop depressive neuroses which are often judged to be understandable reactions to their illnesses. Table 11.1 shows the frequency of psychiatric disorders as reported in 17 investigations which mentioned the number of instances when depression, euphoria or mania were observed.

Thus, excluding papers written specifically to emphasize affective syndromes, the frequency of depression varies from 12.5 to 86 per cent of all patients with psychiatric illnesses. In some investigations it is likely that the frequency of affective and other psychiatric illnesses has been underestimated for, as Bennet *et al.* (1972) comment, "Affective symptoms can be mild, overlooked or misdiagnosed." Richardson (1980) mentions that psychoses occur in 12–50 per cent of patients with SLE and that depression is the most common condition. Similarly, Shearn and Pirofsky (1952), who did not give a breakdown of their patients with mental disturbances, stated that most of them were severely depressed. As in other examples of symptomatic affective disorders, euphoria or mania have been recorded far less often. On the other hand, those diagnosed as schizophrenic by some authors could have been, on the data provided, examples of manic episodes which remitted. For example, Johnson and Richardson (1968) mention that two of their patients with affective disorders were euphoric, but cases 4 and 8 in their paper, listed as schizophrenic-like, could well have been manic.

Aetiology

The overwhelming impression gained from numerous reports is that affective disturbances of psychotic intensity most often develop in conjunction with signs of neurological damage or emerge in the course of brief delirious episodes. Two of B. E. Heine's patients (1969) developed toxic-confusional symptoms but became depressed later. Although relatively few authors give details of family or past personal histories of affective disorders in their patients, it appears that the majority do not have genetic or constitutional loadings for mania or depression. Even when patients have had previous depressive illnesses, it is not always certain that these have been independent of SLE whose more florid physical signs developed later. Bennett *et al.* (1972) specifically state that "mental symptoms can antedate the better known manifestations of SLE by several years", and the two patients reported by McNeill *et al.* (1976) who had suffered from earlier depression, one in the setting of severe personality disorder, could have been manifesting early signs of SLE. The second patient eventually committed suicide when deeply depressed after SLE had been finally diagnosed. One of the patients described by Allen and Pitts (1978) possibly had a positive family history of affective disorder, but she herself had not suffered from depression before SLE developed. Only one of O'Connor's (1959) patients who developed a schizophrenic-like psychosis had a past history of mental disorder, but none of those with depression had records of earlier affective illnesses. In a later survey by O'Connor and Musher (1966) 19 patients had past histories of schizophrenic or personality disorders, but 11 of these did not develop psychiatric symptoms once they became ill with SLE. One of Baker's (1973) seven patients had a past history of "schizophrenia", and another had a family member who had been treated for an affective disorder. Thus, in the majority of cases where details of family history or past personal history are provided, there is no reason for assuming that SLE patients who develop affective

Table 11.1
SLE Patients with Psychiatric and Affective Disorders

Author and Date	No. of Patients	No. of Patients with Psychotic Symptoms (with % of all Patients with SLE)	No. of Patients with Affective Psychoses	No. of Patients with Affective Neuroses	Affective Disorders as a Percentage of All Psychiatric Disturbances	Comments
Shearn & Pirofsky (1952)	34	17 (50)	Not stated	Not stated	—	Most of the psychiatric patients were "severely" depressed
O'Connor (1959)	40	26 (65)	3	2	19	
Stern & Robbins (1960)	53	26 (50)	2	8	38	
O'Connor & Musher (1966)	150	77 (51)	—	19	24	
Guze (1967)	101	36 (36)	10	—	28	Study based on retrospective case records, possibly underestimates psychiatric illness

Reference						
Johnson & Richardson (1968)	24	8 (33)	—	3	34	Two cases listed as schizophrenic could have been manic
Heine (1969)	38	14 (37)	5 + 2	—	50	Two "organics" became depressed later
Bennett et al. (1972)	5	3 (60)	1	1	66	
Ganz et al. (1972)	68	48 (70)	19	—	40	
Baker (1973)	17	7 (41)	6	—	86	
Bennahum & Mersner (1975)	54	22 (41)	9	—	41	
Feinglass et al. (1976)	140	24 (17)	3	—	18.5	
Gibson & Myers (1976)	99	27 (27)	5	—	50	Selected on basis of psychiatr. symptoms
McNeill et al. (1976)	4	4	2	—	50	Selected on basis of psychiatric symptoms
Allen & Pitts (1978)	2	2	2	—	100	
Grigor et al. (1978)	50	25 (50)	11	—	44	Many others with lesser degrees of depression
Bresnihan et al. (1979)	15	12 (80)	3	—	25	

psychoses are predisposed to this kind of illness by virtue of genetic or constitutional loading.

The role of steroids as precipitants of psychosis is not easily determined, for, as O'Connor has pointed out, high doses of steroids are likely to be given when physical and especially neurological symptoms are severe. Consequently, it is not clear how many of those who become psychiatrically ill are doing so because of the disease process or its treatment. Nonetheless, some cases do appear to have become psychotic as a result of steroid therapy, but Stern and Robbins (1960) felt that in only one of their 26 patients with psychoses had the illness been caused by steroids. Baker *et al.* (1973) also considered that steroid treatment was unrelated to their patients' psychiatric disturbances, a point supported by a general review of the problem (*British Medical Journal*, Editorial, 1975). The writer found that about two-thirds of patients with SLE develop lesions of the central nervous system, which most commonly declare themselves as psychotic symptoms ranging from mild affective disorders to severe psychoses. Increasing the dosage of steroids will often result in improvement of physical and mental symptoms.

Organic brain involvement as the basis for all types of mental symptomatology is strongly supported by most of the investigations that have been quoted and is given more precise definition by Bresnihan *et al.* (1979). These authors investigated 15 patients, 12 of whom had a range of psychological abnormalities including four who were depressed. Depression was characterized by abnormal affect, self-deprecation and sleep and appetite disturbances. None of these four patients were psychotically depressed. Cerebral blood flow and immunological investigations revealed that changes in blood flow were most marked in the frontal area. Levels of brain-reactive and lymphocytotoxic antibodies were also measured in these patients. One depressed case had persistently raised antineural antibody titres and marked abnormalities in the brain scan. The authors suggest that self-limiting episodes of cerebral vasculitis in the course of SLE cause changes in cerebral blood flow allowing leakage of serum antibodies into the brain. The consequent brain damage is followed by neuro-psychiatric symptoms and signs. Considering the likely role of frontal lobe structures in the control of affect, the demonstration of abnormalities in this region in patients with SLE could well be relevant to the high incidence of depression in this disease.

Another study demonstrating brain-scan abnormalities in patients with CNS complications in the course of SLE was reported by Tan *et al.* (1978). Twenty of their 25 patients had EEG abnormalities and all had abnormal brain scans. Twenty-one patients had 24 psychotic episodes but their nature was not defined and these authors said little about the localization of the brain scan defects.

Treatment

As already mentioned, continuing treatment with steroids is often successful in controlling neuro-psychiatric, including depressive, symptoms. Other reports have mentioned tricyclic anti-depressants, but the two patients described by Allen and Pitts (1978), who responded poorly to drug treatment, recovered fully with ECT. These authors did not feel that the coexistence of cerebral damage in their patients was a contra-indication to this type of treatment.

Because so many patients with SLE who become depressed or psychotic have signs of cerebral damage, it seems logical to consider this as the direct cause of psychiatric disturbances. Relatively few of the patients who have been described have suffered from earlier episodes of affective disorder and, although it might seem plausible to regard some depressed patients as reacting to a dangerous and debilitating disease, such a judgement will be based more on the observer's intuition than on objective evidence. Some milder affective disturbances could still be caused by brain dysfunction, although this may be aggravated by steroid therapy and the patient's understandable adverse feelings to his illness.

RHEUMATOID ARTHRITIS

During the 1930s, a good deal of uncontrolled speculation about the premorbid personality of patients with rheumatoid arthritis claimed to have shown that psychological predisposition had something to do with the onset of the disease. More recent evidence, however, suggests that any personality changes in rheumatoid arthritis are due more to the effects of the disease and do not precede its onset (Ward, 1971; Crown and Crown, 1973). However, depression is commonly observed, and Labhardt and Müller (1976) found that rheumatoid arthritis can be complicated by severe depression, which is seen both as a result of pain and disability and as part of the rheumatoid syndrome. Basler (1976) compared groups of men and women with rheumatoid arthritis with non-arthritic controls. The patients with rheumatoid arthritis suffered significantly more often from headaches, pressure in the head, insomnia, nervousness, forgetfulness, fatigue and restlessness. Taken together with the additional finding that more of the women arthritic patients considered that life was no longer enjoyable, one might conclude that a syndrome of depression had developed in many of these patients. Robinson *et al.* (1971) felt that depression was an understandable response to pain, but Burry (1976) found an excess of depressive symptoms, as measured by the

Beck Inventory in rheumatoid arthritis patients, compared with patients with other chronic, painful conditions. Zaphiropoulous and Burry (1973, 1974) compared rheumatoid arthritis patients with a control group suffering from a painful non-inflammatory disease of the locomotor system. Forty-six per cent of the rheumatoid arthritis and 18.7 per cent of the controls were depressed with symptoms, which appeared to have come on earlier in men and later in women. The authors did not feel that positive serology or the intensity and duration of the disease were specifically related to their patients' affective disturbances. A short review on the subject (*British Medical Journal*, Editorial, 1969b) considered that emotional factors aggravated the course of the disease and that depression may be sufficiently severe to require psychiatric treatment.

Ganz *et al.* (1972) reported that 47 per cent of rheumatoid arthritis patients were depressed, but not so depressed as SLE patients. Robinson *et al.* (1977), who found a high incidence of depression in their patients, observed that 30 per cent of women and 15.5 per cent of men felt that "they would be better dead". These authors were unable to relate depression to the duration of illness or degree of pain being experienced. However, there was some correlation between depression and joint tenderness, loss of mobility and dependence on others. Rimón (1974), who reviewed the literature on depression and rheumatoid arthritis, treated his patients with anti-depressants. Both joint symptoms and affective states appeared to improve together, a finding also reported by Macdonald Scott (1969) and Dudley Hart (1976). Possibly both the anti-depressant and analgesic effects of the drugs were responsible for this improvement.

It has been claimed that patients in the acute stage of the disease who are seropositive are more likely to be depressed than more chronic patients in quiescent phases of their illnesses. However, Moldofsky and Chester (1970) found that, whereas some patients became less depressed as their pain eased, another group, paradoxically, became more hopeless and distressed as symptoms were improving. They suggested that the mood was, to some degree, independent of the progress of the physical disease.

The causes of depression in rheumatoid arthritis patients have been considered under a number of headings including theories relating the disease to premorbid personality traits or showing that depressed mood is an understandable reaction to pain and disability. Others have examined the role of drugs and their likely effect on cerebral mechanisms. Although Mäkelä *et al.* (1979) state that "cerebral involvement associated with rheumatoid arthritis is rare but well documented", it is unlikely that lesions in the brain will be responsible for affective changes in the disease in more than a small minority of patients. They mention that at autopsy signs of cerebral vasculitis and rheumatoid nodules have been found in the brain and meninges. Conceivably such lesions could cause psychiatric disturbances as well as the neurological symptoms mentioned by Mäkelä and her colleagues. Many of these hypotheses have been reviewed by Rimón (1969), who expressed doubts about the validity of personality theories based on psychometric investigations carried out on patients already afflicted with the disease. He considered that emotional stress could precipitate the illness in some patients, some of whom may show signs of cerebral involvement. On the other hand, the effects of drugs such as gold, steroids, ACTH and anti-malarials should not be neglected as potential causes of psychiatric disturbance.

Rosenblatt *et al.* (1968) examined rheumatoid factor titres in the blood of psychiatric patients and obtained positive results in 63 per cent of depressed, compared with 35 per cent of schizophrenic patients. Examination of the relationship of these results to drug ingestion revealed that 57 per cent of patients who were seropositive were on phenothiazines, barbiturates, chlordiazepoxide and tricyclic antidepressants, but that 65 per cent of patients who had *not* been on medication for six months, also had positive titres. Certainly, when considering depression in the course of rheumatoid arthritis it is worth remembering that some anti-inflammatory drugs and steroids can cause affective disturbances that could erroneously be attributed to the disease being treated.

MISCELLANEOUS DISORDERS

Giant Cell (Temporal) Arteritis and Polymyalgia Rheumatica

The aetiology of this condition is unknown, but it has been described only in subjects aged more than 50. Although typically the external temporal arteries are affected, the intracranial vasculature and blood vessels elsewhere can also be involved. Headaches, fever, malaise and weight loss may be associated with stiffness and aching, predominantly in shoulder girdle muscles. Psychological changes, including depression, are also common. Von Knorring *et al.* (1966) gave details of seven patients, five of whom showed psychiatric disturbances, including one who was depressed. Two of the patients described by Robertson (1947), both men who had no past history of psychiatric illness, were also severely depressed. As the author remarked, both looked "perfectly dejected". Vererker's (1952) patient had been well until two years before his admission, when he became depressed and expressed a wish to die. At that time, he developed symptoms of myocardial ischaemia and only later was his temporal arteritis diagnosed. Vererker considered that, although depression could possibly be secondary to headache, a more likely cause was cerebral arterial disease. Paulley and Hughes (1960) state that mental symptoms such as confusion, depression and dementia are common and may be the only symptoms of the disease. Ross Russell (1959) mentioned that seven of his 35 patients were depressed, but gave no details of the severity or symptomatology of these affective disturbances. Other authors (Hamilton *et al.*, 1971; Hughes, 1977) have observed how psychiatric symptoms often precede the onset of the more characteristic physical signs. Hughes described a good example of this symptom sequence. The patient, an 80-year-old woman, became increasingly depressed and was found to have an ESR in excess of 100 mm in the hour. Typical signs of giant cell arteritis were absent, but a biopsy showed the pathological changes characteristic of the disease. She was treated with steroids and her depressive symptoms cleared completely. Hughes, like other writers, considers that cerebral arterial involvement was responsible for this patient's illness. She had no past history of affective disorder.

Sjögren's Syndrome.

Pittsley and Talal (1980) have found that depression associated with Sjögren's Syndrome can be severe, and in some cases leads to suicide. Evidence of cerebral involvement is usually absent in these depressed patients, who appear to be reacting to intolerable discomforts. In the absence of any investigation designed to examine this issue, it is impossible to reach any conclusion on the origin of affective symptoms involved. Understandably, treatment presents special problems as tricyclic anti-depressants will aggravate the xerostomia, which is one of the more intractable symptoms of Sjögren's syndrome.

12

Mania Secondary to Disease and Drugs, and Depression as a Complication of Schizophrenia

SECONDARY MANIA

The great majority of symptomatic affective disorders so far described have been depressive in nature although there have been references to manic illnesses occurring in patients with cerebral tumours, following major surgery or childbirth, or precipitated by a number of drugs. In many of these cases, a previous history of affective disorder had been recorded. However, Krauthammer and Klerman (1978), in their review of secondary mania, exclude from consideration all cases of mania in a setting of organic brain disease who had suffered from earlier attacks of affective disorder. Consequently, patients who become manic in the course of treatment of depression with anti-depressant drugs were not classed as examples of secondary mania. These authors mention manic episodes following the administration of corticosteroids, isoniazid, procarbazine, L-dopa and bromides, although in the last example (Sayed, 1976) the patient's bromism probably followed the onset of mania which was not attributable to drug toxicity. In any case his serum bromide level of 32.5 mg would hardly have been sufficient to cause a bromide psychosis. In addition to drug-induced mania, Krauthammer and Klerman list cases developing in the course of haemodialysis, following surgery and after a variety of viral infections. Although the post-influenzal case described by Steinberg et al. (1972) was indubitably manic, the upswing in mood appears to have been preceded by a short period of depression. However, the patient had not previously suffered from affective illnesses of this kind.

Other examples of secondary mania were associated with cerebral tumours and epilepsy. Whether the behavioural disturbance of the patient described by Stern and Dancey (1942) could be attributed to the glioma found at autopsy is uncertain. Initially this patient presented with signs of personality change and only some six years later did obvious features of mania appear. The authors considered that the tumour, which impinged on the substantia nigra, thalamus and geniculate bodies on the right side, could have been present for the whole of the nine years of disturbed behaviour, including three years of mania before her death. An additional example of mania in a patient with cerebral neoplasm has been provided by Jamieson and Wells (1979) who describe a 45-year-old man who became manic for the first time of his life when multiple metastatic tumours developed in his brain. The epileptic manic described by Rosenbaum and Barry (1975) who had no earlier episode of mania became ill initially with a basilar artery aneuyrism. Following surgery, he developed epilepsy as a result of surgical trauma to the anterior pole of the right temporal lobe. Mania did not occur until three months after the onset of epilepsy. Rather similar to this case is the patient described by Cohen and Niska (1980), a 59-year-old man with no family history or past personal history of affective disorder who suffered a subarachnoid haemorrhage which caused damage to his right temporal lobe. His mania did not develop until two-and-a-half years later when an EEG showed a focal lesion in the right temporal lobe. He did not experience epileptic attacks.

The topic of epilepsy and mania has been considered by Dalén (1965), who noted the relative rarity of the association. Thirty-five manics aged less than 41 were considered. A number of these had positive family histories of manic-depressive psychosis and others had sustained perinatal brain damage. However, two cases who had no family history of affective disorder developed epilepsy and mania following head injuries, and another two had suffered from serious viral infections. Dalén considered that on rare occasions head injury and viruses can cause mania.

Another apparent example of mania precipitated by organic brain disease is the patient with multiple sclerosis described by Kemp *et al.* (1977). This patient, said to be cyclothymic, became manic when her multiple sclerosis was treated with ACTH. She probably does not fulfil the criteria for secondary mania given by Krauthamer and Klerman (1978). Post-partum mania discussed by Kadrmas *et al.* (1979) was mentioned earlier (Chapter 9, p. 122). Although some of these 21 patients had former episodes of affective disorder this was not invariable; but this important point was not considered in detail by the authors. Young *et al.* (1977) have given details of three patients with coincidental organic brain syndromes who developed mania which was controlled with lithium therapy. However, all these patients appear to have suffered from bipolar affective disorders well before they showed signs of brain damage. The nature of their organic brain diseases is far from clear, but possibly long-term treatment with lithium and phenothiazines could have played a part. Mania induced by treatment of myxoedema with high dosage thyroid preparations was reported by Josephson and Mackenzie (1980). Five of their patients were depressed before treatment, and half the patients had positive family histories or personal histories of unspecified mental disorders. In these cases genetic and constitutional factors probably contributed to manic illnesses precipitated by thyroid treatment.

Mania following head injury is unusual (Lishman, 1978) but Cohn *et al.* (1977) have described a 12-year-old boy whose manic attacks came on shortly after he sustained multiple injuries in a car crash. No mention was made of any family history of affective disorder in this case.

Finally, Shulman and Post (1980) reported the onset of mania in 67 patients aged more than 60 years. All had suffered from affective disorders when younger, but the average length of time between the first attack and the current illness was 20.9 years. Eleven men and five women had evidence of cerebral-organic or neurological disability. Thirty per cent (15) of the 49 female patients had undergone hysterectomy, which is considerably more than the expected figure of 19 per cent of all women aged less than 75 years. The authors considered that this finding supports other studies relating depression to hysterectomy although they did not discuss the possible pathogenesis. In some patients the manic episodes followed closely the onset of cerebral disease or trauma, which in these cases must be regarded as precipitants of affective illnesses to which the patients were predisposed by virtue of earlier attacks.

There are many anecdotal accounts of what might be termed reactive mania; that is, a manic illness following a bereavement or some other major misfortune. For example, I recall a 70-year-old woman who became acutely manic following the accidental death of her husband. She had not suffered from any earlier attacks of affective psychosis. Dunner *et al.* (1979), who assessed the frequency of life events before the onset of affective illnesses, found such incidents in about half their patients. Among 20 manic patients, two became ill during the puerperium, one after an accident and a fourth following an attack of influenza. All these patients had experienced at least one attack of mania in the past and about three-quarters of them had positive family histories of affective disorder. In these cases it appears that the life events, both physical and psychological, acted as triggers setting off fresh attacks of mania in patients already predisposed to this type of illness.

Despite the "organic" basis for these examples of secondary mania, many of them responded well to treatment with lithium carbonate even when, as in Jamieson and Wells' (1979) patient, the tumour thought to be responsible for his symptoms could not be removed. The other patients treated successfully with lithium were discussed by Rosenbaum and Barry (1975), Kemp *et al.* (1977), Weisert and Hendrie (1977) and Cohen and Niska (1980). Oppler's patient (1950) with a meningioma recovered from his mania when the tumour was removed.

SCHIZOPHRENIA AND DEPRESSION

Depression in the course of a schizophrenic illness is not uncommon, but the relationship of the affective to the psychotic symptoms is not fully understood. Bleuler (1950) distinguished between depression as a reaction on the part of the patient to his painful perception of his psychosis and what he referred to as schizophrenic melancholia accompanying acute psychotic agitation, referred to by Strömgren (1969) as somatogenic depression. To these two varieties of affective illness must now be added a third — depression caused by anti-psychotic drugs, notably the long-acting phenothiazines.

McGlashan and Carpenter (1976a), who felt that post-psychotic depression was symptomatically similar to endogenous depression, compared 15 patients with this complication with 15 who were not depressed. The depressed group more often were receiving anti-psychotic medication and the authors noted that drug-induced basal-ganglia syndromes were associated with the affective disorder. In a further study (1976b), these authors commented on the high incidence of physiological disturbances such as sleep reversal, poor appetite and loss of weight in post-psychotic depression. Also, the risk of suicide is high, as not all patients respond to anti-depressive treatment (Bowers and Astrachan, 1967).

Drugs or Disease?

The question of whether drugs or disease cause the depression was discussed by Helmchen and Hippius (1967), who considered that, if depression comes on within 4–8 weeks of starting neuroleptic therapy, the drug rather than the disease is the more likely cause. On the other hand, Planansky and Johnston (1978) found that in the majority of their patients depression was seen early in the course of acute psychoses, a phenomenon which they regarded as being essentially part of the illness. In some of their 65 patients with affective disturbances, depression emerged as a prodromal symptom before the more florid features of psychosis had declared themselves. If depression persisted after the acute symptoms had subsided, this was likely to be a continuation in milder form of the more severe symptoms experienced at the height of the psychosis. The possible contribution of neuroleptic drugs was not considered here by these authors. The major symptoms of depression were feelings of guilt, worthlessness, self-reproach and depressed mood. There were positive associations between these features and suicidal thoughts — but not attempts — and the typical vegetative changes seen in severe endogenous depression. Guilt feelings were sometimes delusional in intensity and association with wishes for bizzare kinds of punishment as atonement for the patient's alleged wickednesses. In 21 patients depression of this kind seemed to be an integral part of the schizophrenic syndrome as it waxed and waned with the remissions and relapses of the psychosis. Palansky and Johnston concluded that their study "identifies a depressive syndrome apparently of an endogenous type, which is an integral component of schizophrenic development". However, in a further analysis of their 115 schizophrenic patients (1980), they compare the records of those who were treated before the phenothiazine era and those who became ill subsequent to the introduction of these drugs. The same type of depressive symptomatology was observed in both groups, but the main impact of anti-psychotic drugs was attenuation or suppression of the existing depressive symptoms which, as shown in the earlier paper (1978), occurred mainly at the height of the psychosis. Thus, the depressive syndrome in schizophrenia appears to be an essential part of the psychosis and to be independent of the action of psychotropic medication.

Roth (1970) has commented on the classically endogenous symptomatology, but one also should consider whether all the patients were schizophrenic or showing atypical mania before depressive symptoms dominated the picture. Steinberg *et al.* (1967) felt that depression was common when the schizophrenic symptoms were remitting, but Donlon and Blacker (1973) observed severe depression in 27 chronic schizophrenics when medication was suddenly replaced with placebo.

The role of medication in some of these cases of post-psychotic depression seems to vary considerably. Simonson (1964) claimed that one-quarter of the cases of depression he was seeing had been caused by phenothiazine medication. Such patients characteristically complained of agitation, crying spells, feelings of inadequacy, guilt, self-deprecation, anorexia, insomnia and loss of libido. However, of the 146 patients with depression, 50 had previously received reserpine. It is not clear what percentage of all these patients was initially diagnosed as schizophrenic, but few would dispute that some patients with endogenous depression are made worse by phenothiazines. May and Van Putten (1978) have described affective changes in the course of a schizophrenic illness under the title of akinetic depression. Of 94 patients, 28 developed akinesia from anti-psychotic drugs, and a further 16 showed akinesia and other extrapyramidal symptoms. Half the akinetic patients became depressed, but they responded rapidly to one dose of trihexiphenidyl. The authors favoured a drug-induced rather than a psychodynamic explanation of the phenomenon.

One might expect severely depressed schizophrenic patients to be more disposed to commit suicide. Virkkunen (1974) compared 82 schizophrenic suicides with 82 non-schizophrenic suicides. The schizophrenic victims had shown more guilt than anxiety but their depressed mood was of shorter duration and characterized by feelings of hopelessness and being a burden on others. Virkkunen found no evidence that neuroleptic drugs had contributed to the affective disorders of these patients. In his review of the problem of depression induced by anti-psychotic drugs, the evidence for and against this side effect appears to be well balanced. Although he does not favour the notion that in some schizophrenic patients depression is caused by the treatment, the evidence for this with respect to his own patients is not as clearly shown as one might wish. Nevertheless, neuroleptics — particularly the depot preparations — appear to be associated with depression and suicide in a minority of patients. The question of how many of these were depressed before medication was given and how many became depressed subsequently is obviously of some importance. If phenothiazines simple aggravate the depressive element in a schizophrenic psychosis, greater care needs to be taken over the use of these drugs in patients with major affective disturbances.

Aetiology

The pathogenesis of depression as an integral part of a schizophrenic illness is unknown. Family studies have not demonstrated a high loading for depressive illness in first degree relatives of schizophrenic patients (Tsuang *et al.* 1980), although there was some increase in the incidence of mania. Roy (1980) found that depressed paranoid schizophrenics more often than non-depressed patients had lost a parent before the age of 17. Twenty of the 30 depressed paranoid schizophrenics developed their affective symptoms coincidentally with their psychoses. These patients appear to belong to the somatogenic category of schizophrenia, but Roy did not analyse their symptoms in detail.

Of considerable interest, from the point of view of the aetiology of depression in the course of schizophrenia, are the observations of Sachar *et al.* (1963). They studied four young male patients who experienced post-psychotic depression and were found to have markedly raised urinary outputs of hydroxycorticosteroids and adrenalin. These findings were later confirmed by Sachar *et al.* (1970). There is an obvious similarity between these observations and the changes in cortisol output in patients with severe depression, but Carroll (1976a), comparing 81 depressed patients with 10 schizophrenics, found that, whereas the depressed patients did not show a fall in plasma and urinary cortisol after dexamethasone, a normal dexamethasone suppression of cortisol output was shown by the schizophrenic patients. Both groups had similar depressive scores on the Hamilton Rating Scale, but it could be argued that the schizophrenic patients were not at the stage of "anaclitic" depression as defined by Sachar and his co-workers. In addition, they were not assessed for feelings of depression, guilt and worthlessness as were Planansky's and Johnston's patients.

At this stage a biochemical or neuro-endocrine basis for depression in the course of schizophrenia has yet to be demonstrated. Depression as a psychological response to a severe illness is understandable and probably accounts for this phenomenon in some patients. Others will be depressed as a consequence of drug treatment, but for a third group of patients whose depression is an integral part of the schizophrenic syndrome some abnormality of cerebral function is likely to be responsible for both affective and psychotic symptoms.

13

Metabolic and Other Disorders

Various metabolic disorders, avitaminoses and related conditions have been alleged to cause depression. Among these, some mention should be made of acute intermittent porphyria, vitamin deficiencies, anaemia, hypertension and myocardial infarction, renal dialysis, Klinefelter's syndrome and anorexia nervosa.

ACUTE INTERMITTENT PORPHYRIA

The psychiatric aspects of this condition have been reviewed by Granville-Grossman (1971) and Lishman (1978). As is usually the case, no single syndrome is characteristic of the condition, but Granville-Grossman reports that in four studies the incidence of mental disturbance ranged from 24 to 80 per cent. Markovitz (1954) stated that 26 per cent of his patients had "hysteria, depression, schizophrenia or paranoia". One patient was treated with ECT for depression some months after the diagnosis of porphyria had been made. In Goldberg's series (1959), 29 of 50 patients had psychiatric symptoms, of whom 14 were depressed, nervous, hysterical, lachrymosal or "peculiar". Seven of the 12 patients described by Ackner *et al.* (1962) were depressed, as were 14 of the 15 patients discussed by Wetterberg (1967). In this series there was a strong family history of depression and Wetterberg felt that there was a genuine acute intermittent porphyria syndrome characterized by depression, with or without confusion, hallucinosis and neurological signs. Stein and Tschudy (1970) reported on 46 patients, 40 of whom were psychiatrically assessed. Seven remained chronically depressed after their illnesses, and one committed suicide. All but 13 of these patients had positive family histories of porphyria, but the authors did not investigate the frequency of affective disorders in the patients' relatives.

One of the difficulties in assessing the incidence of depression *per se* in patients with porphyria is the relative absence of detailed psychiatric reports on patients whose more dramatic physical symptoms and interesting biochemical anomalies tend to over-shadow mental changes. For the most part, little is said about former psychiatric illnesses, and one cannot say whether the metabolic disturbance precipitates affective or other disorders in predisposed patients, or causes them by virtue of the effects of the disease on the brain. Psychiatric disorder could be the consequence of electrolyte changes, loss of pyridoxine or cerebral damage. Stein and Tschudy (1970) carried out neuro-pathological investigations on patients who had died in the course of attacks of acute intermittent porphyria. Loss of neurones had occurred in the supra-optic and paraventricular nuclei of the hypothalamus. The authors consider that lesions in this area of the brain could be responsible for endocrine changes observed in some patients, but they could also play a part in the causation of mental symptoms which develop so frequently.

VITAMIN DEFICIENCIES

Routine measurements of vitamin levels in the body have shown that some patients, particularly the elderly, have psychiatric symptoms that can be relieved or improved by parenteral vitamin therapy. Attention has been concentrated predominantly on folate and B_{12} deficiencies, which appear to cause depression or a picture of dementia, sometimes reversible by treatment.

Folate Deficiency

Carney (1967), in a survey of 423 psychiatric patients, found low folate levels associated with chronicity of illness, drugs, epilepsy, organic psychoses and depression. Thirty-five per cent of the patients with endogenous depression had low serum folate. This deficiency could have been the result of the poor nutritional state of some patients, but folate deficiency causes reduction in the synthesis of catecholamines and 5-HT. In a later paper (Carney and Sheffield, 1970) mention was made of the effects of drugs (barbiturates, phenothiazines and anti-depressants), chronic diseases and malnutrition as causes of low folate and B_{12} levels in psychiatric patients, and Forshaw (1965) clearly regarded depression, alcoholism and gastric disorder as causes rather than the consequences of low folate. Nonetheless, Botez *et al.* (1976) describe a patient who became depressed and fatigued, and who responded to folate treatment along with improvement in her megaloblastic anaemia. Reynolds *et al.* (1968)

described a 20-year-old epileptic patient with a low folate who was prone to bouts of depression. Her depression cleared with vitamin therapy, but her fit frequency increased. Snaith *et al.* (1970) also observed low folate levels in epileptics with mental illness, compared with those not so afflicted. Among the psychotic patients, five were severely depressed, and four of them had low folate levels. Reynolds *et al.* (1970) found that 24 per cent of depressed patients had low serum folate levels which were correlated with higher scores on the Beck Inventory. These authors considered three explanatory hypotheses: that the low folate levels were secondary to depression and inadequate nutrition; that low folate aggravates any tendency to depression; that depression is secondary to reduced catecholamine and serotonin synthesis as a result of the vitamin deficiency. However, it is also clear that severe folate deficiency can cause a variety of neuro-psychiatric syndromes, particularly when associated with chronic diseases. Reynolds *et al.* (1973) have reported on the frequency of neurological disorders associated with folate deficiency in patients who also suffered from alcoholism, diabetes, cancer and a variety of gastrointestinal conditions. Patients with low folate levels were also more anaemic. The multifactorial nature of the causation of neurological damage in these patients is emphasized by these authors, but although it is probable that some of their patients were depressed, this aspect of the syndrome was not discussed. The role of drugs and chronic disease as causes of low folate and neurological syndromes was also emphasized in a short review on the subject (*Lancet*, Editorial, 1976).

Vitamin B$_{12}$ and Pernicious Anaemia

Mental symptoms as a consequence of vitamin B$_{12}$ deficiency can occur even with a normal blood picture (Hunter and Matthews, 1965). Holmes (1956) who reported on 25 patients, found 14 with psychiatric symptoms. Seven were depressed and one patient developed depression (treated with ECT) three years before showing neurological signs. Under the title of Megaloblastic Madness, Smith (1960) described six patients with pernicious anaemia, all of whom were severely depressed. In one patient, depression was attributed to guilt feelings over the death of a relative, and another had been treated by leucotomy for depression in the past. Five of these patients were female, and Smith noted the absence of the typical physical and laboratory findings in some of his patients. Although one patient could have been a case of bipolar affective disorder, it does not appear that the other patients had suffered previously from depression independent of their anaemias. Strachan and Henderson (1965) also commented on how B$_{12}$ deficiency can occur with normal blood and marrow pictures. Hart and McCurdy's patient (1971), a 53-year-old woman, presented with symptoms of pernicious anaemia and a mixed picture of depression, confusion and paranoia. A rather unusual case (Jefferson, 1977) was a depressed man who complained of sexual impotence and numb testicles. He had a macrocytic anaemia and recovered fully with vitamin B_{12} treatment. Neither he nor Hart and McCurdy's patient apparently had suffered from psychiatric illnesses in the past.

Eilenberg (1960) considered that pernicious anaemia was not causally related to psychiatric illness, and Shulman (1967), who examined 27 patients with pernicious anaemia and 21 with iron deficiency anaemia, found that 13 of the former and seven of the latter were depressed. One patient with a family history of affective disorder became self-reproachful and suicidal, but he recovered when the cause of his illness was disclosed to him *before* receiving replacement therapy. Shulman felt that the relationship between B_{12} deficiency and depression was a tenuous one but, as Lishman (1978) points out, about half Shulman's patients reported an increased sense of well-being after treatment. Edwin *et al.* (1967) screened 396 psychiatric patients and found 23 with low B_{12} levels. Only one showed a picture of pernicious anemia, and although no specific diagnosis was associated with B_{12} deficiency, three had manic-depressive psychoses and another four showed depressive reactions. Reading (1975) concluded that B_{12} deficiency, even in the absence of an abnormal blood picture, could cause depression, and went on to speculate about a possible link between mental illness, pernicious anaemia, other auto-immune disorders, cancer and premature greying of the hair.

Shorvon *et al.* (1980) reported their findings on 50 patients with B_{12} deficiency and 34 with folate deficiency, presenting with megaloblastic changes in bone marrow. One-third of the patients had abnormalities of the nervous system, with peripheral neuropathy predominating in patients with B_{12} deficiency. Nineteen of the folate-deficient patients were depressed, but no details of these patients' previous histories were provided. None of these patients had signs of subacute combined degeneration of the cord and there was no clear relationship between haematological and neuro-psychiatric abnormalities.

Although the patient described by Ende *et al.* (1950) was said to be "confused and psychotic", his symptoms were compatible with a severe agitated depression complicated by suicidal behaviour. He recovered with ECT and appropriate treatment of his pernicious anaemia. As in the case of psychosis associated with pernicious anaemia reported by Herman *et al.* (1937), no details of this patient's previous psychiatric history were mentioned. Six of 40 patients with psychoses in the earlier series had affective disorders (five depressed and one manic), and one case, a 76-year-old suicidal depressed man, recovered as his blood picture improved.

Conflicting opinions have been expressed over the significance of iron deficiency anaemia as a cause of depression. Elwood and Hughes (1970) found no differences in a patient's performance on a battery of tests before and after correction of her anaemia, but Lee (1970) considered that a low serum iron was a factor in depression. In elderly patients, iron deficiency is a fairly common finding in patients admitted to psychiatric hospitals, but it may not be the sole or even the principal cause of their symptoms. Nadel and Portadin (1977) found that 11 of 22 patients with sickle-cell anaemia were seriously depressed, four developing their symptoms acutely. They regarded preceding stress as causative of the subsequent physical illness, but it would be difficult to prove this without examining the patients during the stressful period and without adequate controls for comparison.

Other Vitamin Deficiencies

Pellagra

Pellagra as a cause of psychiatric disturbances has long been recognized, but depression is not generally regarded as one of the more common symptoms. However, Wilcocks and Manson-Bahr (1972, p.778) wrote, "In a review of pellagra in an asylum in England it was found that . . . the type of psychosis is a most profound melancholia with suicidal tendencies." Krishnaswamy and Ramanamurthy (1970) reported on 60 patients with pellagra and depression and attempted to relate the mood disorder to changes in serotonin, which was higher in depressed pellagrins compared with non-depressed patients. Nicotinic acid relieved the depression but was said to have caused a fall in serotonin.

Scurvy

John Woodall in his book, *The Surgeon's Mate*, published in 1617 (Keynes, 1967) remarked that "scurvy is a lazy, foul disease: lassitude and depression were in fact symptoms rather than causes". He recommended fresh citrus fruit juice as a means to cure both physical and psychological symptoms of the disease. Coming up to the present century, it is clear that scurvy can still occur. In his account of 11 adult patients with the disease, Cutforth (1951) mentions that more than half were depressed, resentful and rather uncooperative. Shafar (1965) described a patient made scorbutic by being placed on a milk diet for the treatment of a peptic ulcer. He became depressed and made a suicidal attempt but recovered when treated with ascorbic acid. Walker (1968) has given details of patients with severe depression and physical signs of scurvy, and Kinsman and Hood (1971), who produced ascorbic acid deficiency in five healthy volunteers, used the MMPI to record mood changes. As ascorbic acid levels fell the depressive, hypochondriachal, hysterical and social introversion scores rose. However, this is likely to happen in cases of general malnutrition and deprivation of vitamin B complex, so it would be difficult to account for the changes wholly in terms of vitamin C deficiency. Dixit (1979) related depression in scurvy to a decline in activity of dopamine-beta-hydroxylase, a copper-containing enzyme which requires ascorbic acid for its function of converting dopamine to noradrenalin. A fall in this catecholamine as a consequence is considered to be the cause of depressed mood in patients with scurvy.

Vitamin A and Vitamin D Intoxication

Restak (1972) described a patient who became severely depressed with headache and other symptoms suggestive of a cerebral tumour following the ingestion of excessive quantities of vitamin A. She was initially treated by psychotherapy but recovered when vitamin A supplements were omitted from her diet. There was no past history or family history of affective disorders in this patient. In his review of the literature the author mentions two other patients who became depressed when taking large amounts of vitamin A.

According to Chaplin *et al.* (1951) depression is not uncommon in patients who develop vitamin D intoxication when calciferol is given for the treatment of arthritis. Anderson *et al.* (1968) have given details of a female patient who became depressed after the loss of her husband. She had also had a partial gastrectomy and developed steatorrhoea treated with calcium and vitamin D. She then became depressed again in association with hyper-natraemia and potassium and water deficiency. When the calcium and vitamin D were stopped and her electrolyte abnormalities corrected she recovered from her depression. The other patient, who also had a past history of depression and gastrectomy, became depressed when given calcium and vitamin D for osteomalacia. Again, cessation of these substances led to resolution of her depression, although she remained mildly demented, possibly on account of cerebro-vascular disease.

HYPERTENSION AND MYOCARDIAL INFARCTION

Hypertension

Although some hypertensive patients become deeply depressed, usually in response to drug treatment, there is little evidence that in general they are more depressed or anxious than normotensive patients (Wheatley *et al.*, 1975;

Hodes and Rogers, 1976; Friedman and Bennet, 1977; Mann, 1977). The question of premorbid personality in hypertensive patients has been reviewed by B. Heine (1971), and it is far from clear whether hypertension is caused by stress or whether it makes the patient more vulnerable to the effects of stress. In an earlier investigation of 25 depressed patients (B. Heine *et al.,* 1969) a correlation was observed between blood-pressure readings and the duration of affective illness. There was no evidence that the hypertension predisposed patients to the development of affective disorder. An exception to these negative findings was a hypertensive patient whose depression could not be attributed to drugs (Nair, 1971). After surgical treatment of coarctation of his aorta he recovered from his depression.

Most studies of hypertension and depression have relied on rating scales to discover any differences between patients and controls. The fact that some patients achieve high scores on such scales should lead to further clinical examination to discover whether drugs, disease, premorbid personality, genetic predisposition or other factors are responsible. Reliance on rating scales alone cannot solve this problem.

Myocardial Infarction

A high incidence of depression after myocardial infarction has been reported. Wynn (1967) considered that 40 per cent of his patients were depressed, showing typical symptoms of endogenous mood change, with the exception of suicidal thoughts and guilt feelings. Premorbid personality factors seemed to be important variables contributing to depression in men with chronic heart disease. Kavanagh *et al.* (1977), using the MMPI, found that 44 of 100 patients were depressed following a myocardial infarct, although these authors consider the possible bias created by a selected population (older in age) and a variety of drugs that could cause depression. In addition, there were reactive and psycho-social factors, although higher blood pressures and more cardiac pain could have contributed (Kavanagh *et al.,* 1975). Vervoerdt and Dovenmuehle (1964) examined two groups of patients, those aged 35–49 and those aged 60 and over, suffering from cardiac disease. Sixty-four per cent were moderately or severely depressed, but the classic symptoms of endogenous depression were absent. The role of drugs in these patients was not considered. Winshie *et al.* (1971) felt that many of the depressive symptoms seen in patients with myocardial disease were exaggerations of premorbid personalities. There seems to be general agreement that depression in this setting is more frequently a neurotic response to illness than a true endogenous mood change.

Related to this general issue of depression and cardiac disease is the special problem of patients in coronary care units. Hackett *et al.* (1968) observed depression in 29 of 50 patients and regarded it as a reaction to a dangerous illness. Baxter (1974) likewise felt that the depression was understandable, but one would require more details about these patients before assuming that a neurotic rather than an endogenous mood change was being observed. On balance, however, there is little evidence that cardiac disease causes true psychotic depression, although one might anticipate such a development in some patients who, by heredity or constitution, are predisposed to develop affective disorders in the face of physical illness.

RENAL TRANSPLANTATION AND DIALYSIS

According to Levy (1976, p.53), "Depression . . . is the most frequent psychiatric complication of haemodialysis". However, 18 of his 25 patients were depressed before treatment began and, although some patients with renal failure improved, at least initially, in the majority of cases the blood urea and degree of renal failure do not correlate with the depth of depression (Kemph, 1966). The subject of psychiatric illness as a major problem in dialysis and transplantation units has been considered by Cramond *et al.* (1967), who reported that most patients show a mourning reaction. Five of 21 patients were acutely depressed in response to their situation. Rosser (1976) reviewed the many possible causes of depression in dialysis patients, including the total situation and fear of death, electrolyte and other biochemical disturbances, anaemia, hypertensive drugs, sexual problems and psychosocial stresses. She described three severely depressed patients who responded to low dosage of tricyclic antidepressants. Of the 10 patients in dialysis with psychiatric symptoms described by Farmer *et al.* (1979), three had endogenous depression and one a neurotic depressive reaction. None of these patients had a previous history of affective illness and, in general, these patients with psychiatric illnesses more often had additional organic symptoms. Tyler (1976) also observed marked depression with some organic features which could have been the consequence of electrolyte disturbances. Abraham *et al.* (1971), in a study of 3478 chronic dialysis patients, recorded 14 male and 6 female suicides and 15 male and 2 female suicide attempts. This suicide rate was said to be 400 times greater than that prevailing in the general population.

Lowry and Atcherson (1979) examined 58 patients at the start of home dialysis. Thirteen were depressed by DSM III criteria (Spitzer, 1978). A significant association between depression and polycystic kidney was found, but the reason for this is unclear. In this series only one of the depressed patients had a past history of affective disorder, although four patients had positive family histories of psychiatric illness, only one of which was depressive. Most of the patients, whether depressed or normothymic, had been chronically ill for periods of time ranging from six months to two years or longer. The affective symptoms had been present for two weeks to one year. Clearly depression in these patients was not a consequence of dialysis. Lowry (1979) mentions that 47 per cent of a group of dialysis patients had episodes of depression and that 42 per cent had made suicidal attempts, and in a more recent report, Lowry and Atcherson (1980) state that their patients' depressions were not related to the degree of uraemia or cognitive impairment. Once dialysis had started, they improved without psychiatric treatment. However, the cause of depression in these 13 patients is far from clear.

The possible neurological basis for neuro-psychiatric disturbances in dialysis patients has been discussed by Lishman (1978), who mentioned a number of psychiatric symptoms occurring in uraemic patients, including psychotic depression and mania. McCabe and Corry (1978) examined the role of drugs and found that in eight of 20 renal-transplant patients who showed secondary depression this could have been attributed to cortico-steroids or L-dopa. There is no evidence at present relating depressed mood in dialysis patients to aluminium encephalopathy, which more often proceeds to a state of dementia (Alfrey *et al.*, 1976), a condition which is sometimes reversible if aluminium hydroxide by mouth is discontinued and the aluminium content of dialysis fluid reduced (Poisson *et al.*, 1978).

KLINEFELTER'S SYNDROME

Nielson (1969), in a survey of the literature, found that 5.8 per cent of Klinefelter's syndrome patients were reactively depressed and that only 0.2 per cent showed manic-depressive psychoses. In his own 30 patients with sex chromosome abnormalities, eight were regarded as psychogenically depressed. There were eight attempted suicides and one successful suicide. Forty per cent of the Klinefelter's syndrome patients were depressed and 20 per cent had made suicidal attempts. Sørensen and Nielsen (1977) reported psychoses in 20 cases of Klinefelter's syndrome. Despite the alleged rarity of depressive psychosis, they observed four examples and two reactive depressions, and concluded that affective psychosis is not as uncommon as has been stated. Caroff (1978), on the basis of a search of the literature and a case of bipolar affective disorder of his own, also felt that the association of the two conditions was greater than could occur by chance.

Rivieris *et al.* (1979) described two severely depressed examples of Klinefelter's syndrome, neither of whom had previous episodes of affective disorder, who, after responding well to testosterone, remained well over the next six years on maintenance therapy. The authors considered that the hormone enhanced the noradrenergic system by inhibiting monoamine oxidase, which is said to be more active in depressed men and men with a low libido and impotence associated with endocrine dysfunction.

ANOREXIA NERVOSA

In a comprehensive review of 16 studies on anorexia nervosa, Hsu (1980) has drawn attention to the high incidence of affective disorders and suicide during the follow-up period. In six of these investigations where affective illnesses were specifically mentioned, their frequency ranged from 20 to 45 per cent and suicide was a not uncommon cause of death. Precisely what is meant by depression in this context is unclear as Hsu *et al.* (1979) reported that 38 per cent of the patients complained of these symptoms but that only one patient showed major mood swings, which responded to lithium treatment. However, in the study by Cantwell *et al.* (1977) depression included vegetative symptoms, feelings of worthlessness and suicidal ideation. Of 18 patients interviewed, eight exhibited these symptoms. In the whole group of 26 cases, family histories of affective disorders and/or suicidal behaviour were frequent. In addition, many of the patients had had previous episodes of depression.

In his investigation of 94 female patients with anorexia nervosa Theander (1976) reported that seven had first degree relatives with endogenous depression, whereas 21 per cent had positive family histories of depression when second-degree relatives were included. However, the positive family histories of affective disorder were no greater in the depressed than in non-depressed anorexics. Morgan and Russell (1975) reported their findings on 41 patients, 10 of whom, when admitted, were depressed with feelings of guilt present. Two had suffered from earlier episodes of depression and 11 per cent had positive family histories of psychiatric illness in first-degree relatives, but the precise diagnoses were not known. Winokur *et al.* (1980) also found a high incidence of primary or secondary affective disorder in the relatives of their anorexic patients. Twenty-three of their 25 cases had earlier episodes of depression and/or hypomania.

On the evidence it does appear that genetic factors are important contributors to the affective symptomatology of anorexia nervosa, but Dally (1969, p.117) has declared, when discussing comparisons between manic-depressive psychosis and anorexia nervosa, that "there is no evidence from follow-up studies or family histories of such a relationship". In the light of these more recent reports this statement clearly requires modification.

14

Summary and Conclusions

CAUSATION OR PRECIPITATION?

At least two reasonably well-founded conclusions have emerged from the preceding chapters. Firstly, in patients whose affective illnesses develop on a basis of structural brain damage, there is little evidence of predisposition to this kind of disturbance in the form of earlier episodes of depression or mania. Therefore, it seems appropriate to consider the cerebral impairment as being directly responsible for the psychiatric symptoms, which probably follow lesions in areas of the brain thought to be responsible for the experience and display of emotion.

On the other hand, depression or mania following major disturbances of neurotransmitter mechanisms caused by drugs and toxins are far more likely to occur in patients who have genetic or constitutional loadings for affective disorders. Similar illnesses have often followed the previous administration of drugs such as reserpine; and in these patients an innate sensitivity of receptors or enzymes responsible for the formation or destruction of neurotransmitters is probably the essential factor responsible for the onset of an affective illness. In these instances, it is justifiable to regard the drugs as precipitants rather than as absolute causes, as, without the underlying neurochemical pre-disposition, these psychotic disorders have less chance of occurring.

If these conclusions are correct, the frequency of depression in old age as a result of cerebral structural damage and, possibly, inherent biochemical alterations associated with ageing, accords well with the observation of a relatively low incidence of genetic loading and past history of affective disorder in older depressed patients. Similarly, in the case of presenile dementia, it may be that the loss of neurons has greater relevance to affective disorder than the purely biochemical changes such as a decrease in available acetylcholine. Viral infections, which appear to have a particular affinity for limbic brain structures, are frequently followed by major affective illnesses, and one might relate the extensive damage to the frontal lobe in patients with GPI to the depression or euphoria so commonly witnessed in this condition.

EFFECTS OF CEREBRAL DISEASE

Cerebral disease, particularly when the main brunt of the process is borne by the frontal or temporal lobes, causes both depression and mania, without the need for any special predisposition on the part of the patient. The findings in patients with cerebral tumours, for the most part, support this conclusion, although in some instances it seems appropriate to regard depression as an understandable reaction to disability. This may be an apposite interpretation in patients who become depressed after strokes and other cerebrovascular accidents, but it is questionable whether affective changes following head injury, particularly when complicated by epilepsy, fall into the same phenomenological category. Basal ganglia syndromes emerge from a background of structural and biochemical disorganization which seems sufficient to cause major affective illnesses, although similar illnesses secondary to medication more often reflect an inherent predisposition on the part of the patient to this class of reaction. The widespread cerebral damage in those afflicted with multiple sclerosis is probably sufficient to account both for depression and euphoria, although the reactive element in the aetiology of depression may predominate in some cases. However, if depression is to be singled out as a psychogenic symptom, it would be difficult to explain euphoria along similar lines. Euphoria is considered to be the sequel of extensive cerebral impairment, and in some patients depression could just as well be attributed to the same process.

Epilepsy, particularly temporal lobe epilepsy, causes both ictal and inter-ictal affective disturbances. In these patients, dysfunction of parts of the limbic brain is responsible for these phenomena. The accounts of ictal emotions are particularly compelling but, in the absence of careful genetic studies, which have been applied more often to schizophrenia-like psychoses of temporal-lobe epilepsy, it is impossible to say whether the patients who become depressed have any particular propensity for such symptoms. Nonetheless, the sudden onset of profound melancholia as part of an ictus is unlikely to require some innate predisposition to depression for such a symptom to emerge. At present it seems that repeated disruption of brain function is sufficient to cause fairly severe affective disturbances, but whether these are more likely to be associated with discharges originating from one hemisphere rather than the other is a matter that needs further consideration.

OTHER CONDITIONS

Apart from purely neurological disease, other conditions causing brain damage seem to meet the criteria of essental causation when affective symptoms develop as part of a syndrome. In this context, systemic lupus erythematosus causing neurological damage and depression, and giant-cell arteritis affecting intra-cranial as well as extra-cranial blood vessels, do not appear to require any particular tendency on the part of the patient for developing depression or mania. Symptomatic mania as defined by Krauthamer and Klerman (1978), because of its more striking symptomatology, is easier to fit into the concept of affective disturbances caused by cerebral damage. However, when these clinical pictures follow treatment with certain drugs, it is not always possible to consider the association as entirely causal rather than contingent.

Cancer

The observation that in certain patients depression may be the presenting symptom of a hitherto undiagnosed cancer requires further confirmation and, if possible, an elucidation of the possible relationships, which so far have been explained mainly by reference to possible immunological and para-neoplastic mechanisms. Certain features in the symptomatology and, generally, the absence of any past attacks of depression seem to point to a special syndrome which, when present, should demand full investigation in older patients who become severely depressed for the first time in their lives without any obvious antecedent psychological causes. The numerous studies showing that many patients become severely depressed once cancer has been diagnosed cannot differentiate satisfactorily between depression as a response to subtle biochemical or metabolic effects of a developing neoplasm and depression as an understandable reaction to what is likely to be a terminal illness.

Endocrine Disease

The aetiology of the affective syndromes occurring in the course of various endocrinopathies seems to straddle both parts of the hypothesis that is being considered. On the one hand, severe cerebral dysfunction developing in myxoedema, Cushing's disease and hyperparathyroidism could well be the basis for affective symptoms associated with these disorders. Given a derangement of endocrine activity of sufficient intensity, one might suppose that anyone, regardless of innate propensities, might become psychiatrically ill. On the other hand, these endocrine diseases cause major disruption of cerebral biochemistry, and in this respect have some semblance to drug actions causing psychiatric syndromes. Consequently, we find in Cushing's syndrome examples of patients who have become depressed or manic wholly on account of the glandular excesses or deficiencies, whereas others are rendered more susceptible to these changes by virtue of an innate tendency to emotional breakdown following a variety of physical and psychological stresses. In the case of Addison's disease, the apathy, fatigue and inertia which are so frequently observed should not be mistaken for melancholia, although some patients with the condition may well be precipitated into depression if pre-existing tendencies are sufficient for this response to eventuate.

Drugs

In contrast with the preceding syndromes, where brain damage is the essential cause of affective disorder, it does seem that drug-induced psychoses are the outcome of particularly sensitive biochemical mechanisms in the brain. These, one assumes, have a special tendency to respond adversely to a variety of stresses, including the pharmacological as well as direct toxic effects of medication. Consequently, one finds a far greater number of patients with drug-induced depression who have experienced similar earlier episodes and often have positive family histories of affective disorder. In these patients the drugs appear to be *precipitating* symptomatic depression, although to what extent the disease being treated contributes to this outcome is far from clear. Often, stopping the offending drug is sufficient to restore the patient's mood to normal, a finding which suggests that in these cases the drug and not the disease was responsible for the emotional disturbance. This chain of events is commonly observed in patients receiving antihypertensive treatment and, not infrequently, omitting the drug seems to have singularly little effect in the way of adverse consequences for the patient's blood pressure, which now lies within the normal range. It must be said, however, that some drugs, such as reserpine and amphetamines, will probably cause depression in some perfectly normal individuals if they are given for long enough and in sufficient dosage. With amphetamines, of course, the depression occurs when the drug is stopped, and one might suppose that exhaustion of transmitter amines, as well as a temporary loss of sensitivity of previously over-stimulated neuro-receptors, would be responsible for the mood disturbance.

Childbirth and Major Surgery

Affective illnesses during the puerperium or after major surgery seem to share with drug-induced depression a tendency for patients more often to have experienced manic or depressive breakdowns in the past. The evidence from studies of puerperal affective disorder shows that in many instances these are by no means the first, nor the last, attacks of illness. Although psycho-social factors, as well as the physical stresses of childbirth and surgery, may contribute to the subsequent emotional disorder, the inherent qualities of the patient may be more important. At the same time, it is understandable that some vulnerable individuals will react adversely to major crises such as childbirth and surgery, but premorbid qualities of personality usually allow this type of reactive depression to be diagnosed.

Other conditions which appear to have more in common with neurotic depression than with the more severe symptomatic depression are affective disturbances following myocardial infarction or any number of acute or chronic disorders whose emotional significance to the patient may far outweigh the hazards in terms of disability or early death. Yet once again it is essential to take account of the likely contribution of treatment to any mood disturbance developing in the aftermath of an acute illness such as coronary occlusion.

TREATMENT OF SYMPTOMATIC DEPRESSION AND MANIA

In many patients, treatment of the underlying physical disorder or withdrawal of the offending drug or drugs is often sufficient to restore normal mood. This clearly emphasizes the practical importance of recognizing symptomatic affective symptoms and their causes as a means of avoiding unnecessary psychological or psycho-pharmacological treatments. In some patients, however, a good response to anti-depressant drugs or electroconvulsive therapy occurs despite the persistence of the concurrent physical illness. There should be no place for therapeutic pessimism when it comes to managing depressed patients who are physically ill, and it is noteworthy how those who later develop malignant neoplasms have responded well to appropriate anti-depressive treatment months, sometimes years, earlier. In similar fashion, patients who have become deeply depressed following viral infections may have their affective states cut short by anti-depressant drugs or ECT, thus reducing the hazard of suicide, should their illnesses be allowed to run their course to spontaneous remission.

An equally important aspect of affective disorder revealed by this survey is the need for thorough investigation of all patients with depression, particularly when there does not appear to be any obvious psycho-social precipitant of the illness. This requirement applies even more strongly to older patients who, up to the time of their first attack, have shown no obvious manifestations of predisposition or personality traits conducive to this class of reaction.

FUTURE RESEARCH

This review has shown how little we know about the true relationships between physical disorder, drugs and depression, particularly the aetiological aspects which could be of major significance to our understanding of affective illnesses in general. As mentioned in an earlier chapter, we have remarkably little firm information on the frequency of depression after common viral infections such as influenza, hepatitis and infectious mononucleosis. In the case of neurological disease, we need to know more about the location and extent of brain damage, which could be relevant to the neuro-physiological basis of affective disorder, while the major endocrine disorders demonstrate the importance of hormonal and biochemical disturbances as basic factors in the pathogenesis of severe depression. One can but hope that these and other problems will be examined rigorously in the expectation that some of the hypotheses proposed in this review will either be confirmed or refuted.

Finally, let a plea be made for more information on affective disorders developing in association with a large number of physical diseases. Too often one reads that such patients are "depressed" or "emotionally disturbed", but without more exact definition such terms are meaningless. If a cardiologist reported that his patient's pulse was going a little too fast, he would rightly be taken to task for his lack of precision. General physicians and neurologists sometimes show a singular absence of understanding of psychiatric terminology with the result that they overlook significant symptoms; or, if they are recognized, they are too readily attributed to an innate weakness on the part of the patient, who is thought to be reacting adversely to a situation borne with greater fortitude by more robust spirits. Furthermore, if depression as a symptom is detected, it is essential to inquire what other symptoms are present in order to distinguish a transient mood change from a more persistent syndrome. At the same time, it is obligatory for inquiries to be made to ascertain whether the patient has experienced affective disturbances in the past, their nature and treatment, as well as any record of family members suffering similar illnesses. Given all these data the frequency of symptomatic depression or mania might then be estimated with greater precision than is possible at present.

References

Abraham, H. S., Moore, G. L. & Westervelt, M. B. (1971). Suicidal behavior in chronic dialysis patients. *American Journal of Psychiatry, 127,* 1199–1204.

Achté, K. A. (1974). Somatic Symptoms in depression. *In* P. Kieholz (Ed.) *Depression in Everyday Practice,* pp. 285–291. Berne: Hans Huber.

Achté, K. A. Hillbom, E. & Aalberg, V. (1969). Psychoses following war brain injuries. *Acta Psychiatrica Scandinavica, 45,* 1–8.

Ackner, B., Cooper, J. E., Gray, C. H. & Kelly, M. (1962). Acute porphyria: A neuropsychiatric and biochemical study. *Journal of Psychosomatic Research, 6,* 1–24.

Adams, A. R. D. & Maegraith, B. G. (1974). *In* B. G. Maegraith (Ed.), *Clinical Tropical Diseases,* 6th Edn. Oxford: Blackwell.

Adams, G. F. (1967). Problems in the treatment of hemiplegia. *Gerontologia Clinica, 9,* 285–294.

Adams, G. F. & Hurwitz, L. J. (1974). *Cerebrovascular Disability and the Aging Brain.* Edinburgh: Churchill Livingston.

Adams, R. D. (1968). The striatonigral degenerations: *In* P. J. Vinken & G. W. Bruyn (Eds), *Handbook of Clinical Neurology,* Vol. 6, pp. 694–702. Amsterdam: North Holland.

Adams, R. D., Van Bogaert, L. & Van der Eecken, H. (1964). Striatonigral degeneration. *Journal of Neuropathology and Experimental Neurology, 23,* 584–608.

Adolfsson, R., Gottfries, C. G., Roos, B.-E. & Winblad, B. (1979). Changes in the brain catecholamines in patients with dementia of Alzheimer type. *British Journal of Psychiatry, 135,* 216–223.

Akiskal, H. S. & McKinney, W. T. (1975). Overview of recent research in depression. *Archives of General Psychiatry, 32,* 285–305.

Alapin, B. (1976). Psychosomatic and somatopsychic aspects of brucellosis. *Journal of Psychosomatic Research, 20,* 339–350.

Alarcon-Segovia, D. & Fishbein, E. (1957). Patterns of antinuclear antibodies and lupus activating drugs. *Journal of Rheumatology, 2,* 167–171.

Alfrey, A. C., LeGendre, G. R. & Kaehny, W. D. (1976). Dialysis encephalopathy syndrome. *New England Journal of Medicine, 294,* 184–189.

171

Allen, R. E. & Pitts, F. N. (1978). ECT for depressed patients with SLE. *American Journal of Psychiatry, 35,* 367–368.

Almay, B. G., Johannson, F., von Knorring, L. *et al.* (1978). Endorphins in chronic pain. I: differences in CSF endorphin levels between organic and psychogenic pain syndromes. *Pain, 5,* 153–62.

Altschule, M. D. (1975). Depression as seen by the internist. *Disease a Month (D.M.), 24,* 1–46.

American Medical Association Council on Drugs (1968). Evaluation of a new antipsychotic agent: Haloperidol. *Journal of the American Medical Association, 205,* 105–106.

Ananth, J. (1978). Hysterectomy and depression. *Obstetrics and Gynaecology, 52,* 724–730.

Anasstassopoulos, G. & Kokkini, D. (1969). Suicidal attempts in psychomotor epilepsy. *Behavioural Neuropsychiatry, 1* (9), 11–16.

Andersen, J. (1968). Psychiatric aspects of primary hyperparathyroidism. *Proceedings of the Royal Society of Medicine, 61,* 1123–1124.

Anderson, A. E. & McHugh, E. R. (1971). Oat-cell carcinoma with hypercotisolaemia presenting at a psychiatric hospital as a suicidal attempt. *Journal of Nervous and Mental Disease, 152,* 427–431.

Anderson, P. C., Cooper, A. F. & Naylor, G. J. (1968). Vitamin D intoxication with hypernatremia, potassium and water depletion and mental depression. *British Medical Journal, 4,* 744–746.

Anderson, P. O. (1970). Intracranial tumours in psychiatric autopsy material. *Acta Psychiatrica Scandinavica, 46,* 213–24.

Angst, J. (1966). *Zur Atiologie und Nosologie endogener depressiver Psychosen.* Berlin: Springer-Verlag.

Armatruda, T. A. & Upton, J. V. (1974). Hyperadrenocorticism and ACTH releasing factor. *Annals of the New York Academy of Science, 230,* 168–179.

Arnold, B. M., Casal, G. & Higgins, H. P. (1974). Apathetic thyrotoxicosis. *Canadian Medical Association Journal, 111,* 957–958.

Arseni, C., Maretsis, M., Rodin, Z. *et al.* (1968). The role of the pituitary and the central nervous system in the pathogenesis of certain forms of Cushing's Syndrome. *Neuro-Endocrinology, 3,* 257–274.

Asben, M. J. (1975). Psychological aspects of mastectomy: A review of recent literature. *American Journal of Psychiatry, 132,* 57–59.

Ashcroft, G. W., Eccleston, D. & Murray, L. G. (1972). Modified amine hypothesis for the aetiology of affective illness. *Lancet, 2,* 573–577.

Asher, R. (1949). Myxoedematous madness. *British Medical Journal, 2,* 555–562.

Asnis, G. (1977). Parkinson's disease, depression and ECT: A review and case study. *American Journal of Psychiatry, 134,* 191–194.

Assai, G., Zauder, E. & Hadjiantoniou, J. (1957). Les troubles mentaux au cours des tumeurs de la fosse postérieure. *Archives Suisses de Neurologie Neurochurgerie et de Psychiatrie, 116,* 16-27.

Avery, T. L. (1971). Seven cases of frontal tumour with psychiatric presentation. *British Journal of Psychiatry, 119,* 19–23.

Ayd, F. J. (1958). Drug-induced depression: Fact or fallacy? *New York State Journal of Medicine, 58,* 354–356.

Ayd, F. J. (1975). The depot fluphenazines: Reappraisal after ten years' clinical experience. *American Journal of Psychiatry, 132,* 491–500.

Baer, L. (1973). Electrolyte metabolism in psychiatric disorders. *In* J. Mendels (Ed.), *Biological Psychiatry,* 199–234. New York: John Wiley & Sons.

Baer, L., Platman, S. R. & Fieve, R. R. (1970). The role of electrolytes in affective disorders. *Archives of General Psychiatry, 22,* 108–113.

Baker, M. (1973). Psychopathology in systemic lupus erythematosus. I: Psychiatric observations. *Seminars in Arthritis and Rheumatism, 3,* 95–110.

Baker, M., Dorzab, V., Winokur, G. & Cadoret, R. (1971). Depressive illness: The effect of the post partum state, *Biological Psychiatry, 3,* 357–365.

Baker, M., Hadler, M. N. & Whitaker, J. N. (1973). Psychopathology in systemic lupus erythematosus. II: Relation to clinical observation, corticosteroid administration and cerebrospinal fluid C4. *Seminars in Arthritis and Rheumatism, 3,* 111–126.

Baker, P. M., Bartholomeusz, D. B., Siskind, M. & Whitlock, F. A. (1977). Drug-induced depression and attempted suicide. *Medical Journal of Australia, 2,* 322–324.

Baldessarini, R. J. (1975a). Biogenic amine hypothesis in affective disorders: *In* F. F. Flack & S. C. Draghi (Eds), *The Nature and Treatment of Depression,* pp. 347–385. New York: John Wiley & Sons.

Baldessarini, R. J. (1975b). The basis for amine hypothesis in affective disorders. *Archives of General Psychiatry, 32,* 1087–1093.

Ban, T. A. (1978). The treatment of depressed geriatric patients. *American Journal of Psychotherapy, 32,* 93–104.

Bannister, R. & Oppenheimer, D. R. (1972). Degenerative diseases of the nervous system associated with autonomic failure. *Brain, 95,* 457–474.

Bant, W. (1974). Do antihypertensive drugs really cause depression? *Proceedings of the Royal Society of Medicine, 67,* 919–921.

Bant, W. (1978). Antihypertensive drugs and depression: A reappraisal. *Psychological Medicine, 8,* 275–283.

Barbellion, W. N. P. (1919). Diary of a Disappointed Man. London: Chatto & Windus.

Barker, M. G. (1968). Psychiatric illness after hysterectomy. *British Medical Journal, 1,* 91–95.

Barr, A. E. (1979). The Shy-Drager syndrome. *In* P. J. Vinken & G. W. Bruyn (Eds), *Handbook of Clinical Neurology,* Vol. 38, pp. 233–256. Amsterdam: North Holland.

Barraclough, B. M. (1971). Suicide in the elderly. *In* D. W. K. Kay & A. Walk (Eds), *Recent Developments in Psychogeriatrics,* pp. 87–98. Ashford, Kent: Hedley Brothers Limited.

Barton Hall, S. (1929). The mental aspects of epidemic encephalitis. *British Medical Journal, 1,* 444–446.

Bartrop, R. W., Lazarus, L., Luckhurst, E. *et al.* (1977). Depressed lymphocyte function after bereavement. *Lancet, 1,* 834–836.

Basler, H. D. (1976). Untersuchungen zur Psychopathologie der rheumatoiden Arthritis. *Münchener Medizinische Wochenschrift, 118,* 1245–1246.

Bauer, G. E., Croll, F. J. T., Goldrick, R. B. *et al.* (1961). Guanethidine in treatment of hypertension. *British Medical Journal, 2,* 410–415.

Baxter, S. (1974). Psychological problems of intensive care. *British Journal of Hospital Medicine, 11,* 875–885.

Bear, D. M. & Fedio, P. (1977). Qualitative analysis of inter-ictal behaviour in temporal lobe epilepsy. *Archives of Neurology, 34,* 454–467.

Beeson, P. B. & McDermott, W. (1971). Miscellaneous infections (viral), *In: Cecil & Loeb's Textbook of Medicine,* 13th edn. Philadelphia: W. B. Saunders.

Bennahum, D. A. & Mersner, R. P. (1975). Recent observations on central nervous system lupus erythematosus. *Seminars in Arthritis and Rheumatism, 4,* 253–266.

Bennett, R., Hughes, G. R. V., Bywaters, E. G. L. & Holt, P. J. L. (1972). Neuropsychiatric problems in SLE. *British Medical Journal, 4,* 342–345.

Benos, J. (1974). Altersdepressionen und depressive Syndrome in der Frühdiagnose der Pankreaskarzinom, *Aktuel Gerontologie, 4,* 327.

Berger, P. K. & Barchas, J. D. (1975). Biochemical hypothesis of affective disorder. *In* J. D. Barchas (Ed.), *Psychopharmacology.* New York: Oxford University Press.

Bernstein, T. C. & Wolff, H. C. (1950). Involvement of the nervous system in infectious mononucleosis. *Annals of Internal Medicine*, *33*, 1120–1138.

Beskow, J., Gottfries, C. G., Roos, B.-E. & Winblad, B. (1976). Determination of monoamine and monoamine metabolites in the human brain. *Acta Psychiatrica Scandinavica*, *53*, 7–20.

Betts, T. A. (1974). A Follow-up study of a cohort of patients with epilepsy admitted to psychiatric care in an English city. *In: Epilepsy: Proceedings of the Hans Berger Centenary Celebrations*. Edinburgh: Churchill Livingstone.

Betts, T. A., Merskey, H. & Pond, D. A. (1976). Psychiatry. *In* J. Laidlaw & A. P. Richens (Eds), *A Textbook of Epilepsy*, pp. 145–184. Edinburgh: Churchill Livingstone.

Beumont, P. J. V. (1972). Endocrines and psychiatry. *British Journal of Hospital Medicine*, *7*, 485–497.

Beumont, P. J. V.(1979). The Endocrinology of psychiatry: *In* K. Granville-Grossman (Ed.), *Advances in Clinical Psychiatry*, Vol. 3, pp. 185–224. Edinburgh: Churchill Livingstone.

Bianco, P., Anselmi, B. & Michelacci, S. (1965). The effect of indomethicin on pain, fever and vasomotor activity. *In: Recent Additions to the Nonsteroid Antirheumatic Therapy*, pp. 340–344, Milan: Minerva Medica.

Biegon, A. & Samuel, D. (1980). Interaction of antidepressants with opiate receptors. *Biochemical Psychopharmacology*, *29*, 460–462.

Bignami, A., Gerbard, D. & Galla, G. (1961). Sclerosi a placche acute a localizzazione potolomica con sintomologia psychica de tipo malinconico, *Riv Neurologia*, *31*, 240–268.

Bingley, T. (1958). Mental symptoms in temporal lobe epilepsy and temporal lobe gliomas. *Acta Psychiatrica et Neurologica Scandinavica*, Supplement 120, 1–151.

Bird, E. D. (1978). The brain in Huntington's Chorea. *Psychological Medicine*, *8*, 357–360.

Blacher, R. S. (1972). The hidden psychosis of open heart surgery. *Journal of the American Medical Association*, *222*, 305–308.

Blacher, R. S. (1978). Paradoxial depression after heart surgery: A form of survivor syndrome. *Psychoanalytic Quarterly*, *47*, 267–283.

Black, I. B. & Petito, C. K. (1976). Catecholamine enzymes in the degenerative neurological disease, idiopathic orthostatic hypotension. *Science*, *192*, 910–912.

Blazer, D. (1980). The diagnosis of dementia in the elderly. *Journal of the American Geriatric Society*, *28*, 52–58.

Blechman, W. J., Schmidt, R. F., Pavil, P. A. *et al.* (1975). Ibuprofen or aspirin in rheumatoid arthritis therapy. *Journal of the American Medical Association*, *233*, 336–340.

Bleuler, E. (1950). *Dementia Praecox or the Group of Schizophrenias* (Translated by J. Zinkin). New York: International Universities Press.

Blum, A. (1980). Patients at risk of developing severe side effects from depot fluphenazine treatment. *American Journal of Psychiatry*, *37*, 254–255.

Blustein, J. & Seeman, M. V. (1972). Brain tumours presenting as functional psychiatric disturbances. *Canadian Psychiatric Association Journal*, *17*, Supplement 2, SS59–63.

Bochner, F., Burke, C. J., Lloyd, H. M. & Nurnberg, B. I. (1979). Intermittent Cushing's disease, *American Journal of Medicine*, *67*, 507–510.

Bonhoeffer, K. (1909). Exogenous psychoses: *In* S. R. Hirsch & M. Shepherd (1974), *Themes and Variations in European Psychiatry*, Bristol: John Wright & Sons.

Bonhoeffer, K. (1912). Die Psychosen im Gefolge von akuten Infektionen, Allgemeinenkrankungen und inneren Erkrankungen. *In* G. Aschaffenberg (Ed.), *Handbuch der Psychiatrie*. Leipzig and Vienna: Denticke.

Boonstra, C. E. & Jackson, C. E. (1963). Hyperparathyroidism detected by routine serum calcium analysis. *Annals of Internal Medicine*, *63*, 468–474.

Boston Collaborative Drug Surveillance Program (1971). Side effects of non-psychiatric drugs. *Seminars in Psychiatry*, *3*, 406–420.

Botez, M. I. (1974). Frontal lobe tumours: *In* P. J. Vinken & G. W. Bruyn (Eds), *Handbook of Clinical Neurology*, Vol. 17, pp. 234–280. Amsterdam: North Holland.

Botez, M. I., Cadotte, M., Beaulieu, R. *et al.* (1976). Neurologic disorders responsive to folic acid therapy. *Canadian Medical Association Journal*, *115*, 217–223.

Bowen, D. M. & Davison, A. N. (1978). Biochemical changes in the normal ageing brain and in dementia. *In* B. Isaacs (Ed.), *Recent Advances in Geriatric Medicine*. Edinburgh: Churchill Livingstone.

Bowen, D. M., Flack, R. H. A., White, P. *et al.* (1974). Brain decarboxylase activities as indices of pathological change in senile dementia. *Lancet*, *1*, 1247–1249.

Bowen, D. M., Spillane, J. A., Curzon, G. *et al.* (1979). Accelerated ageing or selective neuronal loss as an important cause of dementia? *Lancet*, *1*, 11–14.

Bowers, M. B. & Astrachan, B. M. (1967). Depression in acute schizophrenic psychosis. *American Journal of Psychiatry*, *123*, 976–979.

Bowers, M. B., Goodman, E. & Sim, V. M. (1964). Some behavioural changes in man following anticholinesterase administration. *Journal of Nervous and Mental Disease*, *138*, 383–389.

Boyd, A. E., Reichlin, S. & Turksoy, N. (1977). Galactorrhoea-amenorrhoea syndrome: Diagnosis and therapy. *Annals of Internal Medicine*, *87*, 165–175.

Braceland, F. J. & Giffin, M. E. (1950). The mental changes associated with multiple sclerosis (Interim Report). *Association for Research in Nervous and Mental Disease*, Vol. 28, pp. 450–455, Baltimore, Md.: Williams & Wilkins Co.

Brain, R. & Henson, R. A. (1958). Neurological syndromes associated with cancer, *Lancet*, *2*, 971–975.

Bramwell, B. (1888). Intracranial tumours. Edinburgh: Y. J. Pentland.

Brandon, S. (1979). The organic psychiatry of old age. *In* K. Granville-Grossman (Ed.), *Recent Advances in Clinical Psychiatry*, Vol. 3, pp. 135–159. Edinburgh: Churchill Livingstone.

Bratfos, O. & Haug, J. O. (1966). Puerperal mental disorders in manic-depressive families. *Acta Psychiatrica Scandinavica*, *42*, 285–294.

Brenner, I. (1978). Apathetic hyperthyroidism. *Journal of Clinical Psychiatry*, *39*, 479–480.

Bresnihan, B., Hohmeister, R., Cutting, J. *et al.* (1979). The neuro-psychiatric disorder in SLE: Evidence for both vascular and immune mechanisms. *Annals for the Rheumatic Diseases*, *38*, 301–306.

Brierley, J. B., Corsellis, J. A. N., Hierons, R. & Nevin, S. (1960). Subacute encephalitis of later adult life, mainly affecting the limbic areas. *Brain*, *83*, 357-368.

British Medical Journal, Editorial (1966). Methyldopa and hypertension. *British Medical Journal*, *1* 133.

British Medical Journal, Editorial (1969a). Depression after childbirth. *British Medical Journal*, *1*, 460–461.

British Medical Journal, Editorial (1969b). Mental problems in rheumatoid arthritis. *British Medical Journal*, *4*, 319.

British Medical Journal, Editorial (1969c). Oral contraception and depression. *British Medical Journal*, *4*, 380–381.

British Medical Journal, Editorial (1970a). Psychiatric syndromes of cancer, *British Medical Journal*, *2*, 681.

British Medical Journal, Editorial (1970b). Depression and oral contraception, *British Medical Journal*, *4*, 127–128.

British Medical Journal, Editorial (1975). Cerebral lupus. *British Medical Journal*, *1*, 537–538.

British Medical Journal, Editorial (1976). Low spirits after virus infections. *British Medical Journal*, *2*, 440.

British Medical Journal, Editorial (1978). Epidemic malaise. *British Medical Journal*, *1*, 1–2.

Brockington, I. F. Schofield, E. M., Donnelly, P. & Hyde. C. (1978). A clinical study of post partum psychosis. *In* M. Sandler (Ed.), *Mental Illness in Pregnancy and the Puerperium*, pp. 59–68. Oxford: Oxford University Press.

Brogden, R. H., Speight, T. N. & Avery, G. S. (1974). Baclofen: A preliminary report of its pharmacological properties and therapeutic efficacy in spasticity. *Drugs, 8*, 1–14.

Brogden, R. H., Pinder, R. M., Sawyer, E. R. *et al.* (1975). Low dose clonidine: A review of its therapeutic efficacy in migraine prophylaxis. *Drugs, 10*, 357–365.

Brook, N. M. & Cookson, I. B. (1978). Bromocriptin-induced mania? *British Medical Journal, 1*, 790.

Brown, F. (1966). The relationship between cancer and personality. *Annals of the New York Academy of Science, 125*(3), 865–873.

Brown, G. L., Wilson, W. P. & Green, R. L. (1973). Medical aspects of parkinsonism and their management. *In* J. Siegfried (Ed.), *Parkinson's Disease*, pp. 265–78. Bern: Hans Huber.

Brown, G. M. & Seggie, J. (1980). Neuroendocrine mechanisms and their implications for psychiatric research. *Psychiatric Clinics of North America, 3*(2), 205–221.

Brown, W. A. & Mueller, D. S. (1970). Psychological function in individuals with amyotrophic lateral sclerosis. *Psychosomatic Medicine, 32*, 141–152.

Bruens, A. H. (1974). Psychoses in epilepsy. *In* P. J. Vinken & G. W. Bruyn (Eds), *Handbook of Clinical Neurology*, Vol. 15, pp. 593–610. Amsterdam: North Holland.

Bruyn, G. W. (1968). Complicated migraine. *In* P. J. Vinken & G. W. Bruyn (Eds), *Handbook of Clinical Neurology*, Vol. 5, pp. 59–95. Amsterdam: North Holland.

Bulpitt, C. J. & Dollery, C. T. (1973). Side effects of hypotensive agents evaluated by self-administered questionnaire. *British Medical Journal, 3*, 485–490.

Bunney, W. E. & Davis, J. M. (1965). Norepinephrine in depressive reactions. *Archives of General Psychiatry, 13*, 483–494.

Burnet, F. M. (1976). *Immunology, Ageing and Cancer*. San Francisco, Ca.: W. H. Freeman.

Burkle, F. M. & Lipowski, Z. J. (1978). Colloid cyst of the third ventricle presenting as a psychiatric disorder. *American Journal of Psychiatry, 135*, 373–374.

Burnfield, A. (1977). Multiple sclerosis: A doctor's personal experience. *British Medical Journal, 1*, 435–436.

Burnfield, A. & Burnfield, P. (1978). Common psychological problems in multiple sclerosis. *British Medical Journal, 1*, 1193–1194.

Burr, C. W. (1918). The mental complications and sequelae of influenza. *Medical Clinics of North America, 21*, 709–718.

Burry, H. C. (1976). Depression in rheumatoid arthritis. *In* B. Ansell (Ed.), *Rheumatism and the Psyche*, pp. 20–24. Bern: Hans Hüber.

Cadie, M., Nye, F. J. & Storey, P. (1976). Anxiety and depression after infectious mononucleosis. *British Journal of Psychiatry, 128*, 599–6.

Calder, R. M. (1939). Chronic brucellosis. *Southern Medical Journal, 32*, 451–460.

Caldwell, J. & Sever, P. S. (1974). Biochemical pharmacology of abused drugs. II: Alcohol and barbiturates. *Clinical Pharmacology and Therapeutics, 16*, 737–749.

Canter, A. H. (1951). Direct and indirect measures of psychological deficit in multiple sclerosis. *Journal of General Psychology, 44*, 3 & 27.

Cantwell, D. P., Sturzenburger, S., Burroughs, J. *et al.* (1957). Anorexia nervosa: An affective disorder. *Archives of General Psychiatry, 34*, 1087–1093.

Caplan, L. R. & Nadelson, T. (1980). Multiple sclerosis and hysteria. *Journal of the American Medical Association, 243*, 2418–2421.

Carlson, R. J. (1976). Presenile dementia presenting as depressive illness. *Canadian Psychiatric Association Journal, 21*, 527–531.

Carlson, R. J. (1977). Frontal lobe lesions masquerading as psychiatric disturbances. *Canadian Psychiatric Association Journal, 22*, 315–318.

Carlsson, A., Svennerholm, L. & Winblad, B. (1980). Seasonal and circadian monoamine variations in human brains examined post mortem. *Acta Psychiatrica Scandinavica,* Suppl. 280, 75–83.

Carman, J. S., Post, R. M., Goodwin, F. K. & Bunney, W. E. (1977). Calcium and electroconvulsive therapy of severe depressive illness. *Biological Psychiatry, 12,* 5–17.

Carney, M. W. P. (1967). Serum folate values in 423 psychiatric patients. *British Medical Journal, 4,* 512–516.

Carney, M. W. P. & Harris, M. (1979). Psychiatric disorder and diethylpropion hydrochloride. *Practitioner, 223,* 549–552.

Carney, M. W. P. & Sheffield, B. F. (1970). Association of subnormal serum folate and vitamin B12 and effects of replacement therapy. *Journal of Nervous and Mental Disease, 150,* 404–412.

Carney, M. W. P. & Sheffield, B. F. (1975). Forty-two months' experience of flupenthixol decanoate in the treatment of schizophrenia. *Current Medical Research and Opinion, 3,* 447–452.

Carney, M. W. P. & Sheffield, B. F. (1976). Comparison of antipsychotic depot injections in the maintenance treatment of schizophrenia. *British Journal of Psychiatry, 129,* 476–481.

Carney, P. A. (1977). Recurrence of Gilles de la Tourette's syndrome. *British Medical Journal, 1,* 884.

Caroff, S. N. (1978). Klinefelter's syndrome and bipolar affective illness: A case report. *American Journal of Psychiatry, 135,* 748–749.

Carroll, B. J. (1976a). Limbic system and adrenal cortex regulation in depression and schizophrenia. *Psychosomatic Medicine, 38,* 106–121.

Carroll, B. J. (1976b). Psychoendocrine relationships in affective disorders. *In* O. Hill (Ed.), *Modern Trends in Psychosomatic Medicine,* Vol. 3, pp. 121–153. London: Butterworth.

Carroll, B. J. (1977). The hypothalamic–pituitary–adrenal axis in depression. *In* G. D. Burrows (Ed.), *Handbook of Depression,* pp. 325–341. Amsterdam: Elsevier.

Carroll, B. J., Greden, J. F. & Feinberg, M. (1980a). Neuroendocrine disturbances and the diagnosis and aetiology of endogenous depression. *Lancet, 1,* 321–322.

Carroll, B. J., Greden, J. F., Haskett, R. H. *et al.* (1980b). Neurotransmitter studies of neuroendocrine pathology in depression. *Acta Psychiatrica Scandinavica,* Suppl. 280, 183–199.

Cass, L. J., Alexander, L. & Enders, M. (1966). Complications of corticotropin therapy in multiple sclerosis. *Journal of the American Medical Association, 197,* 173–178.

Castaigne, P., Laplane, D., Morales, R. (1979). Traitement par la clomipramine des douleurs des neuropathies périphériques. *La Nouvelle Presse Médicale, 8,* 843–45.

Castles, J. J., Moore, T. L., Vaughan, J. H. *et al.* (1978). Multicentre comparison of naproxen and indomethacin in rheumatoid arthritis. *Archives of Internal Medicine, 138,* 362–366.

Catel, W. (1957). Das klinische Bild und die Therapie der Toxoplasmose. *Münchener Medizinische Wochenschrift, 99,* 973–991.

Cawley, R. H., Post, F. & Whitehead, A. (1973). Barbiturate tolerance and psychological functioning in elderly depressed patients. *Psychological Medicine, 3,* 39–52.

Celesia, G. G. & Wanamaker, W. M. (1972). Psychiatric disturbances in Parkinson's disease. *Diseases of the Nervous System, 33,* 577–583.

Chacon, C., Mouro, M. & Harper, I. (1975). Viral infections and psychiatric disorder. *Acta Psychiatrica Scandinavica, 51,* 101–103.

Chadwick, D., Jenner, P. & Reynolds, E. H. (1975). Amines, anticonvulsants and epilepsy, *Lancet, 1,* 473–476.

Chambers, W. R. (1955). Neurological conditions masquerading as psychiatric diseases. *American Journal of Psychiatry, 112,* 387–9.

Chaplin, H., Clark, L. D. & Ropes, M. W. (1951). Vitamin D intoxication. *American Journal of Medical Science, 221*, 369–378.

Charcot, J. M. (1877). *Lectures on Diseases of the Nervous System*, Series II. (Translated by G. Siegerson) pp. 194–195. London: New Sydenham Society.

Checkley, S. A. (1978). Thyrotoxicosis and the course of manic-depressive illness. *British Journal of Psychiatry, 133*, 219–223.

Checkley, S. A. (1980). Neuroendocrine study of adreno-receptor function in endogenous depression. *Acta Psychiatrica Scandinavica*, Suppl. 280, 211–217.

Checkley, S. A. & Crammer, J. L. (1977). Hormone responses to methylamphetamine in depression. *British Journal of Psychiatry, 131*, 582–586.

Christian, S. T. (1972). Enzymes. *In* S. J. Mule & H. Brill (Eds), *Chemical and Biological Aspects of Drug Dependence*, p. 449, Cleveland, Oh.: V.R.C. Press.

Christie Brown, J. R. W. (1968). Mood changes following parathyroidectomy. *Proceedings of the Royal Society of Medicine, 61*, 1121–1123.

Church, A. J. (1980). Myalgic encephalomyelitis, "An obscene cosmic joke". *Medical Journal of Australia, 1*, 307–308.

Chynoweth, R. & Abrahams, M. J. (1977). Psychological complications of hysterectomy. *Australian and New Zealand Journal of Obstetrics and Gynaecology, 17*, 40–44.

Chynoweth, R., Tonge, J. I. & Armstrong, J. (1980). Suicide in Brisbane: A retrospective psychosocial study. *Australian and New Zealand Journal of Psychiatry, 14*, 37–45.

Clark, F. (1976). Drugs and vitamin deficiency. *Adverse Drug Reaction Bulletin*, No. 57, 196–199.

Clark, L. D., Curton, G. C., Cobb, S. & Bauer, W. (1953). Further observations on mental disturbances associated with cortisone and ACTH therapy. *New England Journal of Medicine, 249*, 178–183.

Clarke, I. M. C. (1979). The use of psychotropic drugs in the treatment of pain. *Pharmaceutical Medicine, 1*, 106–15.

Clayden, J. R., Bell, J. W. & Pollard, P. (1974). Menopausal flushing: Double-blind trial of a non-hormonal preparation. *British Medical Journal, 1*, 409–412.

Cleghorn, R. A. (1951). Adrenal cortical insufficiency: Psychological and neurological observations. *Canadian Medical Association Journal, 65*, 449–454.

Cleghorn, R. A. (1965). Hormones and humors. *In* L. Martini & A. Pecile (Eds), *Hormonal Steroids: Biochemistry, Pharmacology, and Therapeutics*, Vol. 2, pp. 429–441. New York: Academic Press.

Cleghorn, R. A. (1980). Endorphins: Morphine-like peptides of brain. *Canadian Journal of Psychiatry, 25*, 182–186.

Clineschmidt, B. V., Totaro, J. A., McGuffin, A. C. & Pflueger, A. B. (1976). Fenfluramine: Long-term reduction in brain serotonin (5HT). *European Journal of Pharmacology, 35*, 211–214.

Clower, C. G., Young, A. J., Kepas, D. (1969). Psychiatric states resulting from disorders of thyroid function. *Johns Hopkins Medical Journal, 124*, 305–310.

Cochran, G. M. (1973). A double blind comparison of naproxen with indomethacin in osteoarthritis. *Scandinavian Journal of Rheumatology*, Supplement 2, 89–93.

Cohen, M. R. & Niska, R. W. (1980). Localized right cerebral hemisphere dysfunction and recurrent mania. *American Journal of Psychiatry, 137*, 847–48.

Cohen, S. I. (1980). Cushing's syndrome: A psychiatric study of 29 patients. *British Journal of Psychiatry, 136*, 120–124.

Cohn, C. K., Wright, J. R. & De Vaul, R. A. (1977). Post-head trauma syndrome in an adolescent treated with lithium carbonate: Case report. *Diseases of the Nervous System, 38*, 630–631.

Connell, P. H. (1958). *Amphetamine Psychosis*. London: Chapman & Hall.

Connell, P. H. (1975). Central nervous system stimulants. *In* M. N. G. Dukes (ed.), *Myler's Side Effects of Drugs*, Vol. 8, pp. 1–30. Amsterdam: Excerpta Medica.

Cooper, H. A. (1936). Mental sequelae of chronic epidemic encephalitis and their prognosis, *Lancet, 2*, 677–679.

Coppen, A. (1965). Mineral metabolism in affective disorders. *British Journal of Psychiatry, 111*, 1133–1142.

Coppen, A. (1967). The biochemistry of affective disorders. *British Journal of Psychiatry, 113*, 1237–1264.

Coppen, A. & Shaw, D. M. (1963). Mineral metabolism in melancholia. *British Medical Journal, 2,*1439–1444.

Corbett, L. (1975). Technique of fluphenazine decanoate therapy in acute schizophrenic illness. *Diseases of the Nervous System, 36*, 573–575.

Corsellis, J. A. N. (1962). *Mental Illness and the Aging Brain*. Oxford: Oxford University Press.

Corsellis, J. A. N., Goldberg, J. & Norton, A. R. (1968). Limbic encephalitis and its association with carcinoma. *Brain, 91*, 481–496.

Cottrell, S. S. & Wilson, S. A. K. (1926). The affective symptomatology of disseminated sclerosis. *Journal of Neurology and Psychopathology, 7*, 1–30.

Couch, J. R., Ziegler, D. K. & Hassanein, R. S. (1975). Evaluation of the relationship between migraine headache and depression. *Headache, 15*, 41–50.

Craddock, W. L. & Zeller, N. H. (1952). Use of electroconvulsive therapy in a case of Addison's disease. *Archives of Internal Medicine, 90*, 392–394.

Craig, T. J. & Van Natta, P. A. (1978). Current medication, use and symptoms of depression in a general population. *American Journal of Psychiatry, 135*, 1036–1039.

Crammer, J. L. (1977). Calcium metabolism and mental disorder. *Psychological Medicine, 7*, 557–560.

Cramond, W. A., Knight, P. R. & Lawrence, J. R. (1967). The psychiatric contribution to a renal unit undertaking chronic haemodialysis and renal homotransplantation. *British Journal of Psychiatry, 113*, 1201–1212.

Crémieux, A., Alliez, J., Tonga, M. & Piche, R. (1959). Sclérose en plaque à début per troubles mentaux, Étude anatomo-clinique. *Revue Neurologie* (Paris), *101*, 45–51.

Critchley, M. (1962). Periodic hypersomnia and megaphagia in adolescent males. *Brain, 85*, 627–656.

Cropper, C. F. J. (1973). Hypothyroidism in psychogeriatric patients: Ankle-jerk reaction as a screening test. *Gerontologia Clinica, 13*, 15–24.

Cross, A. J., Crow, T. J., Perry, E. K. *et al.* (1981). Reduced dopamine–beta–hydroxylase activity in Alzheimer's disease. *British Medical Journal, 1*, 93–94.

Crow, T. J. (1978). Viral causes of psychiatric disease. *Postgraduate Medical Journal, 54*, 763–767.

Crowder, K. & Pate, J. K. (1980). A case report of cimetidine-induced depression. *American Journal of Psychiatry, 137*, 1451.

Crown, S. & Crown, J. M. (1973). Personality in early rheumatoid disease. *Journal of Psychosomatic Research, 17*, 189–196.

Cumming, J. & Kort, K. (1956). Apparent reversal by cortisone of an electroconvulsive refractory state in a psychiatric patient with Addison's disease. *Canadian Medical Association Journal, 74*, 291–292.

Curzon, G. (1976). Transmitter amines in brain diseases. *In* A. N. Davison (Ed.), *Biochemistry and Neurological Disease*, pp. 168–227. Oxford: Blackwell.

Cutforth, R. H. (1951). Adult Scurvy. *Lancet, 1*, 454–456.

Cutting, J. (1980). Physical illness and psychosis. *British Journal of Psychiatry, 136*, 109–119.

Dalén, P. (1965). Family history, the electroencephalogram and perinatal factors in manic conditions. *Acta Psychiatrica Scandinavica, 41*, 527–562.

Dally, P. (1969). *Anorexia Nervosa*. London: William Heinemann.

Dalrymple-Champneys, W. (1960). *Brucellosis Infections and Undulant Fever in Man*. London: Oxford University Press.

Dalton, K. (1971a). Puerperal and premenstrual depression. *Proceedings of the Royal Society of Medicine, 64*, 1249–1252.

Dalton, K. (1971b). Prospective study in puerperal depression. *British Journal of Psychiatry, 118*, 689–692.

Daly, D. (1958). Ictal affect. *American Journal of Psychiatry, 115*, 97–108.

Daniels, L. (1934). Narcolepsy. *Medicine, 13*, 1–122.

Davies, D. L. (1949). Psychiatric changes associated with Friedrich's Ataxia. *Journal of Neurology, Neurosurgery and Psychiatry, 12*, 246–250.

Davis, E. E., & Walsh, M. J. (1971). Effect of ethanol on neuroamine metabolism. *In* L. Y. Israel & J. Madrones (Eds), *Biological Basis of Alcoholism*. New York: Wiley Interscience.

Davis, J. L., Lewis, S. B., Gerich, J. E. *et al.* (1977). Peripheral diabetic neuropathy treated with amitriptyline and fluphenazine. *Journal of the American Medical Association, 238*, 2291–2.

Davies, P. & Maloney, A. J. F. (1976). Selective loss of central cholinergic neurones in Alzheimer's disease. *Lancet, 2*, 1403.

De Alarcón, R. (1964). Hypochondriasis and depression in the aged. *Gerontologia Clinica, 6*, 266–277.

De Alarcón, R. & Carney, M. W. P. (1969). Severe depressive mood changes following slow release intramuscular fluphenazine injections. *British Medical Journal, 2*, 564–567.

Debert, R., Van Hooren, J. & Amery, W. (1974). Antinuclear factor, a dysimmunological feature in mental depression: A preliminary communication. *Psychotherapy and Psychosomatics, 24*, 119–122.

Debert, R., Van Hooren, J., Biesbrouck, M. & Amery, W. (1976). Antinuclear factor-positive mental depression: Single disease entity? *Biological Psychiatry, 11*, 69–74.

De Feudis, F. V. (1974). *Central Cholinergic Systems and Behavior*. New York: Academic Press.

Delay, J., Deniker, P. & Barande, R. (1957). Le suicide des épileptiques. *Encéphale, 46*, 401–436.

Denko, J. E. & Kaebling, R. (1962). The psychiatric aspects of hypoparathyroidism. *Acta Psychiatrica Scandinavica, 38*, Supplement 164.

De Paulo, J. R. & Folstein, M. F. (1978). Psychiatric disturbances in neurological patients. Detection, recognition and hospital course. *Annals of Neurology, 4*, 225–228.

Dewhurst, K. (1969). The neurosyphilitic psychoses today. *British Journal of Psychiatry, 115*, 31–38.

Dewhurst, K., Oliver, J., Trick, K. L. K. & McKnight, A. L. (1969). Neuropsychiatric aspects of Huntington's disease. *Confina Neurologia, 31*, 258–268.

Dewhurst, K., Oliver, J. E. & McKnight, A. L. (1970). Sociopsychiatric consequences of Huntington's disease. *British Journal of Psychiatry, 116*, 255–258.

Director, K. L. (1980). Cancer presenting as a delusion of cancer. *Journal of Clinical Psychiatry, 41*, 145–146.

Direkze, M., Bayliss, S. G. & Cutting, J. (1971). Primary tumours of the frontal lobe. *British Journal of Clinical Practice, 25*, 207–13.

Dixit, V. M. (1979). Cause of depression in chronic scurvy. *Lancet, 2*, 1077–1078.

Doberauer, W. & Doberauer, B. (1978). Iatrogene Depressionen in Alter. *Aktuel Gerontologie, 8*, 139–141.

Dollery, C. T., Emslie-Smith, D. & Milne, M. D. (1960). Clinical and pharmacological studies with guanethidine in the treatment of hypertension. *Lancet, 2*, 381–387.

Dominian, J., Serafetinides, E. A. & Dewhurst, M. (1963). A follow-up study of late-onset epilepsy II. *British Medical Journal, 1*, 431–435.

Donald, A. G., Still, C. L. & Pearson, J. M. (1972). Behavioural symptoms with intracranial neoplasms. *Southern Medical Journal, 65*, 1006–9.

Dongier, S. (1959). Statistical study of clinical and EEG manifestations of 536 psychiatric episodes occurring in 516 epileptics between clinical seizures. *Epilepsia, 1*, 117–142.

Donlon, P. T. & Blacker, K. H. (1973). States of schizophrenic decompensation and reintegration. *Journal of Nervous and Mental Disease, 157,* 200–209.

Dorpat, T. L., Anderson, W. F. & Ripley, N. S. (1968). The relationship of physical illness to suicide. *In* H. L. Resnik (Ed.), *Suicidal Behaviour,* Boston, Mass.: Little, Brown & Co.

Drake, F. R. (1957). Neuropsychiatric symptomatology of Addison's disease: A review. *American Journal of Medical Science, 234,* 106–113.

Dudley Hart, F. (1976). Antidepressants in rheumatoid arthritis. *In* B. Ansell (Ed.), *Rheumatism and the Psyche,* pp. 36–37. Bern: Hans Hüber.

Duffy, J. P. & Davison, K. (1968). A female case of the Kleine-Levin syndrome. *British Journal of Psychiatry, 114,* 77–84.

Duhault, J., Malen, C., & Boulanger, M. (1975). Fenfluramine and 5-hydroxytryptophan: Is fluramine or norfenfluramine involved in the decrease of brain 5HT? *Artzneimittel-Forschung, 25,* 1755–1758.

Dunner, D. L., Patrick, & V. Fieve, R. R. (1979). Life events at the onset of bipolar affective illness. *American Journal of Psychiatry, 136,* 508–511.

Easton, H. G. (1978). Epidemic myalgic encephalomyelitis. *British Medical Journal, 1,* 16–96.

Edison, G. R. (1971). Amphetamines: A dangerous illusion. *Annals of Internal Medicine, 74,* 605–610.

Edwin, E., Holten, K., Norum, K. R. *et al.* (1967). Vitamin B12 hypovitaminosis in mental diseases. *Acta Medica Scandinavica, 177,* 689–699.

Egerton, N. & Kay, G. H. (1964). Psychological disturbances associated with open heart surgery. *British Journal of Psychiatry, 110,* 433–439.

Eilenberg, M. D. (1960). Psychiatric illness and pernicious anaemia: A clinical revaluation. *British Journal of Psychiatry, 106,* 1539–1548.

Eldridge, W. W. & Holme, G. A. (1940). The incidence of hyperostosis frontalis interna in female patients admitted to a mental hospital. *American Journal of Roentgenology, 43,* 356–359.

Elian, M. & Dean, G. (1977). Multiple sclerosis and seizures. *In* J. K. Penry (Ed.), *Epilepsy, 8th International Symposium,* pp. 341–344. New York: Raven Press.

Elwood, P. C. Hughes, D. (1970). Clinical trial of iron therapy on psychomotor function in anaemic women. *British Medical Journal, 3,* 254–255.

Ende, M., Klauber, B. & Gendd, B. R. (1950). Electric shock therapy of acute psychosis associated with pernicious anaemia. *Archives of Neurology and Psychiatry, 63,* 110–112.

Evans, N. J. R., Baldwin, J. A. & Gath, D. (1974). The incidence of cancer among patients with affective disorders. *British Journal of Psychiatry, 124,* 518–525.

Ewald, G. (1928). Psychoses in acute infections. *In* O. Bumke (Ed.), *Handbook of Mental Diseases,* Vol. 7, Berlin. Quoted in Slater, E. & Roth, M. (1977). *Clinical Psychiatry.* London: Balliére, Tindall and Cassell.

Extein, I., Potlash, A. L. C., Gold, M. S. *et al.* (1980). Deficient prolactin response to morphine in depressed patients. *American Journal of Psychiatry, 137,* 845–846.

Falloon, I., Watt, D. C., Shepherd, M. (1978). A comparative trial of pimozide and fluphenazine decanoate in the continuation treatment of schizophrenia. *Psychological Medicine, 8,* 59–70.

Farley, I. J., Price, K. S., Hornykiewicz, O. (1977). Dopamine in the limbic regions of the human brain: Normal and abnormal. *Advances in Biochemical Psychopharmacology, 16,* 57–64.

Farley, I. J., Price, K. S. & Hornykiewicz, O. (1978). Monoaminergic systems in the human limbic brain. *In* K. E. Livingstone & O. Hornykiewicz (Eds), *Limbic Mechanisms,* pp. 339–349. New York: Plenum Press.

Farmer, C. J., Snowden, S. A. & Parsons, V. (1979). The prevalence of psychiatric illness among patients on home dialysis. *Psychological Medicine, 9,* 509–514.

Fawcett, J. (1972). Suicidal depression and physical illness. *Journal of the American Medical Association, 219,* 1303–1306.

Feighner, J. P., Robins, E., Guze, S. G. *et al.* (1972). Diagnostic criteria for the use in psychiatric research. *Archives of General Psychiatry, 26*, 57–63.

Feinglass, E. J., Arnett, F. C., Dorsch, C. A. *et al.* (1976). Neuropsychiatric manifestations of SLE: Diagnosis, clinical spectrum and relationship to other features of the disease. *Medicine, 55*, 523–539.

Feldman, S. (1957). Convulsions in multiple sclerosis. *Journal of Nervous and Mental Disease, 125*, 213–220.

Feldstein, A. (1971). Effect of ethanol on neurohumoral amine metabolism. *In* B. Kissin & H. Begleiter (Eds), *Biology of Alcoholism*, Vol. 1, p. 127. New York: Plenum Press.

Feldstein, A. (1973). Ethanol-induced sleep in relation to serotonin turnover. *Annals of the New York Academy of Science, 215*, 71–76.

Fenton, G. W. & Udwin, E. L. (1965). Homicide and temporal lobe epilepsy. *British Journal of Psychiatry, 111*, 304–306.

Ferguson Anderson, W. (1971). The inter-relationship between physical and mental illness in the elderly. *In* D. W. K. Kay & A. Walk (Eds), *Recent Developments in Psychogeriatrics*, pp. 19–24. Ashford, Kent: Hedley Brothers Ltd.

Ferguson Anderson, W. (1978). The early detection and prediction of disease in the elderly. *In* B. Isaacs (Ed.), *Recent advances in Geriatrics*. Edinburgh: Churchill Livingstone.

Findlay, E. M., Martin, N. H. & Mitchell, J. B. (1944). Hepatitis after yellow fever inoculation: Relation to infective hepatitis. *Lancet, 2*, 301–307.

Fink, M. (1966). Cholinergic aspects of convulsive therapy. *Journal of Nervous and Mental Disease, 142*, 475–84.

Fink, M. & Ottosson, J.-O. (1980). A theory of convulsive therapy in endogenous depression: Significance of hypothalamic functions. *Psychiatric Research, 2*, 49–61.

Flanaghan, T. A., Goodwin, D. W. & Alderson, P. (1970). Psychiatric illness in a large family with familial hyperparathyroidism. *British Journal of Psychiatry, 117*, 693–698.

Fleminger, J. J. (1955). The differential effects of cortisone and of ACTH on mood. *Journal of Mental Science, 101*, 123–130.

Fleminger, O. & Seager, C. P. (1978). Incidence of depressive symptoms in users of the oral contraceptive. *British Journal of Psychiatry, 132*, 431–440.

Flor Henry, P. (1969a). Psychosis and temporal lobe epilepsy: A controlled investigation. *Epilepsia, 10*, 363–395.

Flor Henry, P. (1969b). Schizophrenia-like reactions and affective psychoses associated with temporal lobe epilepsy: Aetiological factors. *American Journal of Psychiatry, 126*, 400–404.

Flor Henry, P. (1974). Epilepsy and psychopathology. *In* K. Granville-Grossman (Ed.), *Recent Advances in Clinical Psychiatry*, Vol. 2, pp. 262–295. Edinburgh: Churchill Livingstone.

Folstein, M. F., Maiberger, R. & McHugh, P. R. (1977). Mood disorder as a specific complication of stroke. *Journal of Neurology, Neurosurgery and Psychiatry, 40*, 1018–20.

Ford, C. V., Bray, G. A. & Swerdloff, R. S. (1976). A psychiatric study of patients referred with a diagnosis of hypoglycaemia. *American Journal of Psychiatry, 133*, 291–294.

Ford, J. C. (1943). Infective hepatitis. *Lancet, 1*, 675–678.

Forshaw, J. (1965). Nutritional deficiency of folic acid. *British Medical Journal, 2*, 1061.

Fourman, P., Rawnsley, K., Davis, R. H., Jones, K. K. & Morgan, D. B. (1967). Effect of calcium on mental symptoms in partial parathyroid insufficiency, *Lancet, 2*, 914–915.

Frame, R. (1976). Neuromuscular manifestations of parathyroid disease. *In* P. J. Vinken & G. W. Bruyn (Eds), *Handbook of Clinical Neurology*, Vol. 27, pp. 283–320. Amsterdam: North Holland.

Franz, A. G. (1978). Prolactin. *New England Journal of Medicine, 298*, 201–207.

Fras, I., Litin, E. M. & Pearson, J. S. (1967). Comparison of psychiatric symptoms in cancer of the pancreas with those in some other intra-abdominal conditions. *American Journal of Psychiatry, 123*, 1553–1562.

Frazier, C. H. (1936). Tumours involving the frontal lobe alone. *Archives of Neurology and Psychiatry, 35*, 525–571.

Freyhan, F. A., Gianelli, S., O'Connell, R. A. & Mayo, J. A. (1971). Complications following open heart surgery. *Comprehensive Psychiatry, 12*, 181–195.

Friedman, M., Marshall-Jones, P. & Ross, E. J. (1966). Cushing's syndrome: Adrenocortical activity secondary to neoplasms arising outside the pituitary-adrenal system. *Quarterly Journal of Medicine, 35*, 193–214.

Friedman, M. J. & Bennet, P. L. (1977). Depression and hypertension. *Psychosomatic Medicine, 39*, 134–142.

Frizel, D., Coppen, A. & Marks, V. (1969). Plasma magnesium and calcium in depression. *British Journal of Psychiatry, 115*, 1375–1377.

Fulton, J. F. (1951). *Frontal Lobotomy and Human Behaviour: A Neurophysiological Analysis.* London: Chapman and Hall.

Furhoff, A.-K. (1978). Adverse reaction with methyldopa: A decade's report. *Acta Medica Scandinavica, 203*, 425–428.

Fuxe, A., Hockfelt, T. & Ungerstett, U. (1970). Central monoaminergic tracts. *In* W. G. Clark & J. del Giudice (Eds), *Principles of Psychopharmacology*, pp. 87–96. New York: Academic Press.

Gade, T. N., Hofeldt, F. D. & Treece, G. L. (1980). Diabetic neuropathic cachexia. *Journal of the American Medical Association, 243*, 1160–1.

Gadehold, H. & Madsen, S. T. (1963). Clinical course, complications and mortality in typhoid fever as compared with paratyphoid A. *Acta Medica Scandinavica, 197*, 753–769.

Gaind, R. (1969). Fenfluramine (Ponderax) in the treatment of obese outpatients. *British Journal of Psychiatry, 115*, 963–964.

Gallinek, A. (1954). Syndrome of episodes of hypersomnia, bulimia and abnormal mental states. *Journal of the American Medical Association, 154*, 1081–1083.

Gallinek, A. & Kalinowsky, L. B. (1958). Psychiatric aspects of multiple sclerosis. *Diseases of the Nervous System, 19*, 77–80.

Ganz, H., Gurland, B. J., Demeng, W. E. & Fisher, B. (1972). A study of the psychiatric symptoms of SLE. *Psychosomatic Medicine, 34*, 207–220.

Gatewood, J. V., Organ, C. H. & Mead, B. T. (1975). Mental changes associated with hyperparathyroidism. *American Journal of Psychiatry, 132*, 129–132.

Gelder, M. (1978). Hormones and post partum depression. *In* M. Sadler (Ed.), *Mental Illness in Pregnancy and the Puerperium*, pp. 80–99. Oxford: Oxford University Press.

Geller, I., Purdy, R. & Merritt, J. N. (1973). Alterations in the ethanol preference in the rat: The role of biogenic amines. *Annals of the New York Academy of Science, 215*, 54–59.

Gerner, R. H., Post, R. M., Spiegel, A. M. & Murphy, D. L. (1977). Effect of parathormone and lithium treatment on calcium and mood of depressed patients. *Biological Psychiatry, 12*, 145–151.

Gerner, R. H., Catlin, D. H., Gorelick, D. A. *et al.* (1980). β-endorphin. *Archives of General Psychiatry, 37*, 642–647.

Gibson, A. C. (1961). Psychoses occurring in the senium. *Journal of Mental Science, 107*, 921–925.

Gibson, I. & Myers, A. R. (1976). Nervous system involvement in SLE. *Annals of the Rheumatic Diseases, 35*, 398–406.

Gibson, I. & O'Hare, M. O. (1968). Prescription of drugs for old people at home. *Gerontologia Clinica, 10*, 271–280.

Gifford, S. & Gunderson, J. G. (1970). Cushing's disease as a psychosomatic disorder. *Medicine, 49*, 397–409.

Gifford, S., Murawski, B. J., Klein, N. S. & Sachar, E. J. (1976–77). An unusual adverse reaction to self-medication with prednisone. *International Journal of Psychiatry and Medicine, 7,* 97–122.

Girgis, M. (1971). The orbital surface of the frontal lobe of the brain and mental disorder. *Acta Psychiatrica Scandinavica,* Suppl. 221.

Girgis, M. (1977). The biological basis of emotion. *In* J. Sydney-Smith & L. G. Kiloh (Eds), *Psychosurgery and Society,* pp. 11–17. Oxford: Pergamon.

Girgis, M. (1979). Cholinergic factors in the limbic system. *In* L. G. Kiloh (Ed.), *Biological Psychiatry,* pp. 41–49. Sydney: Geigy Psychiatric Symposium.

Glaser, G. H. & Pincus, J. H. (1969). Limbic encephalitis. *Journal of Nervous and Mental Disease, 149,* 59–67.

Glatt, M. N. (1974). *A Guide to Addiction and Its Treatment.* Lancaster: Medical and Technical Publishing Co.

Gold, P. W., Extein, I., Pickar, D. *et al.* (1980). Suppression of plasma cortisol in depressed patients by acute intravenous methadone infusion. *American Journal of Psychiatry, 137,* 862–863.

Goldberg, A. (1959). Acute intermittent porphyria. *Quarterly Journal of Medicine, 28,* 183–209.

Goldfarb, C., Driesen, J. & Cole, B. (1967). Psychopathologic aspects of malignancy. *American Journal of Psychiatry, 123,* 1545–1552.

Golding, D. (1970). Unusual effect of fenfluramine. *British Medical Journal, 1,* 238.

Goldman, A. L. & Braman, S. S. (1972). Isoniazid: A review with emphasis on adverse effects. *Chest, 62,* 71–77.

Goldney, R. D. & Temme, P. B. (1980). Manic-depressive psychosis following infectious mononucleosis. *Journal of Clinical Psychiatry, 41,* 322–323.

Gonzalez, J. P., Lee, R. L., Sewell, R. D. E. & Spencer, E. S. J. (1980). Antidepressants and pain: A review of some human and animal studies. *Royal Society of Medicine International Congress and Symposium Series, 25,* 59–69.

Goodstein, R. H. & Ferrell, R. B. (1977). Multiple sclerosis presenting as a depressive illness. *Diseases of the Nervous System, 38,* 127–131.

Goodwin, F. K. (1972). Behavioural effects of L-dopa in man. *In* R. I. Shader (Ed.), *Psychiatric Complications of Medical Drugs,* pp. 149–174. New York: Raven Press.

Goodwin, F. K. & Bunney, W. F. (1971). Depression following reserpine: A reconsideration. *Seminars in Psychiatry, 3,* 435–448.

Gordan, G. S. (1974). Hyper- and hypocalcaemia: Pathogenesis and treatment. *Annals of New York Academy of Science, 230,* 181–186.

Gottfries, C. G. (1980). Human brain levels of monoamines and their metabolites: Post mortem investigations. *Acta Psychiatrica Scandinavica,* Suppl. 280, 49–61.

Gottfries, C. G. & Gottfries, I. (1974). Antinuclear factor in relation to age, sex, mental disease and treatment with phenothiazines. *Acta Psychiatrica Scandinavica,* Suppl. 255, 193–201.

Gottfries, C. G., Adolfsson, R., Oreland, L. *et al.* (1979). Monoamines and their metabolites and monoamine oxidase activity related to age and to some dementia disorders. *In* J. Crooks & I. H. Stevenson (Eds), *Drugs and the Elderly.* pp. 189–198. London: McMillan Press.

Gould, J. (1957). Virus diseases and psychiatric ill health. *British Journal of Clinical Practice, 11,* 918–924.

Grad de Alarcón, J. (1971). Social causes and social consequences of mental illness in old age. *In* D. W. K. Kay & A. Walk (Eds), *Recent Developments in Psychogeriatrics,* pp. 75–86. Ashford, Hedley Brothers Ltd.

Grant, E. C. & Pryse-Davies, J. (1968). Effects of contraceptives on depressive mood change and on endometrial MAO and phosphatases. *British Medical Journal, 3,* 777–780.

Grant, I., Adams, K. M., Carlin, A. S. *et al.* (1978). Organic impairment in polydrug users: Risk factors. *American Journal of Psychiatry, 135,* 178–184.

Granville-Grossman, K. G. (1971). *Recent Advances in Clinical Psychiatry*, pp. 202–204. London: Churchill.

Grauer, H. (1977). Depression in the aged: Theoretical concepts. *Journal of the American Geriatric Society*, *25*, 447–449.

Green, A. R. & Costain, D. W. (1979). The biochemistry of depression. *In* E. S. Paykel & A. Coppen (Eds), *Psychopharmacology of Affective Disorders*, pp. 14–40. Oxford: Oxford University Press.

Greenfield, J. G. & Bosanquet, F. D. (1953). Brain-stem lesions in Parkinsonism. *Journal of Neurology, Neurosurgery and Psychiatry*, *16*, 213–226.

Greenfield, N. S., Roessler, R. & Crosby, A. P. (1959). Ego strength and length of recovery from infectious mononucleosis. *Journal of Nervous and Mental Disease*, *129*, 125–128.

Griesinger, W. (1867). *Mental Pathology and Therapeutics*. Translated by C. L. Robertson & C. L. Rutherford. London: New Sydenham Society.

Grigor, R., Edwards, J., Lewkonia, R. *et al.* (1978), Systemic lupus erythematosus. *Annals of the Rheumatic Diseases*, *37*, 121–128.

Gringras, M. (1976). A clinical trial of tofranil in rheumatic pain in general practice. *Journal of International Medical Research*, *4*, Suppl. 2, 41–49.

Grundy, P. F. & Roberts, C. J. (1975). Observations on the epidemiology of post partum mental illness. *Psychological Medicine*, *5*, 286–290.

Guillemin, R., Vargo, T., Rossier, J. *et al.* (1977). Beta-endorphin and adrenocorticotropin are selected concomitantly by the pituitary gland. *Science*, *197*, 1367–1369.

Gunn, J. (1973). Affective and suicidal symptoms in epileptic prisoners. *Psychological Medicine*, *3*, 108–114.

Gurland, B. J. (1976). The comparative frequency of depression in various age groups. *Journal of Gerontology*, *31*, 283–292.

Guy, R. (1759). *An Essay on Schirrous Tumors and Cancer*, London: Churchill.

Guze, S. B. (1967). The occurrence of psychiatric illness in SLE. *American Journal of Psychiatry*, *123*, 1562–1570.

Hackett, T. P. & Weissman, A. D. (1960). Psychiatric management of operative syndromes. *Psychosomatic Medicine*, *32*, 267–282.

Hackett, T. P., Cassein, N. H. & Winshie, H. A. (1968). The coronary care unit: An appraisal of psychologic hazards. *New England Journal of Medicine*, *279*, 1365–1370.

Hafström, T. (1959). Toxoplasmic encephalopathy. *Acta Psychiatrica Scandinavica*, *34*, 311–321.

Haig, R. (1978). The occurrence of depressive symptoms in the influenza epidemic of Spring 1976. (Unpublished Paper).

Hall, R. C. W., Popkin, M. K., Stickney, S. R. & Gardner, E. R. (1979). Presentation of the steroid psychoses. *Journal of Nervous and Mental Disease*, *167*, 229–236.

Hall, R. W., Gardner, E. R., Stickney, S. K. *et al.* (1980). Physical illness manifesting as psychiatric disease. *Archives of General Psychiatry*, *37*, 989–995.

Halonen, P., Rimon, R., Arohonka, K. & Jäntti, V. (1974). Antibodies to herpes simplex type 1, measles and rubella viruses in psychiatric patients. *British Journal of Psychiatry*, *125*, 461–465.

Hambert, G. & Willen, P. (1978). Emotional disturbances and temporal lobe injury. *Comprehensive Psychiatry*, *19*, 441–447.

Hamilton, C. R., Shelley, W. M. & Tumulty, P. A. (1971). Giant-cell arteritis: Including temporal arteritis and polymyalgia rheumatica. *Medicine*, *50*, 1–27.

Hancock, J. C. & Bevilacqua, A. R. (1971). Temporal lobe dysrhythmia and impulsive or suicidal behaviour. *Southern Medical Journal*, *64*, 1189–1193.

Handley, S. L., Dunn, T. L., Baker, A. M. *et al.* (1977). Mood changes in puerperium and plasma tryptophan and cortisol concentrations. *British Medical Journal*, *2*, 18–20.

Harding, T. (1971). Fenfluramine dependence. *British Medical Journal, 3,* 305.

Harding, T. (1972). Depression following fenfluramine withdrawal. *British Journal of Psychiatry, 121,* 338–339.

Harris, D. & Richards, D. A. (1978). Beta-blockers in the treatment of hypertension. *British Medical Journal, 2,* 894.

Harris, H. J. (1950). *Brucellosis.* New York: Paul B. Hoeber.

Hart, R. J. & McCurdy, P. R. (1971). Psychosis in Vitamin B12 deficiency. *Archives of Internal Medicine, 128,* 596–597.

Hawkins, T. D. & Martin, L. (1965). Incidence of hyperostosis frontalis interna in patients at a general hospital and at a mental hospital. *Journal of Neurology, Neurosurgery and Psychiatry, 28,* 171–174.

Hawton, K., Fagg, J. & Marsack, D. (1980). Association between epilepsy and attempted suicide. *Journal of Neurology, Neurosurgery and Psychiatry, 43,* 168–170.

Hays, P. (1980). Relationships between premorbid personalities and unipolar depression. *Canadian Journal of Psychiatry, 25,* 314–318.

Hays, P., Krikler, B., Walsh, L. S. & Woolfson, G. (1966). Psychological changes following treatment of parkinsonism. *American Journal of Psychiatry, 123,* 657–663.

Heath, R. G., Franklin, D. E. & Shraberg, D. (1979). Gross pathology of the cerebellum in patients diagnosed and treated as functional psychiatric disorders. *Journal of Nervous and Mental Disease, 167,* 585–592.

Hécaen, H. & Ajuriaguerra, J. de (1956). Troubles mentaux au cours des tumeurs intracraniennes. Paris: quoted Lishman, W. A. (1978). ibid.

Hegarty, A. E. (1955). Post puerperal recurrent depression. *British Medical Journal, 1,* 637–640.

Heine, B. (1971). Psychosomatic aspects of hypertension. *Postgraduate Medical Journal, 47,* 541–548.

Heine, B., Sainsbury, P. & Chynoweth, R. C. (1969). Hypertension and emotional disturbances. *Journal of Psychiatric Research, 7,* 119–130.

Heine, B. E. (1969). Psychiatric aspects of SLE. *Acta Psychiatrica Scandinavica, 45,* 307–326.

Helmchen, H. & Hippius, H. (1967). Depressive syndrome im Verlauf neuroleptische Therapie. *Die Nervenarzt, 38,* 455–458.

Helmy, B. (1970). Side effects of cycloserine. *Scandinavian Journal of Respiratory Disease,* Suppl. 71, 220.

Hendler, N. & Leahy, W. (1978). Psychiatric and neurologic sequelae of infectious mononucleosis. *American Journal of Psychiatry, 131,* 842–844.

Henriksen, B. Jüül-Jensen, P. & Lund, M. (1970). The mortality of epileptics. *In* R. D. C. Brackenridge (Ed.), *Life Assurance Medicine, Proceedings of the 10th International Conference of Life Assurance Medicine.* London: Pitman.

Herridge, C. F. (1960). Physical disorders in psychiatric illness. *Lancet, 2,* 949–951.

Herzog, A. & Detre, T. (1976). Psychotic reactions associated with childbirth. *Diseases of the Nervous System, 37,* 229–235.

Hertzberg, B. M., Johnson, A. L. & Brown, S. (1970). Depressive symptoms and oral contraceptives. *British Medical Journal, 4,* 142–145.

Hertzberg, B. M., Draper, K. C., Johnson, A. L. & Nicol, G. C. (1971). Oral contraceptives, depression and libido. *British Medical Journal, 3,* 495–500.

Herman, M., Most, H. & Jolliffe, N. (1937). Psychosis associated with pernicious anaemia. *Archives of Neurology and Psychiatry, 38,* 348–361.

Heston, L. L. (1980). Dementia associated with Parkinson's disease: A genetic study. *Journal of Neurology, Neurosurgery and Psychiatry, 43,* 846–848.

Heyck, H. & Hess, R. (1954). Narkolepsiefrage, Klinik und Elektroenzephalogramm. *Fortschritte der Neurologie und Psychiatrie, 22,* 531–579.

References 187

Himmelhoch, G. A., Pincus, J., Tucker, G. & Detre, T. (1970). Subacute encephalitis: Behavioural and neurological aspects. *British Journal of Psychiatry, 116,* 531–538.

Hirsch, S. R., Gaind, R., Stevens, B. C. & Wing, J. C. (1973). Maintenance of chronic schizophrenic patients with long-acting fluphenazine: Double blind placebo trial. *British Medical Journal, 1,* 633–637.

Hodes, C. & Rogers, P. (1976). High blood pressure and psychiatric disorder in general practice. *Journal of the Royal College of General Practitioners, 26,* 178–184.

Hoehn, M. M. & Yahr, M. D. (1967). Parkinsonism: Onset, progression and mortality. *Neurology, 17,* 427–442.

Hoheisel, H. P. & Walch, R. (1952). Über manisch-depressive und verwandte Verstimmungezustände nach Hirnveletezung. *Archiv für Psychiatrie und Nervenkrankheiten, 188,* 1–25.

Holmes, J. M. (1956). Cerebral manifestations of vitamin B12 deficiency. *British Medical Journal, 2,* 1394–1398.

Hopkinson, G. & Ley, P. (1969). A genetic study of affective disorders. *British Journal of Psychiatry, 115,* 917–922.

Horenstein, S. (1970). Effects of cerebrovascular disease on personality and emotionality. *In* A. L. Benton (Ed.), *Behavioural Changes in Cerebrovascular Disease.* New York: Harper and Row.

Horn, S. (1974). Some psychological factors in parkinsonism. *Journal of Neurology, Neurosurgery and Psychiatry, 37,* 27–31.

Hornykiewicz, O. (1966). Dopamine (3–hydroxytryptamine) and brain function. *Pharmacological Reviews, 18,* 925–964.

Hornykiewicz, O. (1971). Neurochemical pathology of brain dopamine and acetylcholine: Rational basis for the current drug treatment of parkinsonism. *In: Recent Advances in Parkinson's Disease,* Vol. 8, 33–65. Philadelphia: F. A. Davis Co.

Hornykiewicz, O. (1977). Biogenic amines in the central nervous system. *In* P. J. Vinken & G. W. Bruyn (Eds), *Handbook of Clinical Neurology,* Vol. 29, pp. 459–483. Amsterdam: North Holland.

Horrobin, D. F. (1977). The role of prostaglandins and prolactin in depression, mania and schizophrenia. *Postgraduate Medical Journal, 53,* Suppl. 4, 160–165.

Hsu, L. K. G. (1980). Outcome of anorexia nervosa. *Archives of General Psychiatry, 37,* 1041–1046.

Hsu, L. K. G., Crisp, A. H. & Harding, B. (1979). Outcome of anorexia nervosa. *Lancet, 1,* 61–65.

Hua, A. A., Kalowski, S., Whitworth, J. A. & Kincaid-Smith, P. (1980). Acebutalol in mild to moderate hypertension. *Medical Journal of Australia, 1,* 226–228.

Hughes, G. R. V. (1977). *Connective Tissue Diseases,* P. 221. Oxford: Blackwell.

Hughes, J., Smith, T. W., Kosterlitz, H. N. *et al.* (1975). Identification of two pentapeptides from the brain with potent opiate agonist activity. *Nature, 258,* 577–579.

Hughues, A., Chauvergne, J., Lissiloir, J. & Lagardi, C. (1963). L'imipramine utilisée comme antalgique majeur en carcinologie: étude de 118 cas. *La Presse Médicale, 71,* 1073–74.

Hunter, R. & Matthews, D. M. (1965). Mental symptoms in B12 deficiency. *Lancet, 2,* 738.

Hunter, R., Blackwood, W., Bull, J. (1968). Three cases of frontal meningioma presenting psychiatrically. *British Medical Journal, 3,* 9–16.

Hunter, R., Barnes, J. & Matthews, D. M. (1969). Effects of folic acid supplement on serum vitamin B12 levels in patients on anticonvulsants, *Lancet, 2,* 666–667.

Huntington, G. (1972). On chorea. *Medical Surgical Reports* (Philadelphia) *26,* 317–21.

Hurst, M. W., Jenkins, C. E. & Rose, R. M. (1976). The relation of psychological stress to onset of medical illness. *Annual Review of Medicine, 27,* 301–312.

Hurwitz, L. J. (1969). Management of major strokes. *British Medical Journal, 3,* 699–702.

Hurwitz, N. (1969). Predisposing factors in adverse drug reactions, *British Medical Journal, 1,* 536–539.

Hurxthal, L. M. & O'Sullivan, S. B. (1959). Cushing's Syndrome: Clinical differential diagnosis and complications. *Annals of Internal Medicine, 51,* 1–16.

Huskisson, E. C., Woolf, D. L., Balme, H. W. *et al.* (1976). Four new anti-inflammatory drugs: response and treatment. *British Medical Journal, 1,* 1048–1049.

Imboden, J. B., Canter, A., Cluff, L. E. & Trever, R. W. (1959). Brucellosis: Psychological aspects of delayed convalescence. *Annals of Internal Medicine, 103,* 406–414.

Imboden, J. B., Canter, A. & Cluff, L. E. (1961). Convalescence from influenza. *Archives of Internal Medicine, 103,* 393–399.

Imlah, M. W. (1970). Unusual effect of fenfluramine. *British Medical Journal, 2,* 178.

Innes, J. A., Watson, M. L., Ford, M. J. *et al.* (1977). Plasma fenfluramine levels, weight loss and side effects. *British Medical Journal, 2,* 1322–1325.

Israel, I. & Mardones, J. (1971). *Biological Basis of Alcoholism.* New York: Wiley Interscience.

Jackson, C. E., Henjke, B. J. & Blumer, D. P. (1978). Medullary thyroid cancer associated with mental illness. *Proceedings of the 60th Meeting of the Endocrine Society of the U.S.A.*

Jackson, J. A., Free, G. B. M. & Pike, H. B. (1923). The psychic manifestations in paralysis agitans. *Archives of Neurology and Psychiatry, 10,* 680–684.

Jacobson, L. & Ottosson, J.-O. (1971). Initial mental disorder in carcinoma of the pancreas and stomach. *Acta Psychiatrica Scandinavica Supplement, 221,* 120–127.

Jacoby, R. J. & Levy, R. (1980). Computed tomography in the elderly (III): Affective disorders. *British Journal of Psychiatry, 136,* 270–275.

Jain, V. K. (1972). A psychiatric study of hypothyroidism. *Psychiatrica Clinica, 5,* 121–130.

James, W. E., Mefferd, R. E. & Kimbell, I. (1969). Early signs of Huntington's Chorea. *Diseases of the Nervous System, 30,* 556–559.

Jamieson, G. R. & Henry, G. W. (1933). Mental aspects of brain tumours in psychiatric patients. *Journal of Nervous and Mental Diseases, 78,* 333–353 and 500–518.

Jamieson, R. C. & Wells, C. E. (1979). Manic psychosis in a patient with multiple metastatic brain tumours. *Journal of Clinical Psychiatry, 40,* 280–283.

Janowsky, D. S., Davis, M. & Sekerke, H. J. (1972). A cholinergic-adrenergic hypothesis of mania and depression. *Lancet, 2,* 632–633.

Jeffcoate, W. J., Silverstone, J. T., Edwards, C. R. W. & Besser, G. M. (1979). Psychiatric manifestations of Cushing's Syndrome: Response to lowering of plasma cortisol. *Quarterly Journal of Medicine, 48,* 465–472.

Jefferson, J. W. (1977). The case of the numb testicles. *Journal of Clinical Psychiatry, 38,* 749–751.

Jefferson, J. W. (1979). Central nervous toxicity of cimetidine: A case of depression. *American Journal of Psychiatry, 136,* 346.

Jeffries, J. J. & Lefebvre, A. (1973). Depression and mania associated with the Kleine-Levin-Critchley Syndrome. *Canadian Psychiatric Association Journal, 18,* 439–444.

Jenkins, R. E. & Groh, R. H. (1970). Mental symptoms in patients treated with L–dopa. *Lancet, 2,* 177–180.

Jensen, I. & Larsen, J. K. (1979). Psychoses in drug-resistant temporal lobe epilepsy. *Journal of Neurology, Neurosurgery and Psychiatry, 42,* 948–954.

Jensen, J. (1959). Depression in patients treated with reserpine for arterial hypertension. *Acta Psychiatrica et Neurologica Scandinavica, 34,* 195–204.

Jimerson, D. C., Post, R. M., Carman, J. J. *et al.* (1979). CSF calcium: Clinical correlates in affective illness and schizophrenia. *Biological Psychiatry, 14,* 37–51.

Jobe, T. H. (1976). Medical theories of melancholia in the seventeenth and early eighteenth centuries. *Clio Medica, 11,* 217–231.

Johannson, F., Von Knorring, L., Sedvall, G. & Terenius, L. (1980). Changes in endorphins and

5–hydroxyindoleacetic acid in cerebrospinal fluid as a result of treatment with a serotonin re-uptake inhibitor (zimilidine) in chronic pain patients. *Psychiatry Research*, *2*, 167–172.

Johnson, D. A. W. (1973). The side effects of fluphenazine decanoate. *British Journal of Psychiatry*, *123*, 519–522.

Johnson, D. A. W. & Malik, N. A. (1975). A double blind comparison of fluphenazine decanoate in the treatment of acute schizophrenia. *Acta Psychiatrica Scandinavica*, *51*, 257–267.

Johnson, J. & Bailey, S. (1979). Cimetidine and psychiatric complications. *British Journal of Psychiatry*, *134*, 315–516.

Johnson, P., Kitchin, A. H., Lawther, C. P. & Turner, R. W. (1966). Treatment of hypertension with methyl–dopa. *British Medical Journal*, *1*, 133.

Johnson, R. T. & Richardson, E. P. (1968). The neurological manifestations of systemic lupus erythematosus: A clinical and pathological study of 24 cases and review of the literature. *Medicine*, *47*, 337–369.

Johnston, E. C. & Whalley, K. (1975). Antinuclear antibodies in psychiatric illness: Their relationship to diagnosis and drug treatment. *British Medical Journal*, *2*, 724–725.

Josephson, A. M. & Mackenzie, T. B. (1980). Thyroid-induced mania in hypothyroid patients. *British Journal of Psychiatry*, *137*, 222–228.

Joynt, R. J. (1974). The brain's uneasy peace with tumours. *Annals of New York Academy of Science*, *230*, 342–347.

Judd, L. L. & Grant, I. (1975). Brain dysfunction in chronic sedative users. *Journal of Psychedelic Drugs*, *7*, 143–149.

Kadramas, A., Winokur, G. & Crowe, R. (1979). Post partum mania. *British Journal of Psychiatry*, *135*, 551–554.

Kahana, E., Lebowitz, W. & Alter, M. (1971). Cerebral multiple sclerosis. *Neurology* (Mineapolis), *21*, 1179–1185.

Kaij, L. & Nilsson, Å. (1972). Emotional and Psychiatric Illness following childbirth. *In* J. G. Howells (Ed.), *Modern Perspectives in Psycho-Obstetrics*, pp. 364–384. New York: Brunner Mazel.

Kanakaratnam, G. & Direkze, M. (1976). Aspects of primary tumours of the frontal lobe. *British Journal of Clinical Practice*, *30*, 220–221.

Kane, F. J. (1970). Carbon disulphide intoxication from overdose of disulfiram. *American Journal of Psychiatry*, *127*, 690–694.

Kane, F. J., Treadway, R. & Ewing, J. A. (1969). Emotional changes associated with oral contraceptives in female psychiatric patients. *Comprehensive Psychiatry*, *10*, 16–30.

Kanof, P. P. & Greengard, P. (1978). Brain histamine receptors as targets for antidepressant drugs. *Nature*, *272*, 329–33.

Karpati, G. & Frame, B. (1964). Neuropsychiatric disorder in primary hyperparathryoidism. *Archives of Neurology*, *10*, 387–392.

Kavanagh, T., Shepherd, R. J. & Tuck, J. A. (1975). Depression after myocardial infarct. *Canadian Medical Association Journal*, *113*, 23–27.

Kavanagh, T., Shepherd, R. J., Tuck, J. A. & Qureshi, S. (1977). Depression following myocardial infarct: The effects of distance running. *Annals of the New York Academy of Science*, *301*, 1029–1038.

Kay, D. W. K. (1959). Observations on the natural history and genetics of old age psychoses: A Stockholm material 1931–1937. *Proceedings of the Royal Society of Medicine*, *52*, 79.

Kay, D. W. K. (1962). Outcome and cause of death in mental disorders in old age: A long-term follow-up of functional and organic psychoses. *Acta Psychiatrica Scandinavica*, *35*, 249–276.

Kay, D. W. K. (1976). The depressions and neuroses of later life. *In* K. Granville-Grossman (Ed.), *Recent Advances in Clinical Psychiatry*, Vol. 2, pp. 52–80. Edinburgh: Churchill Livingstone.

Kay, D. W. K., Roth, M. & Hopkins, B. (1955). Affective disorders arising in the senium I: Their association with organic cerebral degeneration. *Journal of Mental Science, 101*, 302–316.

Kay, D. W. K., Kerr, T. A. & Lassman, L. P. (1971). Brain trauma and the post-concussional syndrome. *Lancet, 2*, 1052–1055.

Kearney, T. R. (1964). Parkinson's disease presenting as a depressive illness. *Journal of the Irish Medical Association, 54*, 117–119.

Keiler, M. H., Taylor, I. & Miller, W. C. (1978). Are all recently detoxified alcoholics depressed? *American Journal of Psychiatry, 136*, 586–588.

Kellett, R. J. & Hamilton, M. (1970). The treatment of benign hypertension with clonidine. *Scottish Medical Journal, 15*, 137–142.

Kelly, D. (1973). Psychosurgery and the limbic system. *Postgraduate Medical Journal, 49*, 825–833.

Kemp, A., Lion, J. R. & Magrum, G. (1977). Lithium and the treatment of a manic patient with multiple sclerosis. *Diseases of the Nervous System, 38*, 210–211.

Kemph, J. P. (1966). Renal failure, artificial kidney and kidney transplant. *American Journal of Psychiatry, 122*, 1270–1274.

Kendell, R. E. (1967). The psychiatric sequelae of benign myalgic encephalomyelitis. *British Journal of Psychiatry, 113*, 833–840.

Kendell, R. E. (1976). The classification of depression: A review of contemporary confusion. *British Journal of Psychiatry, 129*, 15–28.

Kendell, R. E., Wainwright, S., Hailey, A. & Shannon, B. (1976). The influence of childbirth on psychiatric morbidity. *Psychological Medicine, 6*, 297–302.

Kerr, T. A., Schapira, K. & Roth, M. (1969). The relationship between premature death and affective disorders. *British Journal of Psychiatry, 115*, 1277–1282.

Keschner, M., Bender, M. V. & Strauss, I. (1936). Mental symptoms in cases of tumours of the temporal lobe. *Archives of Neurology and Psychiatry, 35*, 572–596.

Keschner, M., Bender, M. B. & Strauss, I. (1938). Mental symptoms associated with brain tumours. *Journal of the American Medical Association, 110*, 714–718.

Keynes, G. (1967). John Woodall, Surgeon: His place in medical history. *Journal of the Royal College of Physicians of London, 2*, 15–33.

Khosla, S. N., Srivastava, S. C. & Gupta, S. (1977). Neuropsychiatric manifestations of typhoid. *Journal of Tropical Medicine and Hygiene, 80*, 95–98.

Kielholz, P. (1959). *Diagnosis and Therapy of the Depressive States.* Basel: J. R. Geigy.

Kielholz, P. (1972). Diagnostic aspects in the treatment of depression. *In* P. Kielholz (Ed.), *Depressive Illness: Diagnosis, Assessment and Treatment.* Bern: Hans Huber.

Kiloh, L. G. (1961). Psuedodementia. *Acta Psychiatrica Scandinavica, 37*, 336–351.

Kiloh, L. G. (1980). Psychiatric disorders and the limbic system. *In* M. Girgis & L. G. Kiloh (Eds), *Limbic Epilepsy and the Discontrol Syndrome*, pp. 231–237. Amsterdam: Elsevier.

Kimball, C. P. (1969). Psychological response to the experience of open heart surgery. *American Journal of Psychiatry, 126*, 96–107.

Kimball, C. P. (1972). The experience of open heart surgery. *Archives of General Psychiatry, 27*, 57–63.

King, R. B. (1980). Pain and tryptophan. *Journal of Neurosurgery, 53*, 44–52.

Kingston, D. (1979). Tetrabenazine for involuntary movement disorders, *Medical Journal of Australia, 1*, 628–629.

Kinsman, R. A. & Hood, J. (1971). Some behavioural effects of ascorbic acid deficiency. *American Journal of Clinical Nutrition, 24*, 455–464.

Kissen, D. M. (1963). Personality characteristics in males conducive to lung cancer. *British Journal of Medical Psychology, 36*, 27–36.

Klaber, M. & Lacey, J. (1968). Epidemic of glandular fever. *British Medical Journal, 3*, 124.

Klee, A. (1968). *A Clinical Study of Migraine with Particular Reference to the most Severe Cases.* Copenhagen: Munksgaard.

Klee, J. G., Lauristen, B. & Oelsen, J. (1979). Parkinsonisime og depression behandlet med elektrostimulation (NCE). *Ugeskr Laeger, 141,* 2393–94. (English abstract).

Klein, D. F. (1976). Differential diagnosis and treatment of the dysphorias. *In* D. M. Gallant & G. M. Simpson (Eds), *Depression: Behavioural Biochemical Characteristics and Treatment Concepts,* 127–154. New York: Spectrum Publication Inc.

Kleinschmidt, H. K., Waxenberg, S. E. & Cucker, R. (1956). Psychophysiology and psychiatric management of thyrotoxicosis: A two-year follow-up study. *Journal of Mount Sinai Hospital, New York, 23,* 131–153.

Klerman, G. L. (1975). Overview of depression. *In* A. M. Freedman, H. I. Kaplan & B. J. Sadock (Eds), *Comprehensive Textbook of Psychiatry,* Vol. 1, 2nd edn. Baltimore: Williams & Wilkins.

Klerman, G. L. Schildkraut, J. J., Hasenbush, L. L. *et al.* (1963) Clinical experience with dihydroxyphenylalanine (dopa) in depression. *Journal of Psychiatric Research, 1,* 289–297.

Kline, N. S., Li, C. H., Lehmann, H. E. *et al.* (1977). Beta-endorphin induced changes in schizophrenia and depressed patients. *Archives of General Psychiatry, 34,* 1111–13.

Knight, A., Okasha, N. S., Salik, M. A. & Hirsch, S. R. (1979). Depressive and extrapyramidal symptoms and clinical effect: A trial of fluphenazine and flupenthixol in maintenance of schizophrenic outpatients. *British Journal of Psychiatry, 135,* 515–523.

Kocher, R. (1976). The use of psychotropic drugs in the treatment of chronic severe pain. *European Neurology, 14,* 458–64.

Kocher, R. (1978). Die Behandlung chronischer Schmerzen mit Psychopharmaka. *Schweitzer Medicinische Wochenschrift, 108,* 686-690.

Kolodny, A. (1928). The symptomatology of tumours of the temporal lobe. *Brain, 51,* 385–417.

Koranyi, E. K. (1979). Morbidity and rate of undiagnosed physical illness in a psychiatric clinic population. *Archives of General Psychiatry, 36,* 414–419.

Korsgaard, S. (1976). Baclofen (Lioresal) in the treatment of neuroleptic-induced tardive dyskinesia. *Acta Psychiatrica Scandinavica, 54,* 17–24.

Kosterlitz, H. W. (1979). Multiple receptors for opiates and opiate peptides in current studies on beta-endorphins and enkephalins. *In* R. Guillemin (Ed.), *Brain Peptides: a New Endocrinology,* pp. 373–383. Amsterdam: Elsevier.

Kraepelin, E. (1921). Manic-Depressive Insanity and Paranoia (Translated by R. M. Barclay). Edinburgh: Livingstone.

Krauthamer, C. & Klerman G. L. (1978). Secondary mania: Manic syndromes associated with antecedent physical illness or drugs. *Archives of General Psychiatry, 35,* 1333–1339.

Kretschmer, H. (1974). Callosal tumours. *In* P. J. Vinken & G. W. Bruyn (Eds), *Handbook of Clinical Biology,* Vol. 17, pp. 490–554. Amsterdam: North Holland.

Krieger, D. T. (1973). Neurotransmitter regulation of ACTH release. *Mt. Sinai Journal of Medicine, 40,* 302–314.

Krishnaswamy, K. & Ramanamurthy, E. S. U. (1970). Mental changes and platelet serotonin in pellagrins. *Clinica Chemica Acta, 27,* 301–304.

Kurtzke, J. F. (1970). Clinical manifestations of multiple sclerosis. *In* P. J. Vinken & G. W. Bruyn (Eds), *Handbook of Clinical Neurology,* Vol. 9, pp. 161–216. Amsterdam: North Holland.

Kutner, S. J. & Brown, W. L. (1972). Depression and contraception: Types of oral contraceptives, depression and menstrual symptoms. *Journal of Nervous and Mental Disease, 155,* 153-162.

Labhardt, F. & Müller, W. (1976). Psychosomatische Aspekte rheumatischer, in besondere, weichteilrheumatische Erkrankungen. *Schweitzer Medizinische Wochenschrift, 106,* 1912–1917.

Ladee, G. A., Scholten, J. M. & Meyer, F. E. P. (1966). Diagnostic problems with regard to acquired toxoplasmosis. *Psychiatria Neurologia Neurochirurgia, 69*, 65–82.

Lambo, T. A. (1966). Neuropsychiatric syndromes associated with human trypanosomiasis in tropical Africa. *Acta Psychiatrica Scandinavica, 42*, 474–484.

Lance, J. W., de Gail, P. & Preswick, G. (1965). Short-term controlled trial of tranylcypromine in multiple sclerosis. *Medical Journal of Australia, 1*, 410–413.

Lancet, Editorial (1976). Folic acid and the nervous system. *Lancet, 2*, 836.

Lawton, P. & Phillips, R. W. (1955). Psychopathological accompaniments of chronic relapsing pancreatitis. *Journal of Nervous and Mental Disease, 122*, 248–253.

Layland, W. R., Lishman, W. D., Matthews, M. L. & Smith, A. J. (1962). Methosperidine (Decasperyl) and depression. *British Medical Journal, 1*, 639.

Learoyd, E. M. (1972). Psychotropic drugs in the elderly patient. *Medical Journal of Australia, 1*, 1131–1133.

Lebensohn, Z. M. & Jenkins, R. M. (1975). Improvement of parkinsonism in depressed patients treated with ECT. *American Journal of Psychiatry, 132*, 283–285.

Lebowitz, S. & Gorman, W. F. (1952). Neuropsychiatric complications of viral hepatitis. *New England Journal of Medicine, 246*, 932–937.

Lee, J. (1970). Anaemia and psychomotor function. *British Medical Journal, 3*, 711.

Lee, R. & Spencer, P. S. J. (1977). Antidepressants and pain: A review of the pharmacological data supporting the use of certain tricyclics in chronic pain. *Journal of International Medical Research, 5*, Suppl. 1, 146–156.

Lee, R., Sewell, R. D. E. & Spencer, P. S. J. (1979). Antinocioceptive activity of d-ala^2-D-leu^5 enkephalin (BW180C) in the rat after modification to central 5–hydroxytryptamine functions. *Neuropharmacology, 18*, 711–714.

Leeton, J. (1974). Depression induced by oral contraceptives: The role of vitamin B6 in its management. *Australian and New Zealand Journal of Psychiatry, 8*, 85–88.

Le Shan, L. & Worthington, R. E. (1956). Some recurrent life history patterns observed in patients with malignant disease. *Journal of Nervous and Mental Disease, 124*, 460–465.

Lesser, R. P. & Fahn, S. (1978). Dystonia: A disorder often misdiagnosed as a conversion reaction. *American Journal of Psychiatry, 135*, 349–352.

Leston, J. M., Rey, J. C., Gonzalez-Montaner, L. J. *et al.* (1970). Psychosomatic reactions to cycloserin in the treatment of tuberculosis. *Scandinavian Journal of Respiratory Disease*, Supplement 71.

Levin, A. (1975). Non-medical use of fenfluramine by drug-dependent South Africans. *Postgraduate Medical Journal, 51*, Supplement 1, 186–188.

Levy, M. B. (1976). Coping with maintenance dialysis: Psychological considerations in the care of patients. *In* S. G. Massey & A. L. Sellers (Eds), *Clinical Aspects of Uraemia and Dialysis*, pp. 53–68. Springfield, Ill.: C. C. Thomas.

Lewin, W., Marshall, T. F. de C. & Roberts, A. H. (1979). Long-term outcome after severe head injury. *British Medical Journal, 2*, 1533–38.

Lewis, A. & Hoghughi, M. (1969). An evaluation of depression as a side effect of oral contraceptives. *British Journal of Psychiatry, 115*, 697–701.

Lewis, A. J. (1934). Melancholia: A clinical survey of depressive states. *Journal of Mental Science, 80*, 277–278.

Lewis, A. J. & Fleminger, J. J. (1954). The psychiatric risk from corticotrophin and cortisone. *Lancet, 1*, 383–386.

Lewis, W. H. (1971). Iatrogenic psychiatric depressive reactions in hypertensive patients. *American Journal of Psychiatry, 127*, 1416–1417.

Libow, L. S. & Durrell, J. (1965). Clinical studies in the relationship between psychosis and the regulation of thyroid activity II, *Psychosomatic Medicine, 27*, 377–382.

Liddon, S. C. & Satran, R. (1967). Disulfiram (Antabuse) psychosis, *American Journal of Psychiatry, 123*, 1284–1289.

Lindemann, E. (1941). Observations on psychiatric sequelae to surgical operations in women. *American Journal of Psychiatry*, *98*, 132–137.

Lindström, L. H., Widerlöv, E., Wahlström, A. & Terenius, L. (1978). Endorphins in human cerebrospinal fluid. *Acta Psychiatrica Scandinavica*, *57*, 153–164.

Lipton, M. A. (1976). Age differentiation in depression: Biochemical aspects. *Journal of Gerontology*, *31*, 293–299.

Lishman, W. A. (1968). Brain damage in relation to psychiatric disability after head injury. *British Journal of Psychiatry*, *114*, 373–410.

Lishman, W. A. (1973). Psychiatric sequelae of head injury: A review. *Psychological Medicine*, *3*, 304–318.

Lishman, W. A. (1978). *Organic Psychiatry*. Oxford: Blackwell.

Liston, E. H. (1977). Occult presenile dementia. *Journal of Nervous and Mental Disease*, *164*, 263–267.

Liston, E. H. (1978). Diagnostic delay in presenile dementia. *Journal of Clinical Psychiatry*, *39*, 599–603.

Liston, E. H. (1979a). Clinical findings in presenile dementia: A report of 50 cases. *Journal of Nervous and Mental Disease*, *167*, 337–342.

Liston, E. H. (1979b). The clinical phenomenology of presenile dementia: A critical review of the literature. *Journal of Nervous and Mental Disease*, *167*, 329–336.

Lloyd, G. G. (1977). Psychological reactions to physical illness. *British Journal of Hospital Medicine*, *18*, 352–358.

Lloyd, K. J. (1978). The biochemical pharmacology of the limbic system: Neuroleptic drugs. *In* K. E. Livingstone & O. Hornykiewicz (Eds), *Limbic Mechanisms*, pp. 263–305. New York: Plenum.

Lloyd, K. J., Farley, I. J., Deck, J. H. N. & Hornykiewicz, O. (1974) Serotonin and 5-hydroxyindoleacetic acid in discrete areas of the brain stem of suicide victims and control patients. *Advances in Biochemical Psychopharmacology*, *11*, 387–397.

Logothetis, J. (1963). Psychotic behaviour as the initial indicator of adult myxoedema. *Journal of Nervous and Mental Disease*, *136*, 561–568.

Logue, V., Durward, M., Pratt, R. T. C. *et al.* (1968). Quality of survival after rupture of anterior cerebral aneurysm. *British Journal of Psychiatry*, *114*, 137–160.

Louria, D. V. (1972). Medical complications of illicit drug use. *In* C. J. Zarafonetis (Ed.), *Proceedings of International Conference on Drug Abuse*, pp. 585–596. Philadelphia: Lea & Febiger.

Lowry, M. R. (1979). Frequency of depressive disorder in patients entering home dialysis. *Journal of Nervous and Mental Disease*, *167*, 199–204.

Lowry, M. R. & Atcherson, E. (1979). Characteristics of depressive disorder on entry into home dialysis. *Journal of Nervous and Mental Disease*, *167*, 748–751.

Lowry, M. R. & Atcherson, E. (1980). A short-term follow-up of patients with depressive disorder on entry into home dialysis training. *Journal of Affective Disorders*, *2*, 219–227.

Lowy, F. (1965). The neuropsychiatric complications of viral hepatitis. *Canadian Medical Association Journal*, *92*, 237–239.

Lurati, M., Bottenberg, E. H., Lützen, K., Archen, J. & Schoefer, M. (1976). Multiple Sklerose und Gesundlichkeits Aspekte. *Archive Psychiatrie und Nervenkrankheiten*, *221*, 303–311.

Lycke, E. & Roos, B.-E. (1968). Effects on the monoamine metabolism of the mouse brain by experimental herpes simplex infection. *Experimentia*, *24*, 687–689.

Lycke, E. & Roos, B.-E. (1972). Monoamine metabolism in viral encephalitides of the mouse II: Turnover of monoamines in mice infected with herpes simplex virus. *Brain Research*, *44*, 602–613.

Lycke, E., Modigh, K. & Roos, B.-E. (1970). Monoamine metabolism in viral encephalitides of the mouse I: Virological and biochemical results. *Brain Research*, *23*, 235–246.

Lycke, E., Norrby, R. & Roos, B.-E. (1974). A serological study on mentally ill patients: With particular reference to the prevalence of herpes virus infection. *British Journal of Psychiatry, 124,* 273–279.

Lying-Tunell, W. (1979). Psychiatric symptoms in normal pressure hydrocephalus. *Acta Psychiatrica Scandinavica, 59,* 415–419.

Maas, J. W. (1972). Adrenocortical steroid hormones, the electrolytes and the disposition of the catecholamines, with particular reference to depressive states. *Journal of Psychiatric Research, 9,* 227–241.

MacDonald Scott, W. A. (1969). The relief of pain with an antidepressant in arthritis. *Practitioner, 202,* 802–807.

Mackay, A. (1979). Self-poisoning: A complication of epilepsy. *British Journal of Psychiatry, 134,* 277–282.

MacLean, P. D. (1955). Limbic system ("visceral brain") and emotional behaviour. *Archives of Neurology and Psychiatry, 73,* 130–134.

Madsen, J. A. (1974). Depressive illness and oral contraceptives: A study of urinary 5–hydroxyindoleacetic acid excretion. *Advances in Biochemical Psychopharmacology, 11,* 249–253.

Maguire, G. P. & Granville-Grossman, K. L. (1968). Physical illness in psychiatric patients. *British Journal of Psychiatry, 114,* 1365–1369.

Maguire, P. (1976). The psychological and social sequelae of mastectomy. *In* J. G. Howells (Ed.), *Modern Perspectives in the Psychiatric Aspects of Surgery,* pp. 390–421. New York: Brunner Mazel.

Maguire, P. (1978). Psychiatric problems after mastectomy. *In* E. C. Brand & P. A. Van Kemp (Eds), *Breast Cancer,* pp. 47–53. Lancaster: MTP Press.

Maguire, P., Lee, F. G., Bevington, D. J. *et al.* (1978). Psychiatric problems in the first year after mastectomy. *British Medical Journal, 1,* 963–965.

Maguire, P., Tait, A., Brooke, M. *et al.* (1980). Effect of counselling on the psychiatric morbidity associated with mastectomy. *British Medical Journal, 2,* 1454–1456.

Mäkelä, A., Lang, H., Sillanpää, M. (1979). Neurologic manifestations of rheumatoid arthritis. *In* P. J. Vinken & G. W. Bruyn (Eds), *Handbook of Clinical Neurology,* Vol. 38, pp. 479–503. Amsterdam: North Holland.

Malamud, N. (1967). Psychiatric disorder with intracranial tumours of the limbic system. *Archives of Neurology, 17,* 113–23.

Malek-Ahmadi, P. & Behrman, P. J. (1976). Depressive syndrome induced by oral contraceptives. *Diseases of the Nervous System, 37,* 406–408.

Malinow, A. C. & Lion, J. R. (1979). Hyperaldosteronism (Conn's Disease) presenting as depression. *Journal of Clinical Psychiatry, 40,* 358–359.

Maneros, A. & Philipp, M. (1978). Zyklothymie und Hirnstamm. *Psychiatria Clinica, 11,* 132–138.

Mann, A. H. (1977). Psychiatric morbidity and hostility in hypertension. *Pscyhological Medicine, 7,* 653–659.

Mann, J. J. & Chiu, E. (1978). Platelet monoamineoxidase in Huntington's Chorea. *Journal of Neurology, Neurosurgery and Psychiatry, 41,* 809–812.

Mapother, E. (1926). Manic-depressive psychosis (discussion). *British Medical Journal, 2,* 872–879.

Mark, V. H. & Ervin, F. R. (1970). *Violence and the Brain.* New York: Harper & Row.

Markovitz, M. (1954). Acute intermittent porphyria: A report of five cases and review of the literature. *Annals of Internal Medicine, 41,* 1170–1188.

Marsden, C. D. & Harrison, M. J. G. (1972). Outcome of investigation of patients with presenile dementia. *British Medical Journal, 2,* 249–252.

Marsh, C. G. & Markham, C. H. (1973). Does levodopa alter depression and psychopathology in Parkinson's disease? *Journal of Neurology, Neurosurgery and Psychiatry, 36,* 925–935.

Marshall, J. (1972). A survey of occlusive disease of the vertebro-basilar arterial system. *In* P. J. Vinken & G. W. Bruyn (Eds), *Handbook of Clinical Psychiatry*, Vol. 12, pp. 447–455. Amsterdam: North Holland.

Martini, G. A. & Strohmeyer, G. (1974). Posthepatic syndromes. *Clinics in Gastroenterology, 3*, 377–390.

Massey, E. W. & Riley, T. L. (1980). Tricyclic antidepressants for peripheral neuropathy. *Journal of the American Medical Association, 243*, 1133.

Masson, J. M., Rigallecin, J., Renoux, G. *et al.* (1976). Incidence de la brucellose. *Psychiatrie Annales Medico-Psychologique* (Paris), *134F*, 804–814.

Matarazzo, E. V. (1976). Permanent depression and temporal lobe epilepsy. *Arquivos de neuropsiquitria* (Sao Paulo), *34*, 172–187.

Matthews, W. B. (1962). Epilepsy and disseminated sclerosis. *Quarterly Journal of Medicine, 31*, 141–155.

Matthews, W. B. (1979). Multiple sclerosis with acute remitting psychotic symptoms. *Journal of Neurology, Neurosurgery and Psychiatry, 42*, 859-863.

Mattingly, D. (1968). Disorders of the adrenal cortex and pituitary gland: *In* D. N. Dawson, N. Compston & A. M. Dawson (Eds), *Recent Advances in Medicine*, 15th edn. London: Churchill.

Mattson, B. (1974). Addison's disease and psychosis. *Acta Psychiatrica Scandinavica*, Supplement 255, pp. 203–210.

Matussek, N., Ackenheil, M., Hippius, H. *et al.* (1980). Effect of clonidine on growth hormone release in psychiatric patients and controls. *Psychiatric Research, 2*, 25–36.

Maudsley (1874). *Responsibility in Mental Disease*. London: Henry S. King & Co.

May, P. R. A. & Van Putten, P. (1978). Akinetic depression in schizophrenia. *Archives of General Psychiatry, 35*, 1101–1107.

Mayer-Gross, W., Slater, E. & Roth, M. (1969). *Clinical Psychiatry,* 3rd edn. London: Ballière Tindall.

McAlpine, D., Compston, N. D. & Lumsden, C. E. (1955). *Multiple Sclerosis*. Edinburgh: E. & S. Livingstone.

McAlpine, D., Lumsden, C. E. & Acheson, E. D. (1965). *Multiple Sclerosis: A Reappraisal*. Edinburgh: Livingstone.

McCabe, M. S. & Corry, R. J. (1978). Psychiatric illness and human renal transplantation. *Journal of Clinical Psychiatry, 39*, 393–400.

McClellan, D. L., Chalmers, R. J. & Johnson, A. H. (1974). A double-blind trial of tetrabenazine, thiopropazate and placebo in patients with chorea. *Lancet, 1*, 104–107.

McCreadie, R. G., Dingwall, J. M., Wiles, D. H. & Heykarts, J. J. D. (1980). Intermittent pimozide versus fluphenazine decanoate as maintenance therapy in chronic schizophrenia. *British Journal of Psychiatry, 137*, 510–517.

McEvedy, C. P. & Beard, A. W. (1970). The Royal Free epidemic of 1955: A reconsideration. *British Medical Journal, 1*, 7–11.

McEvedy, C. P. & Beard, A. W. (1973). A controlled follow-up of cases involved in an epidemic of benign myalgic encephalomyelitis. *British Journal of Psychiatry, 122*, 141–150.

McFie, J. (1960). Psychological effects of stereotactic operations for the relief of Parkinsonian symptoms. *Journal of Mental Science, 106*, 1512–1517.

McGlashan, T. H. & Carpenter, W. T. (1976a). An investigation of the post-psychotic depressive syndrome. *American Journal of Psychiatry, 113*, 14–19.

McGlashan, T. H. & Carpenter, W. T. (1976b). Post-psychotic depression in schizophrenia. *Archives of General Psychiatry, 33*, 231–239.

McHugh, P. R. & Folstein, M. F. (1975). Psychiatric syndromes of Huntington's Chorea. *In* F. Benson & D. Blumer (Eds), *Psychiatric Aspects of Neurologic Disease*, pp. 267–285. New York: Grune & Stratton.

McKenzie, K. R., Martin, M. J. & Howard, F. M. (1969). Myasthenia gravis: Psychiatric concomitants. *Canadian Medical Association Journal, 100*, 988–991.

McLellan, D. L. (1972). The suppression of involuntary movements with tetrabenazine. *Scottish Medical Journal, 17*, 367–370.

McLellan, D. L., Chalmers, R. J. & Johnson, A. H. (1974). A double blind trial of tetrabenazine, thiopropazate and placebo in patients with chorea. *Lancet, 1*, 104–107.

McLelland, H. A. (1973). Psychiatric complications of drug therapy. *Adverse Drug Reactions Bulletin, 40*, 128–131.

McNeill, A. Grennan, D. M., Ward, W. C. & Dick, W. C. (1976). Psychiatric problems in systemic lupus erythematosus. *British Journal of Psychiatry, 128*, 442–445.

Meares, R. Grimwade, J. & Wood, C. (1976). A possible relationship between anxiety in pregnancy and puerperal depression. *Journal of Psychosomatic Research, 20*, 605–610.

Mehta, D. B. (1976). Lithium and affective disorders associated with organic brain impairment. *American Journal of Psychiatry, 133*, 236.

Melody, E. F. (1962). Depressive reactions following hysterectomy. *American Journal of Obstetrics and Gynaecology, 85*, 104–111.

Melzer, H. Y. (1980). The effects of psychotropic drugs on neuroendocrine function. *Psychiatric Clinics of North America, 3/2*, 277–298.

Mendelewicz, J. (1976). The age factor in depressive illness: Some genetic considerations. *Journal of Gerontology, 31*, 300–303.

Mendelewicz, J., Linkowski, P. & Brauman, H. (1977). Growth hormone and prolactin response to levodopa in affective illness. *Lancet, 1*, 652–653.

Mendels, J. (1974). Brain biogenic amine depletion and mood. *Archives of General Psychiatry, 30*, 447–451.

Mendelson, J. H. (1970). Biological concomitants of alcoholism. *New England Journal of Medicine, 283*, 71–81.

Mendelson, J. H., Ogata, M. & Mello, N. K. (1971). Adrenal function and alcoholism. *Psychosomatic Medicine, 33*, 145–157.

Menninger, K. A. (1919a). Psychoses associated with influenza. *Journal of the American Medical Association, 72*, 235–241.

Menninger, K. A. (1919b). Psychoses associated with influenza. *Archives of Neurology and Psychiatry, 2*, 291–337.

Menninger, K. A (1930). The amelioration of mental disease by influenza. *Journal of the American Medical Association, 92*, 630–634.

Merskey, H. & Hester, R. A. (1972). The treatment of chronic pain with psychotropic drugs. *Postgraduate Medical Journal, 48*, 594–598.

Merskey, H. & Woodforde, J. M. (1972). Psychiatric sequelae of minor head injury. *Brain, 95* 521–528.

Meyer, J. S., Stoica, E., Pascu, I. *et al.* (1973). Catecholamine concentrations in CSF and plasma of patients with cerebral infarction and haemorrhage. *Brain, 96*, 277–288.

Meyer, J. S., Welch, K. M. A., Okamato, S. & Shinazu, K. (1974). Disordered neurotransmitter function demonstrated by measurement of NE and 5–hydroxytryptamine in CSF of patients with recent cerebral infarction. *Brain, 97*, 655–664.

Mikkelson, J. & Reider, A. A. (1979). Post-parathyroidectomy psychosis: Clinical and research implications. *Journal of Clinical Psychiatry, 40*, 352–357.

Miller, E. (1977). *Abnormal Ageing*. London: John Wiley & Sons.

Miller, R. (1952). Mental symptoms and myxoedema. *Journal of Laboratory and Clinical Medicine, 40*, 267–270.

Mindham, R. H. S. (1970). Psychiatric symptoms in parkinsonism. *Journal of Neurology, Neurosurgery and Psychiatry, 33*, 188–191.

Mindham, R. H. S. (1974). Psychiatric aspects of Parkinson's disease. *British Journal of Hospital Medicine, 11*, 411–414.

Mindham, R. H. S., Marsden, C. D. & Parkes, J. D. (1976). Psychiatric symptoms during l–dopa therapy for Parkinson's disease and their relationship to physical disability. *Psychological Medicine, 6*, 23–33.

Minski, L. (1933). Mental symptoms associated with 58 cases of cerebral tumours. *Journal of Neurology and Psychopathology, 13*, 330–43.

Misra, S. S., Singh, K. S. & Bhargava, P. (1967). Estimation of 5-hydroxytryptamine (5–HT) levels in cerebrospinal fluid of patients with intracranial or spinal lesions. *Journal of Neurology, Neurosurgery and Psychiatry, 30*, 163–165.

Mitchell–Heggs, N. (1971). Aspects of the natural history and clinical presentation of depression. *Proceedings of the Royal Society of Medicine, 64*, 1171–1174.

Mjönes, H. (1949). Paralysis agitans. *Acta Psychiatrica et Neurologica*, suppl. 54.

Mock, H. E. (1950). *Skull Fractures and Brain Injuries*. Baltimore: Williams Wilkins Co.

Modigh, K. (1976). Long term effects of electroconvulsive shock therapy on synthesis turnover and uptake of brain monoamines. *Psychopharmacology, 49*, 179–185.

Moffic, H. S. & Paykel, E. S. (1975). Depression in medical inpatients. *British Journal of Psychiatry, 126*, 346–353.

Mohr, J. A. & Wilson, J. D. (1973). Psychosis with Chronic Brucellosis. *Oklahoma State Medical Association Journal, 66*, 319–321.

Moldofsky, H. & Chester, W. J. (1970). Pain and mood patterns in patients with rheumatoid arthritis. *Psychosomatic Medicine, 32*, 309–318.

Monroe, R. R. (1970). *Episodic Behavioural Disorders*. Cambridge, Mass.: Harvard University Press.

Monroe, R. R. (1979). Episodic psychoses misdiagnosed as schizophrenia or affective disorder. *In* L. G. Kiloh (Ed.), *Biological Psychiatry* pp. 75–86. Sydney: Geigy Psychiatric Symposium.

Moran, E. A. P. (1969). A Note on Suicide, Homicide and Influenza, (Unpublished paper, A.N.U., Canberra).

Morgan, H. G. & Russell, J. F. M. (1975). Value of family background and clinical features as predictors of long-term outcome in anorexia nervosa: Four-year follow-up study of 41 patients. *Psychological Medicine, 5*, 355–371.

Morgane, P. J. & Stern, W. C. (1974). Chemical anatomy of brain circuits in relation to sleep and wakefulness. *In* E. D. Weitzman (ed.), *Advances in Sleep Research*, 1, New York: Spectrum Publications Inc.

Mulangi, J. R. (1972). Functional or organic psychosis (Four cases of typhoid fever initially presenting as various forms of psychiatric disorder), *African Journal of Medical Science, 3*, 319–326.

Mulder, D. W. & Daly, D. (1952). Psychiatric symptoms associated with lesions of the temporal lobe. *Journal of the American Medical Association, 150*, 173–176.

Munro, A. (1966). Parental deprivation in depressive patients. *British Journal of Psychiatry, 112*, 443–457.

Mûr, J., Kümpel, G. & Dostál, S. (1966). An anergic phase of disseminated sclerosis with psychiatric course. *Confina Neurologia, 28*, 37–49.

Nadel, C. & Portadin, G. (1977). Sickle-cell crises. *New York State Journal of Medicine, 77*, 1075–1078.

Nair, K. A. N. (1970). Depression from a physical symptom. *British Medical Journal, 4*, 234.

Newton, R. W. (1975). Side effects of drugs used to treat tuberculosis. *Scottish Medical Journal, 20*, 47.

Ng, J., Phelan, E. L., McGregor, T. D. *et al.* (1967). Properties of catapres, a new hypotensive drug: A preliminary report. *New Zealand Medical Journal, 66*, 864–870.

Nielsen, J. (1969). Klinefelter's syndrome and the XYY syndrome. *Acta Psychiatrica Scandinavica Supplement* 209.

Nielsen, J., Homma, T., Biøru-Henriksen, T. (1977). Follow-up 15 years after a geronto-psychiatric prevalence study. *Journal of Gerontology, 32*, 544–561.

Niemi, T. & Jääskeläinen, J. (1978). Cancer morbidity in depressive persons. *Journal of Psychosomatic Research*, *22*, 117–120.

Nies, A. S. (1975). Adverse reactions and interactions limiting the use of anti-hypertensive drugs. *American Journal of Medicine*, *58*, 495–503.

Nilsson, A. & Sölvell, L. (1967). Clinical studies on oral contraception: A randomised double blind crossover study of four different preparations. *Acta Obstetrica et Gynaecologica Scandinavica*, *46*, Supplement 8.

Nilsson, A., Jacobson, L. & Ingemansson, C.-A. (1967). Side effects of an oral contraceptive, with particular attention to mental symptoms and sexual adaptation. *Acta Obstetrica et Gynaecologica Scandinavica*, *46*, 537–556.

Noble, P. (1974). Depressive illness and hyperparathyroidism. *Proceedings of the Royal Society of Medicine*, *67*, 1066–1067.

Nordgren, L. & Von Schéele, C. (1976). Myxoedematous madness without myxoedema. *Acta Medica Scandinavica*, *199*, 233–236.

North, R. (1969). Cardiovascular disease. In R. H. Moser (Ed.), *Diseases of Medical Progress*. Springfield, Ill.: C. C. Thomas.

Nott, P. N. & Fleminger, J. J. (1975). Presenile dementia: The difficulties of early diagnosis. *Acta Psychiatrica Scandinavica*, *51*, 210–217.

Oates, J. A., Seligmann, A. W., Clark, N. A. *et al.* (1965). The relative efficiency of guanethidine, methyldopa and pargyline as anti-hypertensive agents. *New England Journal of Medicine*, *273*, 729–734.

O'Brien, W. M. (1968). Indomethacin: A survey of clinical trials. *Clinical Pharmacology and Therapeutics*, *9*, 94–107.

O'Connor, J. F. J. (1959). Psychoses associated with systemic lupus erythematosus. *Annals of Internal Medicine*, *51*, 526-536.

O'Connor, J. & Musher, D. M. (1966). Central nervous system involvement in SLE. *Archives of Neurology*, *14*, 157–164.

O'Dea, J. P. K., Gould, D., Hallberg, H. & Wieland, R. G. (1978). Prolactin changes during electroconvulsive therapy. *American Journal of Psychiatry*, *135*, 609–11.

Öhman, R., Walinder, J., Balldin, J. *et al.* (1976). Prolactin response to electroconvulsive therapy. *Lancet*, *2*, 936–937.

Okava, M., Maeda, S., Nukui, H., Kawafuchi, J. (1980). Psychiatric symptoms in ruptured anterior communicating anurysm: Social progress. *Acta Psychiatrica Scandinavica*, *61*, 306–312.

Oliver, J. E. (1970). Huntington's chorea in Northhamptonshire. *British Journal of Psychiatry*, *116*, 241–255.

Oltman, J. E. & Friedman, S. (1961). Comments on Huntington's Chorea. *Diseases of the Nervous System*, *22*, 1–7.

O'Malley, E. P. (1966). Severe mental symptoms in disseminated sclerosis: A neuropathological study. *Journal of the Irish Medical Association*, *55*, 115–127.

O'Neill, D. (1959). The post-viral state. *Medical World*, *90*, 233–36.

Oppenheim, G., Ebstein, R. P. & Belmaker, R. H. (1979). Effects of lithium on physostigmine–induced behavioural syndrome and plasma cyclic AMP. *Journal of Psychiatric Research*, *15*, 133–138.

Oppenheimer, D. R. (1968). Microscopic lesions in the brain following head injury. *Journal of Neurology, Neurosurgery and Psychiatry*, *31*, 299–306.

Oppler, W. (1950). Manic psychosis in a case of parasaggital meningioma. *Archives of Neurology and Psychiatry*, *64*, 417–430.

Oswald, I. (1974). Fenfluramine and psychosis. *British Medical Journal*, *4*, 103.

Oswald, I., Lewis, S. A., Dunleavy, D. L. F. *et al.* (1971). Drugs of dependence, though not of abuse: Fenfluramine and imipramine. *British Medical Journal*, *3*, 70–73.

Ovesen, L. (1979). Vitamin deficiencies and drugs. *Drugs*, *18*, 278–298.

References 199

Paget, J. (1863). *Lectures on Surgical Pathology.* Revised and edited by W. Turner. London: Longmans Green.

Pai, M. N. (1945). Changes in personality after cerebro-spinal fever. *British Medical Journal, 1,* 289–293.

Papez, J. W. (1937). Proposed mechanism of emotion. *Archives of Neurology and Psychiatry, 38,* 725–743.

Parant, V. (1892). Paralysis agitans: Insanity associated with. *In* D. H. Tuke (Ed.), *Dictionary of Psychological Medicine,* pp. 884–886. London: Churchill.

Pare, C. M. B., Yeung, D. P. H., Price, K. & Stacey, R. S. (1969). 5-hydroxytryptamine, noradrenalin and dopamine in brain stem hypothalamus and caudate nucleus of controls and patients committing suicide by coal gas poisoning. *Lancet, 2,* 133–135.

Pariente, D. (1973).Methyldopa and depression. *British Medical Journal, 4,* 110–111.

Parker, W. (1885). *Cancer: A study of 397 cases of cancer of the female breast.* New York: G. P. Putnam & Sons.

Parry, B. L. & Rush, J. (1979). Oral contraceptives and depressive symptomatology. *Comprehensive Psychiatry, 20,* 347–358.

Pasargiklian, M. & Biondi, L. (1970). Neurologic and behavioural reactions of tuberculous patients treated with cycloserine. *Scandinavian Journal of Respiratory Disease,* Supplement 71, pp. 201.

Paulley, J. W. & Hughes, J. P. (1960). Giant-cell arteritis of the aged. *British Medical Journal, 2,* 1562–1567.

Paykel, E. S., Emms, E. M., Fletcher, G. A. & Rassaby, E. S. (1980). Life events and social support in puerperal depression. *British Journal of Psychiatry, 136,* 339–346.

Payne, C. A. (1974). Thalamic tumours. *In* P. J. Vinken & G. W. Bruyn (Eds), *Handbook of Clinical Neurology,* Vol. 17, pp. 610–9. Amsterdam: North Holland.

Pearce, J. & Miller, E. (1973). *Clinical Aspects of Dementia.* London: Balliére-Tindall.

Pearlman, C. A. (1971). Manic behaviour with l-dopa. *New England Journal of Medicine, 285,* 1326.

Perry, E. K., Perry, R. H., Blessed, L. & Tomlinson, R. E. (1977). Necropsy evidence of central cholinergic deficits in senile dementia. *Lancet, 1,* 189.

Perry, T. L., Hansen, S. & Kloster, M. (1973). Huntington's chorea: deficiency of gamma–aminobutyric acid in brain. *New England Journal of Medicine, 258,* 337–42.

Perry, T. L., Bratty, P. J. A., Hansen, S. *et al.* (1975). Hereditary mental depression and parkinsonism with taurine deficiency. *Archives of Neurology, 32,* 108–13.

Peszke, M. A. & Mason, W. M. (1969). Infectious mononucleosis and its relationship to psychological malaise. *Connecticut Medicine, 33,* 260–262.

Petersen, P. (1968). Psychiatric disorders in primary hyperparathyroidism. *Journal of Clinical Endocrinology, 28,* 1491–1495.

Petite, J. P. & Bloch, F. (1979). Syndrome dépressif à course du traitment par cimétidine. *Nouvelle Presse Médicale, 8,* 1260

Pettingale, K. W., Greer, S. & Tee, E. H. T. (1977). Serum IgA and emotional expression in breast cancer patients. *Journal of Psychosomatic Research, 21,* 395–399.

Pinto O. de S., Polikar, N. & Debono, G. (1972). Results of international trial of lioresal. *Postgraduate Medical Journal, 48* Supplement (October), 18–23.

Pitt, B. (1968). Atypical depression following childbirth. *British Journal of Psychiatry, 114,* 132–135.

Pitt, B. (1973). Maternity Blues. *British Journal of Psychiatry, 122,* 431–433.

Pitts, N. & Guze, S. B. (1961). Psychiatric disorders in myxoedema, *American Journal of Psychiatry, 118,* 142–147.

Pittsley, R. A. & Talal, N. (1980). Neuromuscular complications of Sjögren's Syndrome. *In* P. J. Vinken & G. W. Bruyn (Eds), *Handbook of Clinical Neurology,* Vol. 39, pp. 419–433. Amsterdam: North Holland.

References

Planansky, K. & Johnston, R. (1978). Depressive syndromes in schizophrenia. *Acta Psychiatrica Scandinavica, 57,* 207–218.

Planansky, K. & Johnston, R. (1980). Psychotropic drugs and depressive syndromes in schizophrenia. *Psychiatric Quarterly, 53,* 214–221.

Plantey, F. (1978). Antinuclear factor in affective disorder. *Biological Psychiatry, 13,* 149–150.

Plesser, R. P. & Fahn, S. (1978). Dystonia: A condition often misdiagnosed as a conversion reaction. *American Journal of Psychiatry, 135,* 349–352.

Pletscher, A. (1953). Drug-induced alterations of monoamine metabolism: *In: The Clinical Chemistry of Monoamines,* pp. 191–203, Amsterdam: Elsevier.

Poisson, M., Mashaly, R. & Lebkire, B. (1978). Dialysis and encephalopathy: Recovery after interruption of aluminium intake. *British Medical Journal, 2,* 1610–1611.

Pokorny, A. D., Rawls, W. E., Adams, E. & Mefferd, R. B. (1973). Depression, psychopathy and herpes virus type I antibodies. *Archives of General Psychiatry, 29,* 820–822.

Pollitt, J. (1965). *Depression and its Treatment.* London. Heinemann Medical Books.

Pollitt, J. (1971a). Depression: Emotion of illness? A biological approach. *Proceedings of the Royal Society of Medicine, 64,* 1252–1254.

Pollitt, J. (1971b). Aetiological, clinical and therapeutic aspects of depression. *Proceedings of the Royal Society of Medicine, 64,* 1174–1178

Pollitt, J. (1972). The relationship between genetic and precipitating factors in depressive illness. *British Journal of Psychiatry, 121,* 67–70.

Pommé, B., Girard, J. & Planche, R. (1963). Form dépressive de début d'une sclérose en plaques. *Annales Medico-psychologique* (Paris), *12*/1, 133.

Pond, D. A. (1957). Psychiatric aspects of epilepsy. *Journal of the Indian Medical Profession, 3,* 1441–1451.

Pond, D. A. (1974). Epilepsy and personality disorder. In P. J. Vinken & G. W. Bruyn (Eds), *Handbook of Clinical Neurology,* Vol. 15, pp. 577–592. Amsterdam: North Holland.

Pool, J. L. & Carroll, J. V. (1958). Psychaitric symptoms masking brain tumors. *Journal of the Medical Society of New Jersey, 55,* 4–9.

Post, F. (1962). *The Significance of Affective Symptoms in Old Age.* London: Oxford University Press.

Post, F. (1964). Diagnosis and prognosis of depression. In W. Ferguson-Anderson & B. Isaacs (Eds), *Current Achievements in Geriatrics.* pp. 178–183. London: Cassell.

Post, F. (1965). *The Clinical Psychiatry of Late Life,* Oxford: Pergamon.

Post, F. (1969). The relationship to physical health of the affective illnesses in the elderly. *Eighth International Congress of Gerontology, Proceedings,* Vol. 1, 198–201. Washington, D.C.

Post, F. (1975).Dementia, depression and pseudodementia. In D. F. Benson & D. Blumer (Eds), *Psychiatric Aspects of Neurologic Disease,* pp. 99–120. New York: Grune & Stratton.

Post, F. (1978). The functional psychoses. In A. D. Isaacs & F. Post (Eds), *Studies in Geriatric Psychiatry,* pp. 77–94. Chichester: John Wiley & Sons.

Pottenger, M., McKernon, F., Patrie, L. E. *et al.* (1978). The frequency and persistence of depressive symptoms in the alcohol abuser. *Journal of Nervous and Mental Disease, 166,* 562–570.

Potts, J. T. & Roberts, B. (1958). Clinical significance of magnesium deficiency and its relation to parathyroid disease. *American Journal of Medical Science, 235,* 206–219.

Prange, H. A. (1973). The abuse of antidepressant drugs in elderly patients. *Advances in Behavioural Biology, 6,* 225–237.

Pratt, R. T. C. (1951). An investigation of the psychiatric aspects of disseminated sclerosis. *Journal of Neurology, Neurosurgery and Psychiatry, 14,* 326–336.

Prescott, L. F. (1972). Antipyretic analgesics and drugs used in rheumatic diseases and gout. In L. Myler & A. Herxheimer (Eds), *Side Effects of Drugs,* Vol 7, pp. 138–185; Amsterdam: Excerpta Medica.

References 201

Prichard, B. N. C., Johnston, A. W., Hill, I. D. & Rosenheim, L. (1968). Bethanidine, guanethidine and methyldopa in treatment of hypertension: A within-patient comparison. *British Medical Journal, 1*, 135–144.
Protheroe, C. (1969). Puerperal psychosis: A long-term study, 1927–1961, *British Journal of Psychiatry, 115*, 9–30.
Prout, T. & Epple, J. H. (1959). Early recognition of neurological conditions in a psychiatric hospital. *Bulletin of the New York Academy of Medicine, 35*, 162–166.
Prudhomme, C. (1941). Epilepsy and suicide. *Journal of Nervous and Mental Disease, 94*, 722–731.
Puite, J. K., Schut, T., Van Praag, H. M. & Lakke, J. P. W. F. (1973). Monoamine metabolism and depression in Parkinson patients. *Psychiatrie, Neurologie, Neurochirurgerie, 76*, 61–70.
Pullan, D. T., Clement-Jones, V., Corder, R. *et al.* (1980). Ectopic production of methionine–enkephalin and beta–endorphin. *British Medical Journal, 1*, 758–759.
Purdy, A., Hahn, A., Barnett, H. J. M. *et al.* (1979). Familial fatal Parkinsonism with alveolar hypoventilation and mental depression. *Annals of Neurology, 6*, 523–531.
Quarton, G. C., Clark, L. D., Cobb, S. & Bauer, W. (1955). Mental disturbances associated with ACTH and cortisone: A review of explanatory hypotheses, *Medicine, 34*, 13–50.
Quetsch, R. M., Achor, R. W. D., Litin, E. M. & Fawcett, R. L. (1959). Depressive reactions in hypertensive patients. *Circulation, 19*, 366–375.
Rabinar, C. J. & Willner, A. E. (1976). Psychopathology observed in follow-up after coronary bypass surgery. *Journal of Nervous and Mental Disease, 163*, 295–301.
Rabinar, C. J., Willner, A. E. & Fishman, J. (1975). Psychiatric complications following coronary bypass surgery. *Journal of Nervous and Mental Disease, 160*, 342–348.
Ramsay, A. M. (1978). Epidemic neuromyasthenia. *Postgraduate Medical Journal, 54*, 718–721.
Rand, M. J. & McCulloch, M. W. (1977). Modes of action of antidepressants. *In* G. D. Burrows (Ed.), *Handbook of Depression*, pp. 137–56. Amsterdam: Elsevier.
Reading, C. M. (1975). Latent pernicious anaemia: A preliminary report. *Medical Journal of Australia, 1*, 91–94.
Redlich, F. C., Dunsmore, R. H. & Brody, E. B. (1948). Delays and errors in the diagnosis of brain tumours. *New England Journal of Medicine, 239*, 945–950.
Rees, L. H., Besser, G. M., Jeffcoate, W. J. *et al.* (1977). Alcohol-induced Psuedo-Cushing's Syndrome, *Lancet, 1*, 726–728.
Regenstein, R., Rose, L. I. & Williams, G. H. (1972). Psychopathology in Cushing's Syndrome, *Archives of Internal Medicine, 130*, 114–117.
Reich, T. & Winokur, G. (1970). Post partum psychosis in patients with manic-depressive disease. *Journal of Nervous and Mental Disease, 151*, 60–68.
Relkin, R. (1969). Effect of endocrines on the central nervous system I, *New York State Journal of Medicine, 69*, 2133–2145.
Remington, F. B. & Rupert, S. L. (1962). Why patients with brain tumours come to a psychiatric hospital. *American Journal of Psychiatry, 119*, 256–7.
Restak, R. M. (1972). Pseudotumor cerebri, psychosis and hypervitaminosis. *Journal of Nervous and Mental Disease, 155*, 72–75.
Reynolds, A. R. (1861), *Epilepsy: Its Symptoms, Treatment and Relation to Other Chronic Convulsive Diseases*. London: Churchill.
Reynolds, E. H., Chanaran, L. & Matthews, D. M. (1968). Neuropsychiatric aspects of anticonvulsant megaloblastic anaemia. *Lancet, 1*, 395–397.
Reynolds, E. H., Preece, J. M., Bailey, J. M. & Coppen, A. (1970). Folate deficiency and depressive illness. *British Journal of Psychiatry, 117*, 287–292.
Reynolds, E. H., Rothfeld, E. & Pincus, J. H. (1973). Neurological Disease associated with folate deficiency. *British Medical Journal, 1*, 398–400.
Ribèyre, M. & Facchin, J. Y. (1979). Traitement des douleurs cancéreuses par imipramine à grosses doses. *Lyon Medical, 241*, 703.

Rice, E. & Gendelman, S. (1973). Psychiatric aspects of normal pressure hydrocephalus. *Journal of the American Médical Association, 223,* 409–412.

Richards, P. H. (1973). A post-hysterectomy syndrome. *Lancet, 2,* 983–985.

Richardson, E. P. (1980). Systemic lupus erythematosus. *In* P. J. Vinken & G. W. Bruyn (Eds), *Handbook of Clinical Neurology,* Vol. 39, pp. 273–293. Amsterdam: North Holland.

Rickles, N. K. (1945). Functional symptoms as first evidence of carcinoma of the pancreas. *Journal of Nervous and Mental Disease, 101,* 566–571.

Rieke, J. (1975). Über depressive Psychosen in Verlaufe von Hirntumorenerkrankungen. *Nervenarzt, 46,* 152–9.

Riklan, M., Jacklet, A. C., Orris, S. E. *et al.* (1973). Psychological studies of long range l-dopa therapy in parkinsonism. *Journal of Nervous and Mental Disease, 157,* 452–64.

Rimon, R. (1969). Social and psychosomatic aspects of rheumatoid arthritis. *Acta Rheumatica Scandinavica,* Supplement 13.

Rimon, R. (1974). Depression in rheumatoid arthritis. *Annals of Clinical Research, 6,* 171–175.

Rimon, R. & Halonen, P. (1969). Herpes simplex virus infection and depressive illness. *Diseases of the Nervous System, 30,* 338–340.

Rimon, R., Halonen, P., Anntinnen, E. & Evola, K. (1971). Complement fixation antibody to herpes simplex virus in patients with psychotic depression. *Diseases of the Nervous System, 32,* 822–824.

Rivieris, P. M., Malliaris, D. E., Batrinos, L. & Stefanis, C. N. (1979). Testosterone treatment of depression in two patients with Klinefelter's Syndrome. *American Journal of Psychiatry, 136,* 986–988.

Roberts, J. A., (1977). Dixarit (clonidine hydrochloride) and depression. *Medical Journal of Australia, 1,* 158.

Robertson, K. (1947). Temporal or giant-cell arteritis. *British Medical Journal, 2,* 168–170.

Robins, A. H. (1976a). Are stroke patients more depressed than other disabled subjects? *Journal of Chronic Disease, 29,* 479–82.

Robins, A. H. (1976b). Depression in patients with parkinsonism. *British Journal of Psychiatry, 128,* 141–145.

Robins, E. & Guze, S. B. (1972). Classification of affective disorder: The primary-secondary and the endogenous-reactive and the neurotic-psychotic concepts. *In* T. A. Williams, M. M. Katz & J. A. Niedel (Eds), *Recent Advances in the Psychobiology of the Depressive Illnesses.* Washington: U.S. Government Printing Office.

Robinson, D. S., Nies, A., Davis, J. N. *et al.* (1972). Ageing, monoamines and monoamine oxidase levels. *Lancet, 1,* 290–291.

Robinson, E. T., Hernandez, L. A., Dick, W. C. & Buchanan, W. W. (1977). Depression in rheumatoid arthritis. *Journal of the Royal College of General Practitioners, 27,* 423–427.

Robinson, H., Kirk, R. F. & Frye, R. L. (1971). A psychological study of rheumatoid arthritis and selected controls. *Journal of Chronic Disease, 23,* 791–801.

Robinson, R. G. (1965). Indomethacin in rheumatic disease. *Medical Journal of Australia, 1,* 266–269.

Robinson, R. G. (1966). Indomethacin in rheumatic disease: A reassessment. *Medical Journal of Australia, 1,* 971–972.

Robinson, R. G. & Bloom, F. E. (1977). Pharmacological treatment following experimental infarction: Implications for understanding psychological symptoms of human strokes. *Biological Psychiatry, 12,* 669–80.

Robinson, R. G., Shoemaker, W. J., Schlumpf, M. & Volk, T. (1975). Effect of experimental cerebral infarction on catecholamines and behaviour. *Nature, 255,* 322–324.

Ron, M. A., Toone, B. K., Garralda, M. E. & Lishman, W. A. (1979). Diagnostic accuracy in presenile dementia. *British Journal of Psychiatry, 134,* 161–168.

Rosen, H. & Swigar, M. E. (1976). Depression and normal pressure hydrocephalus. *Journal of Nervous and Mental Disease, 163*, 35–40.

Rosenbaum, A. H. & Barry, B. J. (1975). Positive therapeutic response to lithium in hypomania secondary to organic brain syndrome. *American Journal of Psychiatry, 132*, 1072–1073.

Rosenblatt, S., Oreckes, I., Meadow, H. & Speira, H. (1968). The relationship between anti-gammaglobulin activity and depression. *American Journal of Psychiatry, 124*, 1640–1644.

Rosser, R. (1976). Depression during renal dialysis and following transplantation. *Proceedings of the Royal Society of Medicine, 69*, 832–834.

Ross Russell, R. V. (1959). Giant-cell arteritis. *Quarterly Journal of Medicine, 28*, 471–489.

Roth, B. & Neusimilova, S. (1975). Depression in narcolepsy and hypersomnia. *Schweizer Archive für Neurologie, Neurochirurgie und Psychiatrie, 116*, 291–300.

Roth, M. (1971). Classification and aetiology of mental disorders in old age. *In* D. W. K. Kay & A. Walk (Eds), *Recent Developments in Psychogeriatrics*, pp. 1–18. Ashford: Hedley Brothers Ltd.

Roth, M. (1977). The association of affective disorder and physical somatic problems and its bearing on certain problems of psychosomatic medicine. *In* F. Antonelli (Ed.), *Therapy in Psychosomatic Medicine*, Vol. 1, pp. 189–197. Roma: Edizione L Pozzi SpA.

Roth, M. & Kay, D. W. K. (1956). Affective disorders in the senium II: Physical disability as an aetiological factor. *Journal of Mental Science, 102*, 141–150.

Roth, S. (1970). The seemingly ubiquitous depression following acute schizophrenic episodes: A neglected area of clinical discussion. *American Journal of Psychiatry, 127*, 51–8.

Rowntree, D. W., Nevin, S. & Wilson, A. (1950). Effect of di–isopropylfluorophosphonate in schizophrenia and manic depressive psychosis. *Journal of Neurology, Neurosurgery and Psychiatry, 13*, 47–59.

Roy, A. (1976). Psychiatric aspects of narcolepsy. *British Journal of Psychiatry, 128*, 562–565.

Roy, A. (1980). Depression in chronic paranoid schizophrenia. *British Journal of Psychiatry, 137*, 138–9.

Royal College of General Practitioners (1974). *Oral Contraceptives and Health*. Manchester: Pitman.

Rubin, R. T. & Mandell, A. J. (1966). Adrenocortical activity in psychological emotional states: A review. *American Journal of Psychiatry, 123*, 387–400.

Runge, W. (1928). *In* Bumke's Handbuch der Geisteskrankheiten, Vol. 7, p. 616. Quoted in Surridge, D. (1969).

Rupert, F. B. & Remington, S. L. (1963). Why patients with brain tumours come to a psychiatric hospital: A thirty year survey. *Psychiatric Quarterly, 37*, 253–63.

Rutherford, W. H., Merritt, J. D. & McDonald, J. R. (1977). Sequelae of concussion caused by minor head injuries. *Lancet, 1*, 1–4.

Ryback, R. S. & Schwab, R. S. (1971). Manic response to levodopa therapy. *New England Journal of Medicine, 285*, 788–9.

Sachar, E. J. (1975a). Psychiatric disturbances associated with endocrine disorder. *In* M. F. Reiser (Ed.), *American Handbook of Psychiatry*, Vol. 4, 2nd edn., pp. 299–313. New York: Basic Books.

Sachar, E. J. (1975b). Neuroendocrine abnormalities in depressive illness. *In* E. J. Sachar (Ed.), *Topics in Psychoendocrinology*, pp. 135–56. New York: Grune & Stratton.

Sachar, E. J., Mason, J. W., Couter, H. S. & Lartiss, K. (1963). Psychoendocrine aspects of acute schizophrenic reactions. *Psychosomatic Medicine, 25*, 510–37.

Sachar, E. J., Kanter, S. S., Buie, D. *et al.* (1970). Psychoendocrinology of ego disintegration. *American Journal of Psychiatry, 126*, 1067–8.

Sachar, E. J., Frantz, A. G., Altman, M. & Sassin, J. (1973). Growth hormone and prolactin in unipolar and bipolar depressed patients' responses to hypoglycaemia and l–dopa. *American Journal of Psychiatry, 130*, 1362–7.

Sachar, E. J., Asnis, G., Halbreich, W. *et al.* (1980a). Advances in psychoneuroendocrinology. *Psychiatric Clinics of North America*, 3/2, 311–26.

Sachar, E. J., Asnis, G., Nathan, R. S. *et al.* (1980b). Dextroamphetamine and cortisol in depression. *Archives of General Psychiatry*, *37*, 755–7.

Sachs, E. (1950). Meningiomas with dementia as the first and presenting feature. *Journal of Mental Science*, *96*, 998–1007.

Sachs, O. (1971). *Migraine: Evolution of a Common Disorder*; London: Faber & Faber.

Sachs, O. (1973). *Awakenings*. London: Duckworth.

Sainsbury, P. (1955). *Suicide in London*. London: Chapman & Hall.

Sainsbury, P. (1962). Suicide in later life. *Gerontologia Clinica*, *4*, 161–170.

Sanders-Bush, E., Gallagher, D. A. & Sulser, F. (1974). On the mechanism of brain 5HT depletion by para-chloramphetamine and related drugs and the specificity of their actions. *Advances in Biochemical Psychopharmacology*, *10*, 185–194.

Sartorius, N. (1974). Depressive illness as a worldwide problem. *In* F. Kielholz (Ed.), *Depression in Everyday Practice*. Bern: Hans Huber.

Savage, C., Butcher, W. & Noble, D. (1952). Psychiatric manifestations of pancreatic disease. *Journal of Clinical and Experimental Psychopathology*, *13*, 9–60.

Sayed, A. J. (1976). Mania and bromism: A case report and a look at the future. *American Journal of Psychiatry*, *133*, 228–9.

Schildkraut, J. J. (1965). The catecholamine hypothesis of affective disorder: A review of supporting evidence. *American Journal of Psychiatry*, *122*, 509–22.

Schindler, H. & Schanda, H. (1975). Akute psychiatrische Episode nach Adrenelektomie. *Wiener Klinische Wochenschrift*, *87*, 650–652.

Schmale, A. H. & Iker, H. P. (1966). The psychological setting of uterine cervical cancer. *Annals of New York Academy of Science*, *125*, 807–813.

Schuster, M. M. & Iber, F. L. (1965). Psychosis with pancreatitis. *Archives of Internal Medicine*, *16*, 228–233.

Schwab, J. J., Bialow, M., Brown, J. M. & Holzer, C. E. (1967). Diagnosing depression in medical inpatients. *Annals of Internal Medicine*, *67*, 697–707.

Schwartz, D., Michel, D. & Strian, F. (1973). Depressive Reaktionen unter antihypertensiver Behandlung. *Archive für Psychiatrie und Nervenkrankheiten*, *218*, 41–50.

Selby, G. & Lance, J. W. (1960). Observations in 500 cases of Migraine and allied vascular headache. *Journal of Neurology, Neurosurgery and Psychiatry*, *23*, 23–32.

Selecki, E. R. (1965). Intracranial space occupying lesions. *Medical Journal of Australia*, *1*, 383–90.

Serafetinides, E. A. & Falconer, M. A. (1962). The effects of temporal lobectomy in epileptics. *Journal of Mental Science*, *108*, 584–593.

Shader, R. I. (1972). *Psychiatric Complications of Medical Drugs*. New York: Raven Press.

Shafar, J. (1965). Iatrogenic scurvy. *Practitioner*, *194*, 374–377.

Shapiro, A., Shapiro, E., Wayne, H. *et al.* (1973). Tourette's syndrome: Summary of data on 34 patients. *Psychosomatic Medicine*, *35*, 419–35.

Shaw, D. M., Camps, F. E. & Eccleston, E. C. (1967). 5HT in the hindbrain of depressive suicides. *British Journal of Psychiatry*, *113*, 1407–1411

Shearn, M. A. & Pirofsky, B. (1952). Disseminated lupus erythematosus. *Archives of Internal Medicine*, *90*, 790–807.

Sheldrick, C., Jablinsky, A., Sartorius, N. & Shepherd, M. (1977). Schizophrenia succeeded by affective illness: Catamnestic study and statistical inquiry. *Psychological Medicine*, *7*, 619–624.

Shorvon, S. D., Carney, W. P., Chanarin, I. & Reynolds, E. H. (1980). The neuropsychiatry of megaloblastic anaemia. *British Medical Journal*, *2*, 1036–1038.

Shulman, K. & Post, F. (1980). Bipolar affective disorder in old age. *British Journal of Psychiatry*, *136*, 26–32.

Shulman, R. (1967). Psychiatric aspects of pernicious anaemia: A prospective control investigation. *British Medical Journal, 3,* 266–270.

Sigal, M. (1976). Psychiatric aspects of temporal lobe epilepsy. *Journal of Nervous and Mental Disease, 163,* 348–351.

Silverstein, A. (1978). E.B. Virus Infections of the nervous system. *In* P. J. Vinken & G. W. Bruyn (Eds), *Handbook of Clinical Neurology,* Vol. 34 pp. 185–192. Amsterdam: North Holland.

Silverstone, T. (1974). Intermittent treatment with anorectic drugs. *Practitioner, 213,* 245–252.

Sim, M. (1974). *Guide to Psychiatry,* 3rd edn., pp. 526–527. Edinburgh: Churchill Livingstone.

Sim, M. & Sussman, I. (1962). Alzheimer's disease: Its natural history and differential diagnosis. *Journal of Nervous and Mental Disease, 135,* 489–499.

Simonson, M. (1964). Phenothiazine depressive reactions. *Journal of Neuropsychiatry, 5,* 259–65.

Simpson, F. O. (1973). Antihypertensive drug therapy. *Drugs, 6,* 333–363.

Simpson, F. O. & Waal-Manning, H. J. (1971). Hypertension and depression. *Journal of the Royal College of Physicians of London, 6,* 14–24.

Simpson, F. O., Bolli, P., Bailey, R. R. *et al.* (1977). Initial experience with prazosin in New Zealand. *Medical of Australia, 2,* Special Supplement 1 (August), 23–26.

Sinahan, K. & Hillary, I. (1981). Post-influenzal Depression. *British Journal of Psychiatry, 138,* 131–133.

Siomopoulos, V. (1975). Amphetamine psychosis: Overview and an hypothesis. *Diseases of the Nervous System, 36,* 336–339.

Slater, E. & Glithero, E. (1963). The schizophrenia-like psychoses of epilepsy III: The genetical aspects. *British Journal of Psychiatry, 109,* 130–133.

Slater, E. & Roth, M. (1977). *Clinical Psychiatry,* 3rd edn. London: Balliére, Tindall and Cassell.

Smals, A., Kloppenborg, P. W., Njo, K. T. & Knoben, J. M. (1976). Alcohol-induced Cushingoid Syndrome. *British Medical Journal, 22,* 1298.

Smith, A. T. M. (1960). Megaloblastic madness. *British Medical Journal, 2,* 1840–1845.

Smith, S. (1954). Organic syndromes presenting as involutional melancholia. *British Medical Journal, 2,* 274–77.

Smith, S. L. (1975). Mood and the menstrual cycle. *In:* E. J. Sachar (Ed.), *Topics in Psychoendocrinology,* pp. 19–58. New York: Grune and Stratton.

Smythies, J. R. (1966). *The Neurological Foundations of Psychiatry.* New York: Academic Press.

Snaith, R. P. (1976). Hypotensive drugs in the treatment of depression. *British Journal of Clinical Pharmacology, 3,* Supplement 1, 73–74.

Snaith, R. P. & McCourbie, M. (1974). Antihypertensive drugs and depression. *Psychological Medicine, 4,* 393–398.

Snaith, R. P., Mehta, S. & Raby, A. H. (1970). Serum folate and vitamin B12 in epileptics with and without mental illness. *British Journal of Psychiatry, 116,* 179–183.

Snow, H. (1893). *Cancer and the Cancer Process.* London: J. & A. Churchill.

Snyder, G. H. (1978). The opiate receptor and morphine-like peptides in the brain. *American Journal of Psychiatry, 135,* 645–52.

Sobin, A. & Ozer, M. N. (1966). Mental disorders in acute encephalitis. *Journal of Mount Sinai Hospital New York, 33,* 73–82.

Solomon, G. F. (1969). Discussion. *In:* Second Conference on Psychophysiological Aspects of Cancer. *Annals of the New York Academy of Science, 164,* 633–634.

Solomon, J. G. & Solomon, S. (1978). Psychiatric depression and bronchogenic carcinoma. *American Journal of Psychiatry, 135,* 859–860.

Soniat, T. O. L. (1951). Psychiatric symptoms associated with intracranial neoplasms. *American Journal of Psychiatry, 108,* 19–22.

Sørensen, K. & Nielsen, J. (1977). Twenty psychiatric males with Klinefelter's Syndrome. *Acta Psychiatrica Scandinavica, 56,* 249–255.

Sorkin, S. Z. (1949). Addison's disease. *Medicine, 28,* 371–425.

Sourkes, T. L. (1965). The action of methyldopa on the brain. *British Medical Bulletin, 21,* 66–69.

Sours, F. A. (1963). Narcolepsy and other disturbances in the sleep–waking cycle: A study of 115 cases with a review of the literature. *Journal of Nervous and Mental Disease, 137*, 525–542.

Soutar, C. A. (1970). Tetrabenazine for Huntington's Chorea. *British Medical Journal, 4*, 55.

Sparkes, C. G. & Spencer, P. S. J. (1971). Antinocioceptive activity of morphine after injection of biogenic amines in the cerebral ventricle of the conscious rat. *British Journal of Pharmacology, 42*, 230–41.

Speira, H. (1966). Excretion of tryptophan metabolites in rheumatoid arthritis. *Arthritis and Rheumatism, 9*, 318–324.

Spicer, C. C., Hare, E. H. & Slater, E. (1973). Neurotic and psychotic forms of depressive illness: Evidence for age incidence in a national sample. *British Journal of Psychiatry, 123*, 535–541.

Spillane, J. D. (1951). Nervous and mental disorders in Cushing's Syndrome. *Brain, 74*, 72–98.

Spitzer, R. L. (1978). *Diagnostic and Statistical Manual of Mental Disorders*, 3rd edn. Washington: American Psychiatric Association.

Starkman, M. N. & Schteingart, D. E. (1969). Cushing's Syndrome: A prospective study. *Psychosomatic Medicine, 41*, 72–73.

Starr, A. M. (1952). Personality changes in Cushing's Syndrome. *Journal of Clinical Endocrinology, 12*, 502–505.

Steel, J. M. & Briggs, M. (1972). Withdrawal depression in obese patients after fenfluramine treatment. *British Medical Journal, 3*, 26–27.

Steel, J. M., Munro, J. F. & Duncan, L. J. P. (1973). A comparative trial of different regimens of fenfluramine and phentermine in Obesity. *Practitioner, 211*, 232–236.

Steel, R. (1960). GPI in an observation ward.*Lancet, 1*, 121–123.

Stein, G., Milton, F., Bebbington, P. *et al.* (1976). The relationship between mood disturbance and free and total plasma tryptophan in post-partum women. *British Medical Journal, 2*, 457.

Stein, J. A. & Tschudy, D. P. (1970). Acute intermittent porphyria: A clinical and biochemical study of 46 patients. *Medicine, 49*, 1–16.

Stein, M., Schiavi, R. C. & Camarino, M. (1976). Influence of brain and behaviour on the immune system. *Science, 191*, 435–440.

Steinberg, D., Hirsch, S. R., Marston, S. D. *et al.* (1972). Influenza infection causing manic psychosis. *British Journal of Psychiatry, 120*, 531–535.

Steinberg, H. R., Green, R. & Durell, J. (1967). Depression occurring during the course of recovery from schizophrenic symptoms. *American Journal of Psychiatry, 124*, 699–702.

Steiner, M. (1979). Psychobiology of mental disorders associated with child bearing. *Acta Psychiatrica Scandinavica, 60*, 449–464.

Stendstedt, Å. (1959). Involutional melancholia: An aetiological, clinical and social study of endogenous depression in later life with special reference to genetic factors. *Acta Psychiatrica Scandinavica*, Supplement 127.

Stengel, E. (1943). A study on the symptomatology and differential diagnosis of Alzheimer's disease and Pick's disease. *Journal of Mental Science, 89*, 1–20.

Stengel, E., Zeitlyn, B. B. & Rayner, E. H. (1958). Postoperative psychoses. *Journal of Mental Science, 104*, 389–402.

Stern, K. & Dancey, T. (1942). Glioma of the diencephalon in a manic patient. *American Journal of Psychiatry, 98*, 716–719.

Stern, M. & Robbins, E. S. (1960). Psychoses and systemic lupus erythematosus. *Archives of General Psychiatry, 3*, 205–212.

Stern, S. L., Hurtig, H. I., Mendels, J. *et al.* (1977). Psychiatric illness in relatives of patients with Parkinson's disease: A preliminary report. *American Journal of Psychiatry, 134*, 443–444.

Sternbach, R. A., Janowsky, D. S., Huey, L. Y. & Segal, D. S. (1976). Effects of altering brain serotonin activity on human chronic pain. *Advances in Pain Research and Therapy, 1,* 601–5.

Stewart, M. A., Drake, F. & Winokur, G. (1965). Depression among medically ill patients. *Diseases of the Nervous System, 26,* 479–486.

Stokes, J. F., Owen, J. D. & Holmes, E. G. (1945), Neurological complications of infectious hepatitis. *British Medical Journal, 2,* 642–644.

Storey, P. B. (1967). Psychiatric sequelae of subarachnoid haemorrhage. *British Medical Journal, 3,* 261–266.

Storey, P. B. (1970). Brain damage and personality change after subarachnoid haemorrhage. *British Journal of Psychiatry, 117,* 129–42.

Storey, P. B. (1972). Emotional disablement before and after subarachnoid haemorrhage. In: Physiology, Emotion and Psychosomatic Illness. *Ciba Foundation Symposium, 8,* pp. 337–47. Amsterdam: Elsevier.

Storm-Mathieson, A. (1969). General paresis: A follow-up study of 203 patients. *Acta Psychiatrica Scandinavica, 45,* 118–32.

Strachan, R. W. & Henderson, S. E. (1965). Psychiatric syndromes due to avitaminosis B12 with normal blood and marrow.*Quarterly Journal of Medicine, 135,* 303–317.

Strang, R. R. (1970). The aetiology of Parkinson's disease. *Diseases of the Nervous System, 31,* 381–90.

Strauss, H. (1955). Intracranial neoplasms, and masked depression diagnosed with the aid of electroencephalography. *Journal of Nervous and Mental Disease, 122,* 185–92.

Strauss, I. & Keschner, M. (1935). Mental symptoms in cases of tumour of the frontal lobe. *Archives of Neurology and Psychiatry, 33,* 986–1005.

Strobos, R. J. (1974). Temporal lobe tumours: *In* P. J. Vinken & G. W. Bruyn (Eds), *Handbook of Clinical Neurology,* Vol. 17, pp. 281–95. Amsterdam: North Holland.

Strömgren, E. (1969). Klassifizierung der Depressionen. *Das depressive Syndrom,* 347–56. Berlin; Urban and Schwarzenberg.

Suchenwirth, R. M. A. (1974). Parietal lobe tumours. *In* P. J. Vinken & G. W. Bruyn (Eds), *Handbook of Clinical Neurology,* Vol. 17, pp. 610–619. Amsterdam: North Holland.

Sulser, F., Bickel, M. N. & Brodie, B. B. (1964). The action of desmethylimipramine in counteracting sedative and cholinergic effects of reserpine-like durgs. *Journal of Pharmacology and Experimental Therapeutics, 144,* 321–330.

Summers, W. K. (1979). Psychiatric sequelae to cardiotomy. *Journal of Cardiovascular Surgery, 20,* 471–476.

Surawicz, F. G., Brightwell, D. R. & Weitzell, T. W. (1976). Cancer, emotions and mental illness: The present state of understanding. *American Journal of Psychiatry, 133,* 1306–1309.

Surridge, D. (1969). An investigation into some psychiatric aspects of multiple sclerosis. *British Journal of Psychiatry, 115,* 749–764.

Svanborg, A. (1973). Mental symptoms in Parkinson's disease. *In* J. Siegfried (Ed.), *Parkinson's Disease,* pp. 287–94. Bern: Hans Huber.

Swash, M., Roberts, A. H., Zakho, H. & Heathfield, K. W. G. (1972). Treatment of involuntary movement disorders with tetrabenazine. *Journal of Neurology, Neurosurgery and Psychiatry, 35,* 186–191.

Symonds, C. P. (1937). Mental disorders following head injury. *Proceedings of the Royal Society of Medicine, 30,* 1081–92.

Taft, P., Martin, F. I. R. & Mellick, R. (1970). Cushing's Syndrome: A review of the response to treatment in 42 patients. *Australasian Annals of Medicine, 4,* 295–303.

Takaishi, S., Yamani, H. & Condo, H. (1974).Cerebro-spinal fluid monoamine metabolites in alcoholics: A comparative study with depression. *Folia Psychiatrica Neurologica Japonica, 28,* 347–354.

Tamminga, C., Smith, R. D., Chang, S. *et al.* (1976). Depression associated with oral choline. *Lancet*, *2*, 905.

Tan, R. F., Gladman, D. D., Urowitz, M. B. & Milne, N. (1978). Brain scan diagnosis of C.N.S. involvement in systemic lupus erythematosus. *Annals of the Rheumatic Diseases*, *37*, 357–362.

Targowla, R., Sevin, S. & Ombredane, A. (1928). *Encéphale*. Quoted in Surridge, D. (1969).

Taub, A. (1973).Relief of postherpetic neuralgia with psychotropic drugs. *Journal of Neurosurgery*, *39*, 235–9.

Taylor, A. R. (1967). Post-concussional sequelae. *British Medical Journal*, *3*, 67–71.

Taylor, A. R. & Bell, T. K. (1966). Slowing of cerebral circulation after concussional head injury. *Lancet*, *2*, 178–180.

Taylor, D. C. (1972). Mental state and temporal lobe epilepsy. *Epilepsia*, *13*, 727–765.

Taylor, J. W. (1975). Depression in thyrotoxicosis. *American Journal of Psychiatry*, *132*, 552–553.

Taylor, J. W. (1979). Mental symptoms and electrolyte imbalance. *Australian and New Zealand Journal of Psychiatry*, *13*, 159–60.

Terenius, L., Wahlström, A. & Ågren, H. (1977). Neilosolne (narcan) treatment in depression: Clinical observations and effects on CSF endorphins and monoamine metabolites. *Psychopharmacology*, *54*, 31–3.

Theander, S. (1976). Anorexia nervosa: A psychiatric investigation of 94 female patients. *Acta Psychiatrica Scandinavica Supplement* 214.

Thomas, F. B., Mazzaterri, E. L. & Skillman, T. G. (1970). Apathetic thyrotoxicosis: A distinct clinical and laboratory entity. *Annals of Internal Medicine*, *72*, 679–685.

Thompson, M. & Percy, J. S. (1966). Further experiences with indomethacin in the treatment of rheumatic disorder. *British Medical Journal*, *1*, 80–83.

Thornton, W. E. (1977). Folate deficiency in puerperal psychosis. *American Journal of Obstetrics and Gynaecology*, *129*, 222–223.

Tod, E. D. M. (1964). Puerperal depression, *Lancet*, *2*, 1264–1266.

Todd, J. (1951). A case of Simmond's Disease with mental symptoms. *British Medical Journal*, *2*, 569–571.

Toglia, J., McGlamery, M. & Sambandham, R. R. (1978). Tetrabenazine in the treatment of Huntington's Chorea and other hyperkinetic movement disorders. *Journal of Clinical Psychiatry*, *39*, 81–87.

Tonks, C. M. (1964). Mental illness in hypothyroid patients. *British Journal of Psychiatry*, *110*, 706–710.

Torrey, E. F., Peterson, R., Brannon, W. L. *et al.* (1978), Immunoglobulins and viral antibodies in psychiatric patients. *British Journal of Psychiatry*, *132*, 342–348.

Treadway, C. R., Kane, F. J., Zadeh, A. & Lipton, M. A. (1969). A psycho-endocrine study of pregnancy and the puerperium. *American Journal of Psychiatry*, *125*, 1380–1386.

Trethowan, W. H. & Cobb, S. (1952). Neuropsychiatric aspects of Cushing's Syndrome. *Archives of Neurology and Psychiatry*, *67*, 283–309.

Trimble, M. R. & Cummings, J. L. (1981). Neuropsychiatric disturbances following brain stem lesions. *British Journal of Psychiatry*, *136*, 56–9.

Trouillas, P. & Courgon, J. (1972). Epilepsy with multiple sclerosis. *Epilepsia*, *13*, 325–333.

Tsuang, M. T., Tidball, J. S. & Geller, D. (1979). ECT in a depressed patient with a shunt in place for normal pressure hydrocephalus. *American Journal of Psychiatry*, *136*, 1205–1206.

Tsuang, M. T., Winokur, G. & Crowe, R. R. (1980). Morbidity risk of schizophrenia and affective disorders among first degree relatives of patients with schizophrenia, mania, depression and surgical patients. *British Journal of Psychiatry*, *137*, 497–504

Tuke, D. H. (1892). *Dictionary of Psychological Medicine*. London: Churchill.

Turkington, R. W. (1980). Depression masquerading as diabetic neuropathy. *Journal of the American Medical Association*, *243*, 1147–50.

Turpin, T. J. & Heath, D. S. (1979). The link between hysterectomy and depression. *Canadian Journal of Psychiatry*, *24*, 247–254.

Tyler, H. R. (1966). Neurological disorders seen in renal failure. *In*: P. J. Vinken & G. W. Bruyn (Eds), *Handbook of Clinical Neurology*, Vol. 27, pp. 319–348. Amsterdam: North Holland.

Tyrer, E. (1980). Dependence on benzodiazepines. *British Journal of Psychiatry*, *137*, 576–577.

Van Praag, H. M. (1968). Abuse of, dependence on, and psychoses from anorexogenic drugs. *In* L. Myler & H. M. Peck (Eds), *Drug-Induced Diseases*, Vol. 3, p. 281. Amsterdam: Excerpta Medica.

Van Praag, H. M. (1977). Indoleamines in depression. *In* G. D. Burrows (Ed.), *Handbook of Depression*, pp. 303–23. Amsterdam: Elsevier.

Van Praag, H. M. (1978). Neuroendocrine disorders in depression and their significance for the monoamine hypothesis of depression. *Acta Psychiatrica Scandinavica*, *57*, 389–404.

Van Praag, H. M. & de Haan, S. (1980). Central serotonin deficiency: A factor which increases depression vulnerability. *Acta Psychiatrica Scandinavica*, Suppl. 280, 89–96.

Van Praag, H. M., Korf, J., Lakke, J. D. W. F. & Schut, T. (1975). Dopamine metabolism in depression, psychoses and Parkinson's disease. *Psychological Medicine*, *5*, 138–46.

Varga, E. & Klein, N. S. (1973). Depression, osteoporosis and osteo-arthritis. *Journal of International Medical Research*, *1*, 504–508.

Varsamis, J., Zuchowski, T. & Maini, K. K. (1972). Survival rate and causes of death in geriatric patients. *Canadian Psychiatric Association Journal*, *7*, 17–22.

Vecht, C. J., Van Woerkom, T. C., Teelkan, A. W. *et al.* (1975). 5–hydroxyindoleacetic acid (5HIAA) levels in the cerebrospinal fluid in consciousness and unconsciousness after head injury. *Life Sciences*, *16*, 1179–85.

Verbeist, L., Pignot, J. & Cosemans, A. (1966). Tolerance of ethionamide and PAS in original treatment of tuberculous patients. *Scandinavian Journal of Respiratory Disease*, *47*, 225–235.

Vererker, R. (1952). The psychiatric aspects of temporal arteritis. *Journal of Mental Science*, *98*, 280–286.

Vervoerdt, A. & Dovenmuehle, R. H. (1964). Heart disease and depression. *Geriatrics*, *19*, 856–864.

Virkkunen, M. (1974). Suicides in schizophrenia and paranoid psychoses. *Acta Psychiatrica Scandinavica*, Suppl. 250.

Vlissides, D. N., Gill, D., Castelow, J. (1978). Bromocriptin-induced mania. *British Medical Journal*, *1*, 510.

Von Brauchitsch, H. (1972). Antinuclear factor in psychiatric disorders. *American Journal of Psychiatry*, *128*, 1552–1554.

Von Knorring, J., Erma, M. & Lindström, B. (1966). The manifestations of temporal arteritis. *Acta Medica Scandinavica*, *179*, 691–702.

Waal, H. J. (1967). Propranolol-induced depression. *British Medical Journal*, *2*, 50.

Waggoner, R. W. & Bagchi, B. K. (1954). Initial masking of organic brain changes by psychiatric symptoms. *American Journal of Psychiatry*, *110*, 904–10.

Wagshul, A. M. & Daroff, R. B. (1969). Depression during l-dopa therapy. *Lancet*, *1*, 592.

Wahle, H. (1958). Die erworbene Toxoplasmose. *Fortschritte der Neurologie und Psychiatrie*, *26*, 6–48.

Waitzkin, L. (1966). A survey of unknown diabetics in a mental hospital I: Men under age 50. *Diabetes*, *15*, 97–104.

Wälinder, J. (1977). Hyperostosis frontalis interna and mental morbidity. *British Journal of Psychiatry*, *131*, 155–159.

Walker, A. (1968). Chronic scurvy. *British Journal of Dermatology*, *80*, 625–630.

Wallach, M. B. & Gershon, S. (1972). Psychiatric sequelae to tuberculosis chemotherapy. *In* R. I. Shader (Ed.), *Psychiatric Complications of Medical Drugs*, pp. 201–212; New York: Raven Press.

Wallen, G. D., Connolly, F. H. & Gittleson, N. L. (1972). A case of carcinoma of the pancreas with a psychiatric presentation. *British Journal of Clinical Practice*, *26*, 132–133.

Warburton, J. W. (1967). Depressive symptoms in Parkinson patients referred for thalamatomy. *Journal of Neurology, Neurosurgery and Psychiatry*, *30*, 368–70.

Ward, D. J. (1971). Rheumatoid arthritis and personality: A controlled study. *British Medical Journal*, *1*, 297–299.

Ward, N., Bloom, B. L. & Friedel, R. O. (1979). The effectiveness of tricyclic antidepressants in the treatment of coexisting pain and depression. *Pain*, *7*, 331–41.

Watson, C. G. & Schuld, D. (1977). Psychosomatic factors in the aetiology of neoplasms. *Journal of Consulting and Clinical Psychology*, *45*, 455–464.

Weil, A. (1956). Ichtal depression and anxiety in temporal lobe disorder. *American Journal of Psychiatry*, *113*, 149–157.

Weinstein, F. (1980). Narcoleptic-induced depression? *American Journal of Psychiatry*, *137*, 257–258.

Weisert, K. N. & Hendrie, H. C. (1977). Secondary mania? A case report. *American Journal of Psychiatry*, *134*, 929–30.

Weissman, M. M., Pottinger, M., Klerber, H. *et al.* (1977). Symptom patterns in primary and secondary depression. *Archives of General Psychiatry*, *34*, 854–862.

Wells, C. E. (1975). Transient ictal psychosis. *Archives of General Psychiatry*, *32*, 1201–1203.

Wetterberg, L. (1967). *A Neuropsychiatric and Genetical Investigation of Acute Intermittent Porphyria*. Lund: Scandinavian University Books.

Wheatley, D., Balter, M., Levine, J. *et al.* (1975). Psychiatric aspects of hypertension. *British Journal of Psychiatry*, *127*, 327–336.

Whitlock, F. A. (1970). The syndrome of barbiturate dependence. *Medical Journal of Australia*, *2*, 391–396.

Whitlock, F. A. (1977a). Psychotropic drugs and old age. *Australian Family Physician*, *6*, 52–62.

Whitlock, F. A. (1977b). Depression and suicide. *In* G. D. Burrows (Ed.), *Handbook of Studies on Depression*, pp. 379–403, Amsterdam: Elsevier.

Whitlock, F. A. (1978). Suicide, cancer and depression. *British Journal of Psychiatry*, *132*, 269–274.

Whitlock, F. A. (1981a). Post-influenzal depression. *British Journal of Psychiatry*, *139*, 169–170.

Whitlock, F. A. (1981b). Adverse psychiatric reactions to modern medication. *Australian and New Zealand Journal of Psychiatry*, *15*, 87–104.

Whitlock, F. A. Antidepressant drugs for the treatment of chronic pain. *Current Therapeutics* (in press).

Whitlock, F. A. & Evans, L. E. J. (1978). Drugs and depression. *Drugs*, *15*, 53–71.

Whitlock, F. A. & Siskind, M. (1979). Depression and cancer: A follow-up study. *Psychological Medicine*, *9*, 747–752.

Whitlock, F. A. & Siskind, M. M. (1980). Depression as a major symptom of multiple sclerosis. *Journal of Neurology, Neurosurgery and Psychiatry*, *43*, 861–865.

Whybrow, P. C., Prange, A. H. & Treadway, C. R. (1969). Mental changes accompanying thyroid gland dysfunction. *Archives of General Psychiatry*, *20*, 48–63.

Wilcocks, C. & Manson-Bahr, P. E. C. (1972). *In* C. Wilcocks & P. E. C. Manson-Bahr (Eds), *Manson's Tropical Diseases*, 17th Edition p. 778. London: Balliére, Tindall.

Williams, D. (1956). The structure of emotions in epileptic experiences. *Brain*, *79*, 28–57.

Williams, E. D. (1979). Medullary carcinoma of the thyroid. *In* L. J. de Groot *et al.* (Eds), *Endocrinology*, Vol. 2, pp. 777–796. New York: Grune and Stratton.

Williams, H. L. & Salamy, A. (1972). Alcohol and Sleep. *In* B. Kissin & H. Begleiter (Eds), *Biology of Alcoholism*, Vol. 2, pp. 436–484. New York: Plenum Press.

Williamson, J. (1978). Depression in the elderly. *Ageing*, *7*, Supplement, 35–40.

Winokur, A., Dugan, J. & Mendels, J. *et al.* (1978). Psychiatric illness in relatives of patients with Parkinson's disease: An expanded survey. *American Journal of Psychiatry, 135,* 854–5.

Winokur, A., March, V. & Mendels, J. (1980). Primary affective disorder in relatives of patients with anorexia nervosa. *American Journal of Psychiatry, 137,* 695–698.

Winokur, G., Clayton, P. J., Reich, T. (1969). *Manic-depressive Illness.* St. Louis: C. V. Mosby Co.

Winshie, H. A., Hackett, T. P. & Cassein, N. H. (1971). Psychological hazards of convalescence following myocardial infarct. *Journal of the American Medical Association, 215,* 1292–1296.

Wood, D. I., Othmer, S., Reich, T., *et al.* (1977). Primary and secondary affective disorder. *Comprehensive Psychiatry, 18,* 201–210.

Woodforde, J. M., Dwyer, B., McEwen, B. W. *et al.* (1965). Treatment of postherpetic neuralgia. *Medical Journal of Australia, 2,* 869–72.

Wookey, C. (1978). Epidemic myalgic encephalomyelitis. *British Medical Journal, 2,* 202.

Woolf, S. M., Adler, R. C., Buskirk, E. R. & Thompson, R. H. (1964). A syndrome of periodic hypothalamic discharge. *American Journal of Medicine, 36,* 956–967.

Worden, J. W. & Weissman, A. D. (1977). The fallacy in post-mastectomy depression. *American Journal of Medical Science, 273,* 169–175.

Wynn, A. (1967). Unwarranted emotional distress in men with incidence of heart disease. *Medical Journal of Australia, 2,* 847–851.

Yaskin, J. C. (1931). Nervous symptoms as earliest manifestation of carcinoma of the pancreas. *Journal of the American Medical Association, 96,* 1664–1668.

Young, A. C., Saunders, J. & Ponsford, J. R. (1966). Mental change as an early feature of multiple sclerosis. *Journal of Neurology, Neurosurgery and Psychiatry, 39,* 1008–1013.

Young, E. S. & Whitlock, F. A. (1979). Antinuclear Antibodies and Depression (Unpublished Study).

Young, L. D., Taylor, I. & Holstrom, V. (1977). Lithium treatment of patients with affective illness associated with organic brain symptoms. *American Journal of Psychiatry, 134,* 1405–7.

Yudofsky, S. C. (1979). Parkinson's disease, depression and electroconvulsive therapy: a clinical and neurobiologic synthesis. *Comprehensive Psychiatry, 20,* 579–81.

Zacharias, F. J., Cowen, K. S., Prestt, J. *et al.* (1972). Propranolol in hypertension: A study of long-term therapy, 1964–1970. *American Heart Journal, 83,* 755–761.

Zaphiropoulos, G. & Burry, H. C. (1973). A study of depression in rheumatoid disease. *Annals of Rheumatic Disease, 32,* 593–595.

Zaphiropoulos, G. & Burry, H. C. (1974). Depression in rheumatoid disease. *Annals of Rheumatic Disease, 33,* 132–135.

Zbinden, G. (1962). Pharmacodynamics of tetrabenazine and its derivatives. *In* J. H. Nodine & J. H. Myer (Eds), *Psychosomatic Medicine,* pp. 443-454. Philadelphia: Lea & Febiger.

Ziegler, D. K. (1954). Cerebral atrophy in psychiatric patients. *American Journal of Psychiatry, 111,* 454–458.

Zielinski, J. J. (1974). Epilepsy and mortality rate and cause of death. *Epilepsia, 15,* 191–201.

Index

214

Index

Biochemical changes in the brain
affective disorders and, 9–20
alcohol and, 113
Alzheimer's disease and, 33
cerebral infarction and, 47
Huntington's disease and, 64
old age and, 30–31
oral contraceptives and, 108–109
parkinsonism, fatal familial, 61
Parkinson's disease, 59
Brain damage, epilepsy and, 75
see also Head injuries
Bromocriptine, 116, 125
mania and, 125

Cancer, 131–136
aetiological factors, 134–136
breast cancer, 132–133
see also Mastectomy
cancer-prone personality, 131–132
delusions of, 136
depression preceding, 133–134
pancreas, cancer of, 98, 132
suicide and cancer, 134
thyroid cancer, familial medullary, 87
Cerebral functions, lateralization of, 79–81
Cerebral tumours
affective disorders and, 43, 48–58
cerebellar tumours, 56
corpus callosum tumours, 49
cystic tumours, 55, 56
epilepsy and depression, 56, 58
frontal lobe tumours, 49, 55, 56
mania and hypomania, 49–50, 55
mental symptoms, frequency of, 48, 50, 56
meningiomas, 49, 55, 56–58
missed diagnoses, 48–49, 51, 58
parietal lobe tumours, 49
suicide and attempted suicide, 58
temporal lobe tumours, 49, 56
thalamic tumours, 49
Cerebrovascular disease
cerebral infarction, 47
depression and, 28–29, 43, 46–47
old age and, 28–29
strokes, depression and suicide, 43, 46
subarachnoid haemorrhage, 47
Childbirth and affective disorders, 121–125
see also Post-partum psychoses

Clonidine, 84, 105–106
Contraceptives
see Oral contraceptives
Coronary care units, depression in, 162
Cortisone, effects on mood, 93
Cushing's disease and syndrome, 91–96
alcohol-induced, 92, 113
depression
aetiology of, 93–96
frequency of, 91, 93
ectopic tumours causing, 92
intermittent type, 92, 95–96
psychiatric symptoms, frequency of, 91
psychological stress causing, 95
suicide and attempted suicide in, 92, 93, 94
treatment, effects of, 95

Depression
cancer and, 131–136
cerebrovascular disease and, 28–29, 43, 46–47
Cushing's syndrome and, 91–96
dexamethasone suppression test, 21
drugs and, 99–119
causes or precipitants?, 118–119
drug-induced depression, pathogenesis, 99, 101
frequency of, 118–119
number of drugs causing, 100
see also Drugs and depression
endocrine changes and, 20–22
folate deficiency and, 114, 156–157
growth hormone and, 22
Huntington's disease and, 63–65
hypertension and, 160–161
hysterectomy and, 126–127
myocardial infarction and, 161
narcolepsy and, 82
old age and, 25–34
open heart surgery and, 128–129
Parkinson's disease and, 16, 43, 58–63
physical illness and, 2, 5, 6, 26, 27
nature of relationship, 2
presenile dementia and, 32–34
prolactin and, 22
schizophrenia and, 150–153
sleep disorders and, 81–82
systemic lupus erythematosus and, 138–143

PERSONALITY AND PSYCHOPATHOLOGY
A Series of Monographs, Texts, and Treatises

David T. Lykken, Editor

*Titles initiated during the series editorship of Brendan Maher.

PERSONALITY AND PSYCHOPATHOLOGY

2 3 4 5 6 7 8 9 0 1
A B C D E F G H I J